Facts On File Encyclopedia of

BlackWomen

IN AMERICA

Education

Encyclopedia of
Black Women in America

Facts On File Encyclopedia of

Black Women
IN AMERICA

Education

Darlene Clark Hine, Editor
Valinda Littlefield, Associate Editor

☑® Facts On File, Inc.

Facts On File Encyclopedia of Black Women in America: Education

Copyright © 1997 by Darlene Clark Hine

Facts On File, Inc.
11 Penn Plaza
New York NY 10001

Library of Congress Cataloginig-in-Publication Data
Facts on File encyclopedia of Black women in America / Darlene Clark
Hine, editor ; Kathleen Thompson, associate editor.
p. cm.
Includes bibliographical references and index.
Contents: v. 1. The early years, 1619–1899 — v. 2. Literature —
v. 3. Dance, sports, and visual arts — v. 4. Business and professions —
v. 5. Music — v. 6. Education — v. 7. Religion and community —
v. 8. Law and government — v. 9. Theater, arts and
entertainment — v. 10. Social activism — v. 11. Science, health,
and medicine.
ISBN 0-8160-3424-9 (set : alk. paper)
ISBN 0-8160-3426-5 (Education)
1. Afro-American women—Biography—Encyclopedias. I. Hine,
Darlene Clark. II. Thompson, Kathleen.
E 185.96.F2   1996
920.72′08996073—dc20   96-33268

Facts On File books are available at special discounts when purchased in bulk quantities for businesses, associations, institutions or sales promotions. Please call our Special Sales Department in New York at 212/967-8800 or 800/322-8755.

Text design by Cathy Rincon
Cover design by Smart Graphics

Printed in the United States of America

RRD FOF 10 9 8 7 6 5 4 3 2 1

This book is printed on acid-free paper.

CH   7/97

Contents

How to Use This Volume

SCOPE OF THE VOLUME

This volume, *Education,* includes entries on individuals and organizations relevant to the following professions: teachers, college faculty, college presidents, educators in special fields (e.g., drama), and educational administrators.

RELATED OCCUPATIONS

Related occupations covered in other volumes of this encyclopedia include the following: archivists (*Business and Professions*), librarians (*Business and Professions*), scientists (*Science, Health, and Medicine*), and writers (*Literature*).

HOW TO USE THIS VOLUME

The introduction to this volume presents an overview of the history of black women in education. Women who founded educational institutions are included. A chronology at the end of the volume lists important events in the history of black women as educators and in the history of the education of black women.

Individuals and organizations are presented in alphabetically arranged entries. If you are looking for an individual or organization that does not have an entry in this volume, please check the alphabetically arranged list of the entries for all eleven volumes of this encyclopedia that appears at the end of this book, in addition to the tables of contents of each of the other titles in the series.

Names of individuals and organizations for which there are entries in this or other volumes of the encyclopedia are printed in **boldface**. Check the contents list at the end of this book to find the volume where a particular entry can be found.

Introduction

In 1995, the University of Southern Mississippi received a gift of $150,000 to establish a scholarship fund primarily for African-American students. The donor was not a foundation or a corporation or a government agency. It was Oseola McCarty.

For most of her eighty-seven years, Oseola McCarty did laundry and ironing in Hattiesburg, Mississippi, where the university is located. She didn't have much education—she had to leave elementary school to care for a sick aunt—but she knew it was important. She lived a simple life and started saving a little of the money she got for each bundle of laundry some time after World War II, when her price went up to ten dollars a bundle. (Each bundle contained about a week's washing for a family of four.)

After almost eighty years of hard work and fifty years of saving, McCarty had enough money to do almost anything she wanted to do. What she wanted to do was help African-American children go to college.

What may be most striking about Oseola McCarty's story is that, in the black community, it is not all that unusual. In one way or another and to one degree or another, African Americans have been making extraordinary sacrifices for education for centuries. It is part of a tradition. Since the early days of slavery, education has been seen as "the salvation of the race." The history of black women in American education is the story of the painful, relentless, and often triumphant pursuit of that salvation.

THE EARLY DAYS

In 1772, **Phillis Wheatley**, an African-American woman slave belonging to John Wheatley of Boston, was questioned by such prominent men as John Hancock, future signer of the Declaration of Independence, and Thomas Hutchinson, governor of Massachusetts. At eighteen years of age, Wheatley had written a book of poems. Some of Boston's most respected men had gathered to determine whether it was actually possible for an African-American woman to write poetry or to understand the writings about Greek and Latin mythology referred to in the poetry Wheatley claimed to have written. After questioning Wheatley, the group concluded that she did indeed write the poems without the assistance of a white person.

The story of Phillis Wheatley illustrates one of the two crucial issues that recur in the struggle of African Americans for education. The two are related and, at the same time, contradictory, as are many racist beliefs.

Africans were brought to this country as slaves by people who believed that they were an inferior race. As such, they were thought incapable of learning. Some white people genuinely believed this. Others pretended to believe it in order to justify slavery. The result was the same—there was no point in trying to educate black people. This conviction persisted in the minds of many whites for centuries.

1

Existing alongside that belief was another: that it was dangerous to educate black people. Many slave owners feared that educated blacks, such as Nat Turner, would instigate or lead slave rebellions. At best, education spoiled a good field hand.

Much of white America managed to hold both of these beliefs at the same time. Black people couldn't be taught, and it was dangerous to teach them. However, there was a regional difference in the strength of the beliefs and therefore in the tasks faced by those seeking education for black Americans.

In the North, slavery was never the tremendous economic force that it became in the South. Slaves were usually house servants or farm workers. Some slaves who worked inside, rather than in the field, learned to read and write by listening to lessons being given to the slave owner's children. Often they then passed on their knowledge to others in the slave community. Some, like Phillis Wheatley, were taught by their more enlightened owners.

It was difficult to convince white Northerners that African Americans had the ability to learn, but there were many who came around. And the fear that education would lead to rebellion was not strong. In the early 1700s, therefore, schools for black Americans were established.

In 1704, for example, Elias Neau, a white New Yorker, founded the Catechism School for slaves at Trinity Church. Both Puritans and Quakers established other such schools in the years that followed. The founders of these schools were white, but black women often were assistants in the classroom. In some of the later schools, they also were teachers. By the late 1700s and early 1800s, black women had begun to found their own schools.

Catherine Ferguson, who was born around 1774, started an integrated Sunday school in her home in 1793 in New York. She offered both religious instruction and basic education. Living in a poor neighborhood, Ferguson taught children whose families, both black and white, were unable to care for them. In order to provide assistance to the poor, she worked as a caterer for wealthy white families and provided laundry services for delicate materials such as lace items.

Ferguson also found homes for many of the children and accepted some in her own home as well. With the help of others, she continued to teach and supervise the school for forty years. Her school was New York's first Sunday School.

In the early 1830s, **Sarah Mapps Douglass**—who came from a well-to-do family and had been educated at home—opened a high school for black girls in Philadelphia, the first of its kind in the country.

These successes did not come easily. Opposition to the education of black people was still strong in many places in the North. In 1833, Prudence Crandall, a white Quaker woman, attempted to admit a *respectable* black girl, seventeen-year-old Sarah Harris, into a school she was conducting for white girls. The community of Canterbury, Connecticut, where the school was located, strenuously objected. White parents removed their children from her school. They argued that she was fostering social equality and intermarriage between whites and blacks.

Crandall closed the school and reopened it for black girls only. The objections did not cease. Community members were still outraged. Crandall was shunned, her well was filled with manure, and her house set afire. Her family was not allowed to visit and was threatened with fines of $100 for the first offense and $200 for the second offense. Crandall was arrested and twice tried. After months of being terrorized, she gave up her attempt to educate African-American students.

Gaining a public education on a level of equality with white students was a battle fought by African Americans even in the North. In 1787, a group of Boston blacks led by Masonic organizer and abolitionist Price Hall petitioned the legislature for equal school facilities. Over a century later, blacks still were struggling for equal educational opportunities. In 1837, the *Colored American* charged that separate school systems "so shackled the intellect of the colored youth, that an education acquired under such circumstances, was, comparatively, of little advantage." Frederick Douglass demanded court action to allow students to attend all schools without discrimination. But in 1848, Boston officials barred Sarah Roberts from attending a white neighborhood school. In order to attend a black school, Sarah was required to pass five white schools. Her father filed the first school integration suit. In *Sarah C. Roberts* v. *City of Boston*, the Massachusetts state supreme court upheld the local school board's decision. This ruling is the first recorded use of the "separate but equal" doctrine. And in 1770, Lucy Terry Prince argued on behalf of her son's admission to Williams College for three hours before the college trustees, quoting the law and the Bible, but to no avail. They refused, in principle, to admit an African American.

In the South, the situation was even grimmer. Slavery, by the middle of the 1700s, was becoming more and more critical to the Southern economy. Racist beliefs, and the division between blacks and whites, had hardened. Fear undeniably was the overriding factor in denying education to slaves and even to free blacks. As early as 1740, South Carolina made it illegal to provide education to African Americans, slave or free. Reactions to Nat Turner's rebellion in 1831 would increase the number of such laws throughout the slaveholding states.

Still, African Americans managed to learn, and to teach. When it was necessary to hide their activities, they did so, but they would not give up. In 1819, for example, a black woman from Santo Domingo named Julian Froumountaine opened a free school for African Americans in Savannah, Georgia. According to historian Linda Perkins, it was one of many. When restrictive laws were passed in the 1830s, Froumountaine went underground. Throughout that decade she taught secretly. Another black woman, known only as Miss Deveaux, started an underground school in 1838 and taught in secret for twenty-five years.

Elizabeth Lange had some success in this area by working under the protection of the Roman Catholic Church. Born and reared in a French colony in the Caribbean, Lange came to the United States in 1817 and settled in Baltimore in 1827. There she opened a school for French-speaking black immigrants. Her accomplishments led Pope Gregory XVI to allow her to found a religious order dedicated to education, the **Oblate Sisters of Providence**. According to one report, the black nuns were stoned when they first appeared on the street in their habits. But they persevered.

After the death in 1843 of the priest who had encouraged their founding, Father Jacques Hector Nicholas Joubert, the Oblate Sisters received little or no support from the church. They were forced to take in laundry and sewing to keep their school going. Four years later, they found another sponsor priest and continued their work under less impoverished circumstances.

Ann Marie Becroft, one of the Oblate Sisters, came to the order at the age of twenty-seven after having worked for black education for twelve years. When she was only fifteen years old, in 1820, Becroft founded a day school for black girls in Georgetown. She ran the school for almost eight years, until she was asked by a priest to open a school sponsored by the Catholic Church. She moved to larger facilities and operated the school as a boarding and day school until 1831, when she left to join the Oblate Order.

North or South, the efforts of black women to learn and to teach were ceaseless. Yet, in addition to race, there was another obstacle to be overcome.

TRUE WOMANHOOD AND BEYOND

While North America was being settled, women were involved in most aspects of life. Their labor was needed to clear the wilderness, to farm, to build towns, and, eventually, to create the United States. Black women, of course, were defined as laborers, having been brought to these shores for the sole purpose of working.

Then, in the early nineteenth century, the situation began to change. As life became somewhat more civilized—and as England's Queen Victoria began her morally stringent reign—the role of women became more limited. The view of the proper role of a woman in society was that of mother and wife. Whites, especially the middle class, adhered to the notion of "true womanhood." Women were to be pious, submissive, domestic, and pure. As a result, only the rudiments of education—reading and writing—were considered necessary. It was widely believed that educating a woman caused an inability to reproduce, thus making her undesirable for her natural roles in life of wife and mother.

In the view of white society, however, black women did not fit the profile of "true womanhood." It was very important for white people, especially slave owners, to believe in a very different concept of black womanhood.

For one thing, black women were expected to do hard manual labor. They plowed, planted, and harvested. They worked long days in the field and came home to clean, cook, and care for their own families in the slave quarters. Delicacy was something neither they nor their owners could afford.

Sexual purity was even less possible under the economic requirements of slavery. Black women were expected to bear children to maintain the work force. Their role in reproduction was therefore often forced, not voluntary. They were also frequently sexually abused by male slave owners. In order to justify this, white society conjured an image of black women that involved sexual "impurity." Black women were, in this view, naturally sexual and lacking in moral worth.

Both views of women, as weak and pure, on the one hand, and as strong and impure, on the other, were destructive. However, the latter was clearly more destructive, at least in the short run. For that reason, even while the majority of black women were doing harsh physical labor on Southern plantations, there were others who accepted the Victorian ideal for themselves. Respectability was extremely important to free black women who were trying to gain acceptance or at least tolerance from the dominant culture. They would not jeopardize this by defying the definition of ideal womanhood. So, the limitations that applied to white women of their class applied largely to them as well.

For example, **Oberlin College**, in 1833, allowed admission without regard to race or gender. It was the first college in the United States to do so. But there was a separate curriculum for women, called the Young Ladies' Course. The more demanding College Course, which led to a bachelor's degree, was also called the "gentleman's course." It was not until 1862 that a black woman graduated from the College Course at Oberlin.

In the area of education, however, black women could not afford to accept the dominant groups' definition of true womanhood. And there were some leaders who recognized this. In 1832, **Maria W. Stewart** stressed the importance of education for the women of her race. Because African Americans were at the bottom of the economic ladder, the labor of black women was needed to sustain families. Stewart argued that in order for the race to advance and survive, women, as well as men, needed an education. She made a plea to "let our girls possess whatever amiable qualities of soul they may . . ." because without an education, "it is impossible for scarce an individual of them to rise above the condition of servants."

Stewart's appeal fell on receptive ears because of the importance African Americans had long given education. Families made tremendous sacrifices for the education of their children. In the decades immediately before the Civil War, free blacks relocated entire families or sent children away from home in order to obtain education for their sons and daughters.

Lucy Ellen Moten's parents moved from Fauquier County, Virginia, to Washington, D.C., in the 1850s so that their daughter could receive an elementary education in a private black school. When public schools for African Americans opened in the District of Columbia in 1862, she was enrolled. After elementary school, she attended **Howard University**'s normal and preparatory departments for two years. Moten began a teaching career in 1870 at Washington's O Street School, a public grammar school. She also served as principal of Miner Normal School in Washington, D.C., from 1883 to 1920.

When Blanche Harris was rejected by a seminary for white women in Michigan, her family moved to Ohio so that she could attend Oberlin. She graduated from the Ladies' Course in 1860. Her sister graduated ten years later.

The first black woman to graduate with a bachelor's degree from any recognized American college was **Mary Jane Patterson**. Her parents moved to Ohio from Raleigh, North Carolina, so that the Patterson children could go to school at Oberlin. Mary Jane entered the College Course and graduated in 1862. She later became the first black principal of Dunbar High School in Washington, D.C.

Fannie Jackson Coppin also received the help of her family and her community. The second African-American woman to receive a college degree, she was purchased from slavery by her aunt when she was a child. In the early 1850s, she moved to Newport, Rhode Island, to live with relatives, going to work in the home of the prominent Calvert family. Out of her wages she hired a tutor, who taught her one hour a day, three days a week. During the last of the six years she worked for the Calverts, she attended a black public school. From there she went on to Rhode Island State Normal School in Bristol and finally, in 1860, to Oberlin College.

Coppin received financial assistance from her aunt, a scholarship from Bishop Daniel Payne of the African Methodist Episcopal Church, and aid from Oberlin. She also worked while attending college. Coppin became the principal of the **Institute for Colored Youth** in Philadelphia in 1869, and served in the position for almost forty years.

The stories of Moten, Harris, Patterson, and Coppin are typical. And the pursuit of education only became more intense as the years passed. As objections to education for women in general began to lessen in the second half of the nineteenth century, black women began to catch up with and eventually surpass their male counterparts.

Most black families understood the importance of women's contributions to the race, and many valued education for their daughters more than for their sons. While sons could probably find a manual-labor job that required very little education, if any, women needed an education in order to secure jobs such as teaching or nursing that would improve their status in the community while simultaneously enabling them to contribute to the family income and making them self-supporting in case they did not marry. Such emphasis placed on educating women also included the indoctrination of social responsibility, and most of these daughters were expected to use their education to teach the masses.

Important as formal schooling was in the early story of education for black women, another aspect of life in the black community was almost as significant in the decades before the Civil War.

LADIES WHO LUNCH

Although women were denied access to higher education until the second half of the nineteenth century, literary interests were not discouraged. Indeed, it was considered quite acceptable for respectable women to gather together over tea to discuss the English poets, or even that daring young Nathaniel Hawthorne. Among black women, the groups looked and sounded much the same, but the agenda was different.

In the cities of the Northeast and even in some Southern cities, black women founded a multitude of "literary societies." There was the Minerva Literary Association of Philadelphia, founded in 1834; the Ladies Literary Society, founded the same year in New York City; the Female Literary Society, founded two years later in New York City. There was the Ladies Literary and Dorcas Society of Rochester, founded in 1836, and the Young Ladies Literary Society of Buffalo, founded in 1837. These were only a few of the hundreds of such groups that flourished before the Civil War.

What made the black woman's literary society so different from her white counterpart's was the underlying motivation. According to historian Brenda E. Stevenson, "Even at the most fundamental level, African-American women who were active in literary groups believed that their goals supported abolition and black rights activism, maintaining that the intellectual acuity and high moral standards demonstrated by their work undermined racist notions of innate black inferiority and debasement."

In other words reading, writing, or even understanding a poem constituted evidence in the continuing struggle to prove black equality. But the women of these groups went much further in using their literary accomplishments for the good of their people. They contributed regularly to abolitionist journals and newspapers, such as the *Liberator*, the *Christian Recorder*, *The Anglo-African* magazine, and others. In fact some of them developed significant literary careers through their activities in the societies and the abolitionist press.

The **Forten sisters**—Margaretta, Sarah, and Harriet—were members of the free black community of Philadelphia. They were founders, with their mother and other women both black and white, of the **Philadelphia Female Anti-Slavery Society** in 1833. All made significant contributions to the abolitionist cause, but it was Sarah who became known as a writer. Historian Janice Sumler-Edmond writes: "Her poems and essays poignantly described the humanity of the bondsmen while attacking the hypocrisy of slavery in a nation founded on the concept of individual liberty."

Another member of the prominent Forten family, **Charlotte Forten [Grimké]**, received her education at Higginson Grammar School in Salem, Massachusetts, where in 1854 she was the only nonwhite student. She then went on to the Normal School at Salem. Forten was an active member of the Salem Female Anti-Slavery Society, the first all-woman abolitionist group founded by black women. She took a job as a teacher after

graduation and regularly contributed poems to abolitionist periodicals. Soon, her reputation as a poet was equal to her reputation as an abolition activist. Later, her account of teaching on the Sea Islands in the early years of the Civil War became a classic of African-American literature.

There were other women who came out of the literary and anti-slavery societies to establish literary careers, including **Frances Ellen Watkins Harper,** the most-published African-American writer of the nineteenth century. But the greatest significance of these societies was almost certainly their contribution to the education of thousands of free black women, who in turn passed on their knowledge to their children, their students, and the black community at large. These free black women were ready when the greatest educational challenge in African-American history presented itself.

FREE TO LEARN

> Above all let us who have had an opportunity, who have educational advantages, modify our caste line—stoop down now and then and lift up others.
>
> Margaret Murray Washington, 1898

When the Civil War ended, there were millions of African Americans freed from slavery and ready to become full citizens of the United States. And almost all of them were illiterate. The underground slave schools, slave-quarters tutors, and occasional compassionate owners had educated only a tiny minority of the slave population.

The drive to educate this mass of humanity began even before the war ended. In

It is well known that thousands of white women journeyed to the South during and after the Civil War to teach newly emancipated slaves. It is less well known that black women also played a crucial role in the massive task of educating freed people. This is a schoolroom, circa 1902. (LIBRARY OF CONGRESS)

September of 1861, Mary Chase opened a day school for "contrabands"—the term given to slaves who escaped or were otherwise freed during the course of the war—in Alexandria, Virginia. Weeks later, the American Missionary Association (AMA) hired **Mary Peake** to teach at Fortress Monroe. Peake was a free black woman who had been teaching in Hampton, Virginia.

In 1862, Union forces took over the Sea Islands of South Carolina. Plantation owners fled, abandoning their homes and crops. Also left behind were thousands of slaves. The federal government sent agricultural supervisors to help harvest the crops and teachers to educate the new citizens.

Charlotte Forten was the only African American in the first group of teachers in what became known as the Port Royal Experiment. She remained on St. Helena until her health forced her to leave in 1864. Her account of teaching on the islands, published in the *Atlantic Monthly* in 1864, describes her approach, which included visiting homes, instructing people in health and cleanliness rules, and providing health care to the sick. The children responded:

> Coming to school is a constant delight and recreation for them. They come here as other children go to play. The older ones, doing the summer work in the field from early morning until eleven or twelve o'clock, and then come to school after their hard toil in the hot sun, as bright and anxious to learn as ever.

In the century to come, black teachers would often find themselves playing multiple roles. Frequently the only educated person in a small, rural community, the teacher was healer, letter-writer, arbiter of disputes, and counselor. She would teach sanitation along with geography and food preparation along with algebra. This may be one of the reasons teaching was considered a calling, rather than just a job.

It may also be one reason that education came to represent so much more to African Americans than learning letters or getting a degree. It was the road to freedom. It *was* freedom. Viewed by many whites as being immoral, lazy, and intellectually inferior, African Americans looked to education to counter such perceptions and to prepare themselves for the future and their newly earned freedom. Through education, blacks hoped to improve their economic, political, and social status.

The last two stanzas of the poem entitled "Learning to Read" by Frances Ellen Watkins Harper speaks in the voice of a woman of sixty and reveals what literacy meant to the old as well as the young.

> So I got a pair of glasses,
> And straight to work I went,
> And never stopped till I could read
> The Hymns and Testament.
>
> Then I got a little cabin
> A place to call my own—
> And I felt as independent
> As the queen upon her throne.

Booker T. Washington recalled, "It was a whole race trying to go to school. Few were too young and none were too old to make the attempt to learn."

In the late nineteenth century, most African Americans lived in the South. W. E. B. DuBois' 1901 study of the Negro Common School revealed that two years after the Civil War, fewer than 100,000 African-American children were enrolled in Southern schools. However, by 1900 more than 1.5 million were enrolled. Providing the opportunity for these education-hungry people to learn was an enormous task.

The Freedmen's Bureau, established by Congress in 1865 to coordinate aid and relief efforts for African Americans, was one of the first governmental institutions to support educational opportunities for blacks. Black and white missionary organizations also established elementary and secondary schools and colleges.

The American Missionary Association (AMA), was one of the largest organizations to establish such institutions. According to historian Robert C. Morris, there were many black women among the teachers the AMA sent all over the South. For example, in 1864, in Norfolk, Virginia, Blanche Harris, Clara C. Duncan, **Sara G. Stanley**, and Mary Watson were among the teachers employed by the AMA. Later, Edmonia Highgate left a better-paying job as principal of a high school in Binghamton, New York, to join the crusade to educate newly freed slaves.

There were black women among the teachers in AMA schools in other parts of the South as well. Mary Weston, daughter of a prominent Charleston family, taught free black girls in her home just before the war. She was arrested twice under antiliteracy laws. After the war, she became an AMA teacher. Frances Rollin, a women's rights activist and later wife of black legislator William J. Whipper, also taught for the AMA.

Black organizations and communities also were extremely instrumental in providing educational support. According to DuBois, between the years 1868 and 1870, blacks contributed $785,700 to their own education. Black women often were the driving force behind the establishment and maintenance of educational institutions.

In 1896, the **National Association of Colored Women** was founded in Washington, D.C. This organization, which by 1901 had chapters in twenty-six states, addressed issues as varied as health, education and Jim Crow laws. They gave continuing support to black schools and black teachers.

In 1900, the Women's Convention, an auxiliary to the National Baptist Convention, was formed. One of the Convention's major concerns was equal funding for black education. In his 1918 publication, *Darkwater*, W. E. B. DuBois wrote that three-fourths of the property of black churches resulted directly from the fund-raising efforts of

black women. He considered black women to be "the main pillars of those social settlements which we call churches." **Nannie Burroughs, Mary Mcleod Bethune**, and others were relentless fund-raisers for their churches to support the education of African Americans.

While many organizations were involved in supporting this crucial work financially, there was an even greater need: the need for teachers. Free black women from privileged families in the North could not fill that need for long. And white teachers, helpful as they were in the struggle, were not the answer. There must be more black teachers.

FREE TO TEACH

In 1865, it was estimated that at least 22,000 black teachers were needed immediately to work for the education of the newly freed. And they must be good teachers. Fanny Jackson Coppin, the first African-American woman to head an institution of higher learning, declared that "first-class pupils are possible only when we have first-class teachers, who are the great soul artists in the schoolroom, the makers of men and women." To gather this sort of force, three things would be needed: schools, motivation, and powerful leaders.

Coppin was one of the leaders, and she clearly stated the motivation. In an 1879 commencement address at the Institute for Colored Youth, she told her graduating students, "You can do much to alleviate the condition of our people. Do not be discouraged. The very places where you are needed most are those where you will get least pay. Do not resign a position in the South which pays you $12 a month as a teacher for one in Pennsylvania which pays $50." Teaching was a sacred profession, a service to the race.

As for the schools, private elementary and secondary institutions established after the Civil War educated the majority of African-American teachers. A number of black institutions of higher learning were established. By 1868, fifteen colleges had been chartered. Historian Linda Perkins notes that more than 70 percent of the teacher training took place in private black institutions. And most were supported by religious denominations.

Another of the leaders was **Anna Julia Haywood Cooper**. A feminist, educator, author, and lecturer, Cooper, born the daughter of slaves, was the first member of her family to attend school beyond the primary grades. She wrote that she decided to become a teacher shortly after kindergarten. She earned an A.B. in 1884 from Oberlin, became principal of M Street High School in Washington, D.C., and became the second president of Frelinghuysen University, also in Washington, D.C.

In 1925 Cooper graduated from the Sorbonne in France, becoming the fourth African-American woman to earn a Ph.D. She was sixty-six years old at the time. She was known for her staunch support of education for women. "Not the boys less, but the girls more," she argued in 1892.

Lucy Ellen Moten developed a first-rate teacher-training school for African Americans in Washington, D.C. But she had to overcome her own appeal as a woman to get the opportunity:

In 1883, the principalship of the Miner Normal School was vacant. Mr. Frederick Douglass, a member of the Miner Board, recommended Miss Lucy Moten for the position of principal. The Board acknowledged the excellent scholastic and personal fitness of Miss Moten for the position but feared that she was too youthful and far too fascinating to fill the position. Mr. Douglass called on Miss Moten and stated the Board's objections. He then asked her if she would be willing to give up going to the theatre, playing cards, and dancing to be favorably considered for the appointment. She accepted his advice and agreed to the terms. Mr. Douglass then recommended her a second time and upon his statement that, he himself, would stand

Anna Julia Haywood Cooper was a feminist, educator, author, and lecturer. Born the daughter of slaves, she was the first member of her family to attend school beyond the primary grades. She received her Ph.D. from the Sorbonne at the age of sixty-six.
(SCURLOCK STUDIO)

surety for her promise, the Board approved her appointment.

Moten served as principal for twenty-five years. Under her leadership, Miner Normal School gained the reputation as one of the top teacher-training institutions in the United States.

In an attempt to reach as many students as possible, black women initiated educational reform efforts in their institutions. When Fanny Jackson Coppin was elected principal of the Institute for Colored Youth in Philadelphia in 1869, she instituted curriculum changes to ensure that the institution reached the masses of African Americans. She established a normal school (where teachers and ministers were educated) and an industrial department where boys learned such trades as bricklaying, plastering, and carpentry, and girls learned dressmaking, millinery, and typing. Coppin was a pioneer of industrial education while Booker T. Washington was still a student.

Black woman educators often attempted to address specific issues that concerned African-American girls. Some believed, as **Lucy Laney** wrote: "To woman has been committed the responsibility of making the laws of society, making environments for children. She has the privilege and authority, God-given, to help develop into a noble man or woman the young life committed to her care. There is no nobler work entrusted to the hands of mortals."

Lucy Laney was among the first African-American women educators to establish a high school for girls. She attended AMA schools and graduated from the first normal class of Atlanta University. She founded the **Haines Normal and Industrial Institute** in Augusta, Georgia, in 1886 with the help of

the Presbyterian Board of Missions. Shortly after its founding, the institution became coeducational because of the need for a high school for both boys and girls.

Because of limited funding and the desire to provide education to as many as possible, African Americans usually established coeducational institutions. However, several founders were successful in establishing and maintaining all-female institutions.

In 1881, two white missionaries from New England, Sophia B. Packard and Harriet E. Giles, opened a school for young African-American girls in the basement of Atlanta's Friendship Baptist Church. It was called the Atlanta Baptist Female Seminary and offered an elementary education. In 1883, it expanded to offer a college preparatory course. In 1886, nurse's training was added, and in 1897, this became a college course. The school later became **Spelman College**. In 1901 it granted its first college degrees to Jane Anna Granderson and Claudia Turner White.

In 1888 Hartshorn Memorial College, founded in Richmond, Virginia, became the first educational institution in the United States to be chartered as a college for black women. In 1892, Mary Moor Booz, Harriet Amanda Miller, and Dixie Erma Williams graduated with B.S. degrees.

THE WOMEN OF TUSKEGEE

For despite their achievements, the world has not been willing to accept the contributions that women have made.

Mary McLeod Bethune

Too often, black women educators have not received credit for their contributions to education. Nowhere is this more true than in the case of Tuskegee Institute. Founded by Booker T. Washington, the Institute came to represent the industrial education movement. Washington's name was firmly linked to both the movement and the school. And yet, a great deal of the success of Tuskegee should be credited to two women who worked beside him as partners as well as helpmeets. **Olivia Davidson Washington** and, later, **Margaret Murray Washington** were both critically important contributors to the accomplishments of Tuskegee Institute.

Booker T. Washington considered Olivia Davidson the cofounder of Tuskegee. Perhaps history would have made the same judgment if she had not, many years later, married her colleague and been saddled with the label "Washington's second wife."

Born free in Mercer County, Virginia, Davidson began teaching school at sixteen in Ohio. She also taught during the summer in Mississippi and Arkansas. She entered the senior class at Hampton Institute in 1878. After Hampton, she completed two years of study at the Framingham, Massachusetts, State Normal School.

With nearly six years of teaching experience in several states, and training at Hampton and at Framingham, Davidson was well prepared for her role at Tuskegee. In 1881 she went to Alabama and, finding "literally nothing" at Tuskegee, worked tirelessly to build an institution. Booker T. Washington acknowledged that "the success of the school, especially during the first half dozen years of its existence, was due more to Miss Davidson than any one else."

Davidson was teacher, curriculum specialist, lady principal, and fund-raiser. She

Margaret Murray Washington was critically important to the success of Tuskegee Institute. (LIBRARY OF CONGRESS)

continued to raise funds for Tuskegee and to serve in many ways, even when her health did not permit her to work full time. She married Washington after the death of his first wife in 1886. Davidson's early death at the age of thirty-five is attributed to poor health and overexertion.

Booker T. Washington did not make colleagues of his wives. Instead, he made wives of his colleagues. Margaret Murray was first teacher and then lady principal at Tuskegee before she consented to marry Washington. Both before and after her marriage, she was a major figure in the life of the Institute.

Born to Lucy Murray, a black washerwoman, and a white father who died when she was seven, Margaret Murray entered Fisk University's preparatory school in 1881. After completing both her secondary work and college degree, she went to teach at Tuskegee in 1889. In 1900, she became the director of the department of domestic sciences ("laundering, cooking, dressmaking, plain sewing, millinery and mattress making"). She was integrally involved in the construction of Dorothy Hall, a housing facility for girls' industries.

She also served on the fifteen-person executive committee of Tuskegee. Booker T. Washington often was away from the institute fund-raising, sometimes for months at a time, and this committee was responsible for the day-to-day activities of the institution. Eventually, Murray became the dean of women.

In addition to providing leadership on the campus, she also provided outreach opportunities to the local black community. As were other woman educators during this period, Murray was the prime force behind social service programs. She formed the Tuskegee Woman's Club in 1895. Its purpose was to promote the "general intellectual development of women." By 1897 the club was actively involved in the community. It supported such projects as a public library and reading room, and a night school for working adults unable to attend school during the day.

On Saturdays, Murray devoted her time to mothers' meetings, which included sewing and racial uplift discussions. By 1904, such meetings were attracting nearly three hundred women.

Although there were a few efforts at single-sex education for black girls and women, coeducation was the norm for black education. Here, students in a Tuskegee Institute history class learn the story of Pocahontas. (LIBRARY OF CONGRESS)

The leadership, fund-raising, and outreach efforts provided by Davidson and Murray to the institution and the community insured the success of Tuskegee. Without such tireless support, it is doubtful whether Tuskegee Institute could have survived.

EFFECTS OF JIM CROW

Black women such as Cooper, Thompson, Yates, Moten, Laney, and the Washingtons attempted to educate the race at a perilous time. After 1877, the social, political, and economic climate for African Americans, especially in the South, had begun to worsen. Access to the political system for improvement of conditions became increasingly difficult for African Americans. During the 1890s, Jim Crow laws were being developed and enforced. Beginning in 1890, the "Mississippi Plan," created to eliminate black voters, was adopted by other Southern states.

Also in 1890, the Blair Bill, intended to reduce illiteracy among the Southern poor by providing federal funds for education, failed to pass in the U.S. Senate. In 1894, Congress repealed an 1870 Enforcement Act Provision that would have provided federal marshals and election supervisors to ensure that election practices in local communities did not violate blacks' right to vote.

Lynching of African Americans, the terrible weapon white Southerners used to deter black activism and advancement, averaged 103 per year from 1890 to 1900.

Furthermore, in 1896 the Supreme Court gave credence to "separate but equal" accommodations in the *Plessy* v. *Ferguson* case. And, in the Supreme Court's 1899

Pauli Murray survived her early educational experiences to become (to cite the subtitle of her autobiography) "a Black Activist, Feminist, Lawyer, Priest, and Poet." (SYLVIA JACOBS)

decision in the case of *Cumming* v. *School Board of Richmond County, Georgia,* blacks were denied the right to public secondary education.

The nationwide illiteracy rate among African Americans was 44.5 percent at a time when 90 percent of the African-American population of approximately nine million lived in the South. More than 60 percent lived in Georgia, Mississippi, Alabama, the Carolinas, and Louisiana.

Historian James D. Anderson, in *Black Education in the South, 1860–1935,* notes that, after 1900, the proportion of funding to black schools in the South dropped significantly and that from 1900 to 1920, although tax appropriations for building schoolhouses sharply increased in every Southern state, these states designated virtually none of this funding for the building of black schools.

This was the situation black teachers had to face at the end of the nineteenth and the beginning of the twentieth century. And, by the late nineteenth century, black women had become the majority among teachers in the educational system for blacks in the South. In 1890 the U.S. Census identified 15,100 black educators, of whom 7,864 were women and 7,236 were men. By 1900, there were 13,524 black women and 7,734 black men. And by 1910, more than two-thirds of the black educators in the United States were women.

Most were determined to make an impact on the deplorable conditions their students faced, such as these described by **Pauli Murray** in *Proud Shoes: The Story of an American Family*:

On one side of this road were long low warehouses where huge barrels of tobacco shavings and tobacco dust were stored. All day long our nostrils sucked in the brown silt like fine snuff in the air. West End looked more like a warehouse than a school. It was a dilapidated, rickety, two-story wooden building which creaked and swayed in the wind as if it might collapse . . . Outside it was scarred with peeling paint from many winters of rain and snow. At recess we [were] herded into a yard of cracked clay, barren of tree or bush, and played what games we could improvise like hopscotch or springboard, which we contrived by pulling rotted palings off the wooden fence and placing them on brickbats. . . .

The floors were bare and splintery, the plumbing was leaky, the drinking fountains broken and the toilets in the basement smelly and constantly out of order. We'd have to wade through pools of foul water to get to them. . . .

Murray's description was of a Southern school, but it could easily have applied to a black school almost anywhere in the country. During this same period, Daniel A. Brooks, a teacher and principal in Philadelphia, described some black Northern schools as "old, frame buildings, gas-lighted with coal stoves in many rooms, and outdoor water-closets." In 1916, a Northern Philadelphia black community petitioned the school superintendent for a new building to replace the existing structure built in 1866. Although the superintendent promised to "look into the matter," major repairs were not made until 1925.

The attempt of Northern states to provide adequate educational facilities to a growing urban population, including a large number of black Southern migrants, is complex. After 1920, an increased number of African Americans migrated from the South in search of economic opportunities for themselves and educational opportunities for their children. However, most Northern states, like their Southern counterparts, reacted to the "Negro problem" by creating public schools for blacks that generally were inferior to those for whites. Increased segregation, overcrowding, and an increase in the number of older children in elementary schools were the results.

It is important to understand a common belief of African Americans that an individual's education belongs to the community. It allows one to comprehend both the struggle of black women to obtain an education and their struggle to uplift the race by becoming educators. Black women often were socialized to see teaching as being the single most important thing they could do for their people. A part of that socialization was the belief that the ultimate goal of educating the race could be reached despite obstacles such as the kind of small, poorly built, dilapidated, unfurnished, unsanitary buildings as the one described by Pauli Murray.

Mary Pauline Fitzgerald Dame, a rural schoolteacher in North Carolina, wrote that "I walked four miles from my mother's country home to school, through rain, snow and fair weather. I was young and healthy and often waded through snow up to my knees. I would have to keep on my wet clothes all day and walk back home in the same way." She described one of her schools as a "one room log cabin with only benches made from a split log with holes bored in the end and small trees sawed so as to make legs, no backs and no desks. The children had to sit on them and swing their legs over the side, leaving their books and lunch pails on the floor."

Inadequate facilities were only one of the many difficulties that black women faced every day of their teaching lives. They usually taught a larger number of students and a larger number of older students in elementary grades. Most black women taught in rural elementary schools, which meant that, like their students, they usually walked to and from school, sometimes two or three miles. They were more than likely to teach in one- and two-teacher schools, as compared to white teachers who taught in schools with three or more teachers.

A 1930 survey revealed that eleven Southern states spent an average of $12.57 per black child, as opposed to $44.31 to educate a white child. At that time, the average expenditure for the nation was $99.00 per child. As late as 1937, 64 percent of schools for Southern African Americans were one-teacher schools, and 19 percent were two-teacher schools. Also, black educators were more likely than white educators to teach or supervise a group of children with a wider range of ages and cognitive skills. And in addition, black women were paid less than black and white men and also less than white women.

Black educators also were forced by law and custom to work with preconceptions as to what education should be for black children. Those preconceptions brought pressure on teachers from many different directions. The black women who taught in one-room schoolhouses, and those who ran larger educational institutions, all became adept at embracing the ideals of the dominant group and simultaneously molding these ideals to fit the needs of their communities.

Industrial education presents a case in point. Originally, educating black young people for the jobs that would be available to them in a racist society seemed a practical thing to do. At the same time, limiting black education to that sort of vocational training started a vicious circle. Both Northern philanthropists and Southern whites saw the validity of the first point, but not the second. A great deal of pressure was put on African Americans to embrace industrial education and to accept their appointed place in society as cooks, maids, and field hands. However, black teachers managed to use these preconceptions to their own advantage.

Although many embraced industrial education, they also encouraged academic and higher education. And they used the practical lessons of sewing, cooking, and cleaning to improve the conditions of their communities and their schools, and even to fund the kind of wider education that the dominant society frowned upon for African Americans. They deliberately concealed their activism for educational improvements under the cloak of industrial education.

Such invisibility created a dual perception. On the one hand, these educators were viewed as doing exactly what they were told, as evidenced by the writings of such historians as Horace Mann Bond and Carter G. Woodson. And on the other hand, they were quite visible in the black community, raising funds for educational needs and working tirelessly to improve the living conditions of the race.

Black women often taught in rural schools, under wretched conditions, but their accomplishments were tremendous, especially considering that they worked during periods of intense hostility toward women and men of color. Recognizing obstacles such as racism and sexism, poverty, and often indifference concerning funding for the education of African Americans, black women resolved to "make the most of it" by adhering to the philosophy that one individual can make a difference.

JEANES SUPERVISORS

During the heyday of industrial education reform, the experiences of a group of teachers called the Jeanes Supervisors paint a vivid picture of the struggle to uplift the race. They also reveal the importance of a holistic education, one in which teachers are active participants in the community and the school. One Jeanes teacher in Georgia described her role as learning to do the "next need thing." People from the community called upon her to "Improve my soil, add my account at the commissary, feed my children, take me to the hospital, bury my mother, write my son, read this letter, mend my steps, find a minister or justice of the peace to get me married, show me how to build a sanitary privy."

Jeanes supervisors were paid primarily from a fund established in 1907 by Anna T. Jeanes, a white Quaker woman interested in contributing to the education of African Americans in rural areas. Established with a donation of $1,000,000, the **Jeanes Fund** was meant to encourage "the rudimentary education of Colored people residing in rural districts" in the Southern states of Delaware, Maryland, Virginia, West Virginia, North Carolina, South Carolina, Georgia, Florida, Alabama, Mississippi, Louisiana, Texas, Arkansas, Missouri, Kentucky, and Tennessee.

The **Jeanes Teachers** program was modeled after the work of **Virginia Randolph**, an African-American teacher in Honrico County, Virginia, who became the first Jeanes teacher. In discussing the importance of education to her family, Randolph noted that her mother worked outside the home three days of the week, washed at home for five families, and washed and ironed sometimes all night in order for her four children to attend school. Randolph herself began teaching at sixteen and developed a way of combining academic subjects with practical education and of working with the community that foreshadowed the methods of more contemporary groups such as the Peace Corps.

Jeanes Supervising Industrial Teachers were a vital force in black education from 1908 to 1968. At an average salary, in the early 1900s, of $45 per month for seven months, they visited schools and encouraged teachers to teach sanitation, sewing, cooking, basket making, chair caning, and mat making. They were expected to encourage industrial education and community involvement.

Jeanes teachers organized men and women into "Improvement Leagues" or "Betterment Associations," whose purpose was to improve the "living conditions among the colored people." Under the leadership of the Jeanes teachers, communities painted or whitewashed schoolhouses, homes, and outhouses. They raised money to build better schoolhouses and to lengthen the school terms. They organized home and school gardens, tomato clubs, and corn clubs. In general, they "promote[d] higher standards of living, integrity of character, honesty, and thrift among all people."

In addition, they improved the quality of instruction in county group meetings, reading circles, study groups, extension courses, libraries, and summer schools, and organized programs dealing with health and industrial arts. They taught in Moonlight Schools, which were established to teach illiterate adults how to read and write. These

Jeanes Fund teachers did everything from write letters to advise on sanitary conditions. This photo shows an "Annual Exhibit of Jeanes School/Jeanes Fund Work" in Faquier County, Virginia. The Jeanes teacher in the photo is Esther Williams Tyler. (DONNA HOLLIE)

schools usually were in session at night, and often teachers were not compensated financially for their services. After working during the day, these women labored tirelessly at night to educate the parents and grandparents of their day students.

As noted by historian Cynthia Neverdon-Morton, in *Afro-American Women of the South and the Advancement of the Race, 1895–1925*, Jeanes teachers initially encountered resistance in some African-American communities. Parents objected to the curriculum, which stressed industrial education, because they felt it was being forced on them by whites. The attempts of Jeanes teachers to balance industrial and academic education and their genuine concern for the betterment of the community—illustrated by a supervisor using money won at a state fair for an industrial exhibit to extend the term for seventh graders—overcame the initial objections and endeared them to communities.

In addition to teaching reading, writing, and arithmetic, teachers taught students and parents how to grow and preserve foods such as peaches, apples, corn, beans, and tomatoes. The Jeanes teachers raised money in churches and through the sale of livestock and produce from gardens. In 1928, Jeanes teachers raised more than $41,000 for the improvement of rural education.

During this period many African Americans and whites lived in unhealthy conditions. Chamber pots and a few outhouses or privies were the norm. Houses often were dilapidated. Hookworm disease, tuberculosis, and syphilis were prevalent, and doctors scarce. Few institutions were organized to care for the poor and the ill. Jeanes teachers, and African-American woman teachers in general, often took on such responsibilities.

These powerful black women helped community members to form cooperatives to purchase land for schools and families. And they worked with parents in parent-teacher associations to purchase school buses and playground equipment, and to improve schools, buildings, and grounds.

Julius Rosenwald, president of Sears, Roebuck and Company, provided funding for rural schoolhouses called Rosenwald Schools. The Rosenwald contract stipulated that African-American community members match or exceed the amount requested from the Fund. Black woman educators were extremely instrumental in securing financial and in-kind funding for these schools. They organized meetings, solicited funding, and oversaw the operation of these schools.

Black woman educators constantly encouraged community members to contribute to educational systems, even if it meant creating a debt. In 1915, African-American citizens in a Southern county mortgaged their property and borrowed $3,500 from a local bank. "They had to do this as it is hard to raise money at this time of year," wrote Mrs. P. L. Bryd, a black teacher in Wake County, North Carolina. The parents pledged this amount and promised to pay those who had borrowed the money in November. She noted that the parents had raised the required amount of $4,100 for a Rosenwald school and requested from the St te Board of Education the initiation of the plans for the building.

Also during 1915, blacks in one Southern county deeded to the county board of education a large, nearly completed building containing "four classrooms, and nine acres of land." They also volunteered to raise $500 to pay part of the salary of a black farm demonstrator; $200 to help pay for the salary of a teacher; and $150 to complete the school building.

In an effort to explain why state and local funding was not being provided for black education, many whites argued that blacks were not willing to support education. Clearly this was not the case. With few resources but strong convictions, African Americans made tremendous sacrifices. And there were some black women who devoted their entire lives, virtually every waking moment, to the cause of education. They stand out in African-American history like beacons.

THE FOUNDERS

One of the most significant contributions of African-American women to education has been made through the founding of educational institutions. Mary McLeod Bethune is an example of an institution-builder during this period who worked against tremendous odds.

Bethune was born in 1875 in South Carolina and attended Scotia Seminary in North Carolina. After graduating, she planned to serve as a missionary in Africa. Like others during this time, Bethune was interested in saving souls in other countries. However, the Presbyterian Church rejected her application, refusing to send African-American missionaries to Africa. Instead, Bethune taught in Georgia and Florida.

In 1904, she opened the Daytona Educational and Industrial Institute in a rented house with five woman students. By 1918, it was a four-year high school, Daytona Normal and Industrial Institute, with one of its missions being the training of African-American teachers for Florida's public schools. In 1923, the school was merged with Cookman Institute (founded in 1872), and became **Bethune-Cookman College**. When Bethune gave up the presidency of the College in 1942, the institution had cash receipts of more than $155,000 and a $600,000 physical plant that included thirty-four acres, fourteen buildings, and a farm.

Another African-American woman educator actively involved in racial uplift urged her students to "Work, Support Thyself, to Thine Own Powers Appeal." This was the first motto of the **National Training School for Women and Girls**, founded in 1909 in Washington, D.C., by Nannie Helen Burroughs. In the first twenty-five years of its existence, the school served more than 2,000 women from across the United States, Africa, and the Caribbean.

Like Bethune, Burroughs experienced a disappointment in her early years. Soon after graduation from high school, her domestic science teacher failed to keep a promise to hire her as an assistant. It was thought that her dark skin color and social class kept her from attaining this position. Provoked by this experience, Burroughs devoted her life to religious and educational work to improve the social, political, and economic status of her race, especially that of women.

Charlotte Hawkins Brown was only nineteen when she founded the Alice Freeman Palmer Memorial Institute in Sedalia, North Carolina. Like Bethune, Burroughs, and others, she encountered hardships along the way. She helped to finance her school by giving music recitals and recitations at New England resorts. She also had an intense pride and was proud of the number of times she was ejected from Pullman berths and first-class railway seats in the South.

Brown spent forty years building Palmer Memorial Institute from an elementary school serving local children to a high

Bethune-Cookman College is the only historically black college founded by a woman that continues to thrive today. Its founder, Mary McLeod Bethune, is seen here with the school's choir. (LIBRARY OF CONGRESS)

school and junior college enrolling black students from the United States and abroad. It became one of the foremost finishing schools in the country.

Many black women of this era looked upon the teaching profession as a service and a calling and went about their task of educating as did ministers in savings souls. Lack of funds, lack of training, and lack of supplies inspired an independent resourcefulness among these educators. They were high achievers because tremendous responsibilities at a very early age prepared them for larger-

than-life roles. Such personal characteristics, as exemplified by Brown and other educators, would continue to be sorely tested in the late 1940s, into the 1950s, and beyond.

CONFRONTATION, CONTINUITY, AND CHANGE

I'm a Negro, born black in a white man's land. I am a teacher. I have spent my whole life teaching citizenship to children who really aren't citizens. They have fulfilled all the requirements for citizenship; many of their fathers and brothers have died for their country; but this is not enough to qualify them to vote, to receive a decent education. . . . I can no longer aid in their education, because I joined in the movement to help them to claim their citizenship.

Septima Poinsette Clark, 1958

Separate and unequal schools have been one of the most destructive forms of segregation. In the 1940s, the majority of African-American classrooms, public or private, elementary or secondary, did not contain rows of uniform seating, a blackboard, a teacher's desk, classroom equipment, and a collection of books and papers. Lola Solice, a black schoolteacher in North Carolina during this period, noted that the only supplies black teachers received from the county were a "broom and a bucket."

Teachers were required to use their salaries to purchase chalk, pencils, and other supplies. Textbooks for the black schools were rented by their parents, and these were usually secondhand books from the white schools. Most African Americans felt that they had to take a stand against an inferior educational system, and they either openly or secretly confronted the system.

In 1938, for example, Pauli Murray unsuccessfully attempted to be admitted to the graduate school at the University of North Carolina, Chapel Hill. On December 14, 1938, the dean of the graduate school wrote, "members of your race are not admitted to the University."

After lengthy correspondence and much publicity, Murray gave up her attempt to enter UNC. The university based its decision on the fact that she was an out-of-state resident. Ironically, Murray's white great-aunt, Mary Ruffin Smith, had left part of her estate to the university and created a permanent trust fund for the education of students. All of her grandmother Murray's immediate white male family had attended UNC, and her grandfather had served on the Board of Trustees.

In 1946, Murray applied to Harvard University Law School for an advanced degree. This time she was denied admission because the school did not admit women. She was admitted to the University of California at Berkeley and earned an LL.M. degree in 1945. And in 1965, she became the first black person to receive a doctor of juridical science degree from Yale University Law School.

Septima Clark (shown here on the left with a "civil rights group") became the director of the Highlander Folk School's workshop program in 1956. The Highlander workshops provided a valuable forum where individuals could share their experiences, address common problems, and develop strategies and tools for achieving change in their communities.
(STATE HISTORICAL SOCIETY OF WISCONSIN)

In 1946, Murray applied to Harvard University Law School for an advanced degree. This time she was denied admission because the school did not admit women. She was admitted to the University of California at Berkeley and earned an LL.M. degree in 1945. And in 1965, she became the first black person to receive a doctor of juridical science degree from Yale University Law School.

Some organizations, such as the **National Association for the Advancement for Colored People** (NAACP), sought relief on behalf of individuals through the courts. In an attempt to dismantle the unequal educational systems provided to African Americans, the NAACP brought several suits before the Supreme Court during the late 1940s.

One such suit involved **Ada Lois Sipuel [Fisher]**, a black woman who applied for admission to the University of Oklahoma Law School in 1946. She was denied admission to law school solely on the basis of her race, and the NAACP entered a lengthy court battle. In 1948, in *Ada Lois Sipuel* v. *Board of Regents*, the Supreme Court ordered the university to admit Sipuel and sent the case back to the Oklahoma high court. The Oklahoma court ordered the university to admit Sipuel, open a separate school for her, or to suspend the white law school until it opened one for blacks.

The university responded by creating, overnight, a separate law school, roping off a small section of the state capitol in Oklahoma City for "colored students" and assigning three law teachers to instruct Miss Sipuel. Sipuel was outraged, of course, and so were some students and professors at the University, who staged a protest rally. Thurgood Marshall took the case back to the

Supreme Court. In the summer of 1949, Sipuel was admitted to the law school. By that time, she was married and pregnant with her first child. In spite of the added challenge, she graduated in 1951.

After the Sipuel case, states could not require African Americans to wait until they established separate graduate or professional schools. This was one of dozens of cases the NAACP sponsored that attacked the "separate but equal" doctrine. As each court's decision came in, it became clearer and clearer that the doctrine was becoming legally indefensible. Finally, the Legal Defense Fund team decided to attack the situation head on.

Marshall, **Constance Baker Motley**, and other NAACP lawyers prepared *Brown* v. *Board of Education*, the landmark school desegregation case. The Supreme Court ruled in 1954 that there really was no such thing as "separate but equal" in education. Schools had to desegregate.

From the first suit, *Sarah C. Roberts* v. *City of Boston* in 1848, to a little over a century later in *Brown* v. *Board of Education*, black women had been at the center of confrontations. Although the suit on Sarah Robert's behalf did not force changes, Linda Brown's suit provided a landmark case that held laws enforcing segregation in public schools to be unconstitutional. But the fight was not over. In some ways, it had just begun.

Most Southern states actively searched for and found ways to avoid integration, even after the Brown decision. In this, they were aided by the Eisenhower administration's failure to back up the Supreme Court's ruling. The result was a wave of civil rights protests that swept across the country and far beyond the bounds of the schoolroom.

The pivotal action in terms of school desegregation came in 1957. Nine black students in Little Rock, Arkansas, were enrolled in a local all-white high school. Arkansas' Governor Orval Faubus, with an eye on reelection by white constituents, called out the Arkansas National Guard to prevent the students' admission into the school. Even after the guard was withdrawn, white supremacists blocked the students' entry. Finally, President Eisenhower federalized the National Guard and ordered them to protect the students.

In the court case that arose out of the Little Rock incident, *Cooper* v. *Aaron*, the Supreme Court ruled that the *Brown* decision must be enforced by state governments. Also resulting from the incident was the Civil Rights Act of 1957, the first real attempt by the federal government to assume responsibility for the enforcement of civil rights. However, the Act of 1957 was toothless. Not until 1964 was legislation passed that allowed the federal government to take legal action and offer federal assistance in the cause of school desegregation.

The need for further action is clear from the statistics. In 1964, a full ten years after the *Brown* ruling, only 2.3 percent of Southern black students were attending integrated schools. The law of the land clearly was not being followed. The Civil Rights Act of 1964 was passed to change that situation, in other areas as well as in education.

The Civil Rights Act of 1964 was quickly followed by the Elementary and Secondary Education Act (ESEA) of 1965. This landmark legislation made the doctrine of equal educational opportunity a national priority and backed up that stand with federal funds to implement it. There were five "titles," or specific areas of concern. Title I allocated funds for the education of the children of low-income families. Title I became Chapter I when the ESEA was reauthorized in 1981, and 47 percent of the children helped by the plan have been African American.

Still, desegregation was not moving swiftly. Voluntary integration simply didn't work. For example, volunteer integration for students went into effect in 1965 in the Durham, North Carolina, county school system, and yet, as late as January 1970, ten blacks out of a total of 2,700 had agreed to attend a white school, and no white students out of a total of 8,600 had agreed to attend a black school.

In 1965, only 7.5 percent of African-American students in the South were in integrated schools. In 1966, the figure had risen to 12.5 percent. A report from the U.S. Commissioner of Education in 1966 stated that "American public education remains largely unequal in most regions of the country, including all those where Negroes form any significant part of the population." By 1968, still only 32 percent of Southern black students were in integrated classrooms. The Supreme Court, in *Green* v. *County School Board* in 1968, decided that was not good enough. Immediate desegregation was ordered.

In the meantime, individual teachers were at the center of the battle. First they fought for change and then they became crucial to making it work. When forced integration was implemented in the 1970s, mixed feelings—anger, anxiety, pessimism, optimism, and a general bewilderment on the part of many students, black and white, were the result. Because they belonged to two groups that had few positive ties, (the teachers and the black community), black teachers often served as linchpins in this new system. They were interpreters of culture and mediators.

Some white teachers requested help from black teachers with their problems dealing with black students, or sought suggestions about a more inclusive curriculum. Similarly, black students with problems with white teachers often sought out black teachers.

Black women in administrative roles also facilitated the change, often by confronting myths. Elizabeth Schmoke Randolph recalled an incident in the 1960s when she served as principal of a school in Charlotte, North Carolina:

I never will forget one principal who called me on the first day of bussing, and she was going to get some black kids in her school. She called me and asked me how she was going to treat the parents. "How am I going to act when these parents bring their kids to school?" And I said, "Well, how do you act when white parents bring their kids to school?" I said, "There's absolutely no difference. You just act the same way, as all your other students." So at the end of the day she called me and thanked me for what I had told her to do. "Really, there's absolutely no difference, the parents brought their kids to school, wanted to meet the teacher, I took them around and showed them the school, the parents and the children and the teachers, and nothing happened." I said, "Well, I didn't expect anything to happen!" I said, "I am so glad that you learned a lesson today."

During the initial period of integrating schools, the success or failure of the system depended mainly on educators, and to a greater extent, black woman educators. The outcome of a long, hard fight for equal education opportunities, fought in the court systems, now rested mainly on the shoulders of these teachers and students.

There were definitely negative aspects to the change. A National Educational Association (NEA) study in 1972 revealed that African Americans had lost 30,000 teaching positions since 1954 in seventeen Southern and border states because of desegregation and discrimination. Some lost their jobs because of their participation in the battle for educational equality.

Septima Clark began teaching in 1916 at the age of eighteen. Forty years later, in 1956, her teaching contract with the South Carolina education board was not renewed. On April 19, 1956, the South Carolina legislature passed a law that barred city employees from affiliating themselves with any civil rights organization. Because Clark had openly confronted an unequal system, becoming an agitator for civil rights, requesting equal salaries for black teachers, and refusing to dissociate herself from the NAACP, she was fired.

Jo Ann Robinson, a crucial organizer and initiator of the Montgomery Bus Boycott of 1955–56, kept a low profile as long as possible in order to maintain her teaching position at Alabama State College. Robinson and other members of the **Women's Political Council of Montgomery, Alabama,** were responsible for producing and distributing the leaflets announcing the boycott. They also organized carpooling services and provided grassroots organizational structures to sustain the boycott for an entire year. Even though Robinson worked for a black university, the reaction of those in power to her participation in civil rights activities resulted in her resignation.

The challenges Clark and Robinson presented to the system resulted in their being forced out of their respective educational institutions. And they were not alone in paying for their convictions. Still other black women lost their jobs when black and white schools were combined. Fewer teachers were needed for one school than for two, and black women were the first to be terminated.

Also when schools were combined, it was usually the black schools that were closed, and the high schools became elementary schools. White families were not willing to allow their kids to attend many of black schools because of the condition they were in.

Losing schools and black teachers in their communities was a terrible blow to African Americans. For one thing, when the schools closed, black people lost community centers, since the schools often served in this capacity. Schools provided space for programs of all kinds, from athletic to artistic and cultural, allowing educational opportunities for the entire community.

More important, the community lost the black woman teacher, she who had been so much more than a classroom instructor. Besides her leadership, the community also lost its educational mediator. For decades she had interpreted and shaped educational doctrines to meet the needs of individual communities, schools, and students. She had used the resources of industrial education to provide solid academic instruction. She had found ways to use any funds she could get her hands on to serve the specific requirements of her students, their parents and grandparents, and everyone in the community who needed education. Suddenly, in far too many schools, she was gone.

Soon, a cry went up for decentralization, local control. The black community is still trying to regain what it lost in the necessary but often wrong-headed move toward desegregation.

As segregation under law, de jure, was rooted out in the South, there was another problem in the North. Legally, there was no segregation. In fact, de facto, it was rampant. In 1971, because of legal rulings and federal enforcement actions, 79 percent of black students in the South were attending integrated schools. In the same year, in the North, only 43 percent of black students were in integrated schools.

No one knew exactly what to do about de facto segregation in 1971, and the situation has not significantly improved since then. Two of the methods tried were magnet schools and metropolitan redistricting.

Magnet schools were established in order to draw students from all parts of a school district. Often they provided a certain academic emphasis, such as fine arts or mathematics and science. The result was often a high quality of education and a racial mix in these particular schools. In smaller cities, magnet schools have been quite successful. But in the largest cities, they have provided little increased opportunity for those who need it most. Entrance standards often keep out all but middle-class black students.

Metropolitan redistricting, combining urban and suburban school districts, has had a checkered history. Where the courts have been able to enforce it, it has been effective. Indeed, it has been the most useful tool for defeating de facto segregation for the past three decades. However, a 1995 Supreme Court ruling concerning the Kansas City school system set a disturbing new precedent. It stated, in effect, that the state of Missouri was not responsible for the segregated condition of the Kansas City school system and therefore was not obligated to pay for magnet schools or legislate metropolitan redistricting.

One of the most effective programs to improve educational opportunities has been the Head Start program. Operated by the Office of Economic Opportunity since 1965, it has provided preschool training for poor children aged three to five. Head Start also works with parents to prepare them to handle their responsibilities vis-à-vis their children's educations. Many studies have demonstrated that the Head Start program clearly is useful.

Clarity is a rare commodity in discussions of American education, especially where questions of race and gender are concerned. But two things are obvious. First, there are serious and continuing problems. Second, they are not going to go away by themselves.

In 1983, the National Commission on Excellence in Education published a report that stated that "the education foundations of our society are presently being eroded by a rising tide of mediocrity that threatens our very future as a nation and a people." The report went on to say that the poor and minority groups were most at risk.

Perhaps sometimes we need commissions to tell us what we already know. Other times, we need to be told clearly and without mitigation what we ought to know. In 1989, the National Research Council issued a report that stated that virtually all of the progress that has been made in increasing equality between blacks and whites in this country has been the result of "purposeful actions and policies by government and private institutions." If those actions stop, the report contends, progress almost certainly will stop as well.

FOR THE SAKE OF THE CHILDREN

We ignore the needs of Black children, poor children, and handicapped children in this country.

Marian Wright Edelman

A black girl today has a 1-in-7 chance of dropping out of school before her high school graduation; a 2-in-5 chance of having a child before she reaches her twentieth birthday; a 1-in-21 chance of being the victim of a violent crime during her teen years. That same black girl has a less than 1-in-21,000 chance of receiving a Ph.D. in mathematics, engineering, or the physical sciences; a 1-in-891 chance of becoming a physician; and a 1-in-356 chance of becoming a lawyer.

One in four black male children drops out of high school before graduation.

Two out of three black public school children attend schools where the majority of the students are from ethnic minorities.

Black high school graduates are about half as likely as white graduates to have taken advanced courses in science and mathematics.

Black students are about half as likely as white students to complete college.

Nearly one third of the increase in the earnings gap between blacks and whites between 1976 and 1990, according to the National Bureau of Economics Research, can be accounted for by the inability of black workers to use computers.

Life for a black child in the United States is not easy. The educational statistics are bad; other statistics are much worse. Those statistics paint a picture of gangs, killings, children born to teenagers, infant mortality, unemployment, desperate poverty. Black women have always known that those two sets of statistics go together. They have long considered education to be their most important contribution to the uplift of the race. They founded and paid for public high schools at a time when states would not support them. They built institutions by raising funds a penny at a time. Through the eighteenth, nineteenth, and twentieth centuries, they have agitated for equality and supported educational opportunities for young and old.

Support for education often comes from women with seemingly the least to give. In the 1790s, Katie Ferguson washed laundry and catered food in order to support a school for poor blacks and whites. In 1886, **Ida B. Wells** was unable to pay her landlady, Mrs. Powell, due to the common practice of irregular payment of teachers. Wells wrote in her diary that she was upset because Mrs. Powell was determined to "hire herself out" in order to earn money so that Wells could continue living with her and most importantly, remain in the community and teach. Lucy Ellen Moten, after a life as an educator, left more than $51,000 to her alma mater, Howard University.

Who, today, is working for the children? **Marva Collins** is. An innovative, nationally known black educator, she openly challenged a system that failed to educate all its children with equal commitment and success. In 1975, she established the Westside Preparatory School, an alternative system for black children on Chicago's West Side. Her success received national attention, and she has served as a consultant in establishing similar schools for other cities. Like **Virginia Randolph**, she understands the needs of the community and has improvised and developed programs to educate the neglected. And, like Bethune, she established an institution in order to meet those needs.

Willa Player was one of the first of such leaders when she became president of Bennett College in 1955. She was the first black woman president of a college since Mary McLeod Bethune founded Bethune College. Committed to civil rights and equal opportunities for women, after retiring from Bennett she became the director of the Division of Institutional Development in the Bureau of Postsecondary Education in D.C. She established Title III, which served as a major source of support for historically black and other minority institutions of higher education.

Mary Frances Berry became known for her uncompromising position in the "struggle for African-American liberation and justice." She was the first African-American woman to serve as the chancellor of a major research university, the University of Colorado at Boulder. Historian Berry also served as assistant secretary for education in the Department of Health, Education, and Welfare from 1977 to 1979.

Visionaries such as **Marguerite Ross Barnett**, who served as vice chancellor of academic affairs at the City University of New York from 1983 to 1986, worked tirelessly to establish programs for high school students from poor families. Barnett's programs smoothed their transition from high school, to college, to the labor force. In 1990, Barnett was appointed president of the University of Houston. She was the first woman president of the University. In 1992, she died, due to complications from cancer. But her model for linking minority high school students and colleges serves as an example for present and future educators. Like Mary Mcleod Bethune, Barnett and others were successful fund-raisers, organizers, and believers that higher education could solve social problems in their communities.

Regina Goff was appointed in 1961 as the Assistant Commissioner in the Office of Disadvantaged and Handicapped, Office of Education, HEW. She also was responsible for the Head Start program. **Barbara Ann Sizemore** served as the Superintendent of Washington D.C., public schools from 1973 to 1975. Marian Wright Edelman became the first black person, and the second woman, to chair the Spelman College Board of Trustees in 1980. And, in 1987, **Johnnetta Betsch Cole** became the president of Spelman College.

In the last few decades, the tradition of service and commitment has begun to pay off in terms of responsibility and authority. There are now more than three dozen African-American woman presidents of colleges and universities.

Marian Wright Edelman continues to make the Children's Defense Fund, founded in the 1970s, the nation's most effective advocate for children. And Oseola McCarty donated the savings of a lifetime of hard work to fund a scholarship.

VALINDA LITTLEFIELD

A

American Teachers Association

"We Win Battles by Social Action, Education Will Win Social War: The American Teachers Association and Black Women Educators . . . Support Freedom through Education."

These statements headed an advertisement in the *Negro History Bulletin* for a joint membership in the American Teachers Association (ATA) and the **Association for the Study of Negro Life and History (ASNLH)** in 1965, one year before the ATA merged with the National Education Association (NEA). For the twenty-six years of its existence, the ATA represented black schoolteachers struggling to achieve parity with their white counterparts while simultaneously educating young black men and women to have pride in their race and its achievements. This dual struggle, for equity and autonomy, marked the transition from the separate institutions of the segregated South to integrated institutions.

Although black women have been in the forefront of the struggle for education, their role in that history has been relegated to biographical sketches of prominent educators and school founders such as **Mary McLeod Bethune, Charlotte Hawkins Brown, Fanny Jackson Coppin,** and **Nannie Helen Burroughs**. However, by the last decade of the nineteenth century their numbers had begun to exceed those of black male teachers. By 1900, black women teachers outnumbered black men two to one and

represented a major force in the teaching profession. In many school districts married women were barred from teaching until the 1920s, and those women who did find jobs tended to work in rural schools for wages that fell below those of white male and female teachers and black male teachers. Despite these barriers, black women increasingly moved into teaching because it offered status and autonomy for educated women within the bounds of the community's accepted norms of women's roles. The history of these black women schoolteachers and their struggle for autonomy is reflected in the institutional history of the organizations in which they were active, as well as their individual biographies.

The ATA represents one such organization. In 1939, the National Association of Teachers in Colored Schools (NATCS), an organization of black schoolteachers founded in 1904, became the ATA. Carter G. Woodson's ASNLH worked closely with the NATCS and later the ATA to promote the teaching of black history in America's schools. In addition to publishing the *Journal of Negro History,* Woodson began in 1937 to publish the *Negro History Bulletin* specifically for the many public school teachers and administrators who were establishing local branches of ASNLH. This latter publication publicized the activities of NATCS members as well as ATA plans and programs. Mary McLeod Bethune wrote in 1938 on the importance of teaching black history:

"Through accurate research and investigation, we serve so to supplement, correct, re-orient, and annotate the story of world progress as to enhance the standing of our group in the eyes of all men. In the one hand, we bring pride to our own; in the other, we bear respect from the others." This statement, and the work of ATA (and NATCS) in conjunction with ASNLH to promote "Negro history," reflects the dual goal of empowering black students and educating the white community about the accomplishments and needs of black people.

In July 1926, an interracial committee of the NEA and the NATCS was formed to investigate issues surrounding black education. Originally titled "A Committee on Problems in Colored Schools," in 1928 it was reorganized and became the "Committee to Cooperate with the National Association of Teachers in Colored Schools." The committee's three major areas of study were the portrayal of black people in textbooks, the unequal distribution of federal funds for education along racial lines, and the development of materials on race relations for teacher training and classroom usage. Several of the NATCS members on the committee also served on the White House Conference on Child Health and Protection during the early 1930s and brought issues of black child health to the attention of the NEA. In addition the committee put together plans for a film that would portray black history in America, focusing on black people's successes in literature, art, business, education, and music.

The joint committee of the NATCS and NEA, by working together, forged a relationship that initiated the overall process of integration. For example, after World War

II, two publications designed by Ambrose Caliver, a member of the joint committee and a prominent black educator from Washington, D.C., were circulated in cooperation with the Commission on the Defense of Democracy through Education: "Education of Teachers for Improving Majority-Minority Relationships" and "Sources of Instructional Materials on Negroes." These publications were typical of the joint committee's materials designed to broaden educators' knowledge of race relations and black history.

A five-year program that expanded and consolidated the NEA after World War II accelerated the organization's efforts to enlist black teachers among its ranks. Mildred Fenner, in her 1945 history of the NEA, recalls a founding principle of the organization when writing of this program: "What we want is an Association which embraces all the teachers of our whole country."

In 1947, the joint committee officially called for the integration of black teachers into the NEA. In the past, individual black teachers, as well as delegates from local associations, had participated in annual conventions; however, it was not until 1947 that state associations permitted direct affiliation with the NEA, following rules changes. Thus black teachers were able to participate in the NEA before southern schools were desegregated, marking a transition from separate professional associations to a more integrated national system. The ATA's work in bringing racial issues to the forefront of the NEA agenda was central to this transformation.

In 1955, the NEA agreed to work for school desegregation in accordance with the *Brown* v. *Board of Education* decision a year before. Reporting to the annual NEA convention, the joint committee stated in 1955: "All efforts toward cooperative work were encouraged among teachers on common professional problems in those states where segregated teachers associations exist." However, it was not until after the Civil Rights Act of 1964 was passed that the merging of the ATA and NEA was accomplished, on June 28, 1966.

Although ATA was wooed initially by the American Federation of Teachers (AFT) for a possible merger after the passage of the Civil Rights Act, its long-term relationship with the NEA made a better match. Because the joint committee had developed a plan for such a merger years before, the transition itself was relatively smooth. The NEA accepted all ATA life members as life members of the NEA, transferred the assets of the ATA into a fund to promote the civil rights of black teachers, and accepted two of the ATA staff as employees of the NEA. At the time of the merger the ATA had a membership of 41,000; however, over 90 percent of these ATA members also held NEA membership in the dual affiliates of previously segregated southern states.

Two years after the merger, a black educator from North Carolina, **Elizabeth D. Koontz**, was elected president of the NEA. Mary L. Williams, a black woman from West Virginia, had acted as president of the ATA from 1941–44, as had Lillian Rogers Johnson from Mississippi in 1955, and Leila A. Bradby from South Carolina in 1961. These women, who rose to positions of relative power within the ATA, symbolized the thousands of female rank-and-file members who worked among the segregated classrooms of the North and South.

The first one hundred years of post-emancipation education focused on the empowerment and uplifting of the race within a segregated system. Separation gave black educators the room to explore cultural differences, through organizations such as the ASNLH, that in an integrated atmosphere became threatening to the status quo. Thus desegregation represented an answer to the call for equity but also marked the end of an era. In 1958, when prominent educator **Anna Julia Cooper**, at the age of one hundred, was asked about her reaction to the *Brown* v. *Board of Education* decision, she said she opposed it because during segregation black children were taught race pride and black history.

Cooper's remark places her within a lifetime of struggle that focused on empowerment within the black community. The nature of this search for empowerment was at times contradictory. Hence, the ATA brought the inequities of segregation to the attention of powerful organizations such as the NEA. Ironically, however, the move toward group empowerment and social integration did not eliminate all contradictions, because the NEA both assisted in the education of black Americans and yet often proved institutionally removed from the black community. The ATA brought the inequities of segregation to the attention of powerful organizations such as the NEA, and so empowered the black community to make the demands that brought about integration.

EARL LEWIS
VICTORIA WOLCOTT

Association for the Study of Afro-American Life and History

The Association for the Study of Negro Life and History (ASNLH), now the Association

The prominent black leader Mary McLeod Bethune served as president of the Association for the Study of Negro Life and History from 1936 to 1951. She is seen here at a WAC center luncheon during a National Civilian Advisory Committee inspection tour in 1945. (NATIONAL ARCHIVES)

for the Study of Afro-American Life and History, was organized in Chicago by Dr. Carter G. Woodson on September 9, 1915. In attendance at the meeting were George Cleveland Hall, W. B. Hartgrove, and J. E. Stamps. The purpose of the organization, according to Dr. Woodson, was to collect sociological and historical data on the Negro, to study the peoples of African ancestry, to publish books in the field, and to promote harmony between the races by acquainting one with the achievements of the other.

In January 1916, four months after the founding of the association, Dr. Woodson began to publish the *Journal of Negro History*, and in 1937 he inaugurated the popular magazine the *Negro History Bulletin*. For a number of years, **Mary McLeod Bethune** (both as a member of ASNLH and as president) had encouraged Woodson to devise new ways to reach primary and secondary school teachers, children, and the masses of African Americans; the *Negro History Bulletin* was designed to accomplish this end. Following the publication of the first edition of the *Journal of Negro History*, scholars such as W. E. B. DuBois, Frederick Jackson Turner, F. W. Shepardson, Oswald Garrison Villard, and major newspapers such as the *New York Evening Post*, the *Boston Herald*, and the *Southern Workman*, were enthusiastic in their praise of the *Journal*. The *Boston Herald* concluded in its comments: "Hitherto, the history of the Negro race has been written chiefly by white men; now the educated Negroes of this country have decided to search and tell the historic achievements of their race in their own way and from their own point of view. Judging from the first issue of their publication, they are going to do it in a way that will measure up to the standards set by the best historical publications of the day."

In 1940, on the occasion of the twenty-fifth anniversary of the association, Professor W. B. Hesseltine of the University of Wisconsin concluded that the association had made a major contribution to scientific history in two respects. By doing scholarly research on the Negro, the association had prompted a reconsideration and a consequent revision of the older concepts of the Negro's role in American history and furnished an example of the interrelationship between history and sociology. The first enriched the content of American history and the second improved the methods of scientific research.

Recognizing the difficulties faced by black scholars in getting their work published, Carter Woodson organized Associated Publishers in 1920 as the publishing arm of the association. Dr. Charles Wesley, coauthor with Dr. Woodson of *The Negro in Our History* (1992), quotes Woodson as saying that "The Negro faces . . . a stone wall when he presents scientific productions to the publishing houses. If the Negro is to settle down to publishing merely what others permit him to bring out, the world will never know what the race has thought and felt and attempted and accomplished and the story of the Negro will perish with him."

In February 1926, Dr. Woodson inaugurated Negro History Week, to coincide with the birthdays of Abraham Lincoln and Frederick Douglass. This celebration enlarged the scope of Woodson's work beyond the circle of scholars to school systems and school curricula. The observance of Negro History Week led to the demand for books, literature, and pictures on the Negro. In 1976, in honor of the nation's bicentennial observance, the week was expanded to National Black History Month. The association, through Associated Publishers, continues to establish the theme for each year's celebration.

Since the association's founding, women have played a significant role in virtually every aspect of the organization. Two women, Mary McLeod Bethune (1936–51) as president and Lorraine Williams (1974–76) as editor, worked at the *Journal of Negro History*—the only women who have served in these positions. During Lorraine Williams' years as editor, the editorial board became more reflective of women and younger scholars. Women have served as vice president (Jeannette Cascone and Darlene Clark Hine), secretary (Janet Sims-Wood), and treasurer (Janette Hoston Harris and Mauree Ayton) of the organization, on its executive council, and on the editorial boards of the *Journal of Negro History* and the *Negro History Bulletin*.

Lucy Harth-Smith, a school principal from Lexington, Kentucky, was the first woman named to the executive council, in 1935. Later, Wilhelmina Crosson, Vivian Cook, and Edith Ingraham served on the council.

For a number of years, **Lois Mailou Jones**, the well-known artist, illustrated books for Associated Publishers, and **Dorothy Porter Wesley** lent her considerable skills as an author and archivist to numerous activities of the association, including working with the Committee for the *Encyclopedia Africana*. W. Leona Miles, after more than forty-five years at the association in a variety of positions, oversees the affairs of Associated Publishers as managing director.

Women also have been represented as authors and as subjects in the *Journal of Negro History*. As of 1950, more articles by women authors had appeared in the *Journal of Negro History* than in any other historical journal. During the twenty years from 1958 to 1978, 12 percent of the articles in the *Journal of Negro History* were contributed by women. Among the black women represented were **Merze Tate**, Bettye Gardner, Bettye Collier-Thomas, and Martha Cobb.

The Association for the Study of Afro-American Life and History continues the work begun by Carter G. Woodson, with Black History Month, an annual convention, and two Ford Foundation–funded projects.

BETTYE J. GARDNER

Association of Black Women Historians, Inc.

In 1977, recognizing the need for a uniquely focused organizational structure within their profession, three black women historians spearheaded the move to recruit other black women nationwide. Rosalyn Terborg-Penn, **Eleanor Smith**, and Elizabeth Parker initiated a series of meetings held in South Hadley, Massachusetts, and in two California cities, Los Angeles and San Francisco.

After Parker's death, Terborg-Penn and Smith sustained the first organizational efforts by convening a steering committee in Cincinnati, Ohio. Gloria Dickerson, Juanita Moore, **Darlene Clark Hine**, and Janice Sumler-Lewis (later Sumler-Edmond) met with Terborg-Penn and Smith in February 1979 to create a governance and structural framework for the new organization. The committee selected the name Association of Black Women Historians (ABWH) and unanimously endorsed Dickerson's suggestion to call their newsletter *Truth*. It was decided that membership should be reserved for trained black women historians and other persons interested in black women's history and in the professional development of black women historians. Smith agreed to ask noted artist Gilbert Young to create a logo for the new organization.

In October 1979, approximately fifty black women attended ABWH's first annual gathering in New York City. A business meeting and an address by **Gwendolyn Baker** of the U.S. Department of Education marked the official beginning of the ABWH organization. While still in New York, the membership asked Marquita James to draft the ABWH constitution, which was later approved by the group's executive council when it met in Chicago in spring 1980.

The ABWH constitution outlines four organizational goals: to establish a network among the membership; to promote black women in the profession; to disseminate information about opportunities in the field; and to make suggestions concerning research topics and repositories. Apart from amendments concerning dues, the constitution has undergone few revisions since its adoption.

Starting with the 1979 gathering in New York, ABWH annual meetings have been held every fall in conjunction with the convention of the Association for the Study of Afro-American Life and History (ASALH). This consolidation of meetings saves ABWH members additional travel expense. Over the years ABWH-sponsored sessions have become an integral part of the ASALH convention. At the second ABWH annual meeting in New Orleans, the membership elected Terborg-Penn as the group's first national director, a position she held for two consecutive terms. In 1980, with a view toward the organization's continued stability and growth, Terborg-Penn and other members of the executive council instructed National Treasurer Bettye J. Gardner to incorporate ABWH under the laws of the District of Columbia.

In 1980, ABWH collaborated with the Organization of American Historians and the Fund to Improve Post-Secondary Education to complete a Black History Project. The following year, ABWH members coordinated their efforts with the American Historical Association to develop a *Directory of Women Historians* (1981). During the summer of 1983, ABWH members organized a conference on women in the African diaspora held at **Howard University**. Other ABWH projects and activities are local in character and focus. The four regional areas, consisting of a far west region, a midwest region, a southern region, and an eastern region, comprise the ABWH organizational framework. The four regional directors plan miniconferences, luncheons, and seminars for the members in their regions.

First initiated in 1981, the ABWH annual luncheon, featuring a keynote address, takes place on the afternoon of the general membership meeting and serves as an organizational fund-raiser and opportunity for networking. Publication prize awards, created in 1983 to honor the now-deceased black historian Letitia Woods Brown, recognize excellence in scholarship. The Brown Prize recipients receive their awards during the luncheon.

In 1987, the ABWH Executive Council announced the Lorraine Anderson Williams Leadership Award, to be given to distinguished black women leaders. This award honors Williams, professor emeritus of Howard University and mentor to many black women historians. The Drusilla Dunjee Houston Scholarship is reserved for outstanding black women graduate students. The Houston award, created in 1989 as a collaborative effort between ABWH and the Black Classic Press of Baltimore, Maryland, celebrates the life and work of **Drusilla Dunjee Houston** (1876–1941), a teacher, journalist, and self-taught historian.

Through the various awards and activities, emphasizing excellence in scholarship and leadership, the ABWH remains committed to strengthening networks among historians and to its founders' goals as set forth in its constitution.

JANICE SUMLER-EDMOND

Association of Deans of Women and Advisers to Girls in Negro Schools

On black college campuses in the early twentieth century, black women were virtually absent from boards of trustees, administrations, and faculties; they were paid less than their male counterparts for comparable work; and they were subjected to deplorable living conditions as students. Determined to confront this situation, **Lucy Diggs Slowe,** the first permanent dean of women at **Howard University** in Washington, D.C., and founder of the National Association of College Women (NACW), convened a conference of deans and advisers to girls in Negro schools on March 1–2, 1929. This conference, initiated by the NACW committee on standards, gave birth to the Association of Deans of Women and Advisers to Girls in Negro Schools and to twenty-five years of advocacy for black women in the academy.

Attending the meeting at Howard were women representing ten black colleges and public schools. Among the participants were Helen Brown, Carol Cotton, Otelia Cromwell, Marian Cuthbert, Sadie Daniels, Hilda A. Davis, Johanna Houston (Ransom), Juanita Howard (Thomas), Ruth Howard (Beckham), Bertha McNeil, Anna Payne, Ruth Rush, **Lucy Diggs Slowe, Georgiana** Simpson, Aletha Washington, Tossie Whiting, and Gertrude Woodard. By the close of the conference, five problems had been identified in black institutions: the underrepresentation of black women on boards of trustees and college administrations; the need for academically qualified and equitably salaried deans of women and advisers to girls; the lack of adequate and properly equipped housing for female college students; the absence of wholesome extracurricular and well-planned recreational activities for female college students; and the need for separate housing as well as developmentally appropriate regulations and activities for girls attending high school on college campuses.

This photograph is identified in the Moorland-Spingarn photo collection as showing a "meeting with colored deans." Lucy Diggs Slowe is the sixth from the left. (MOORLAND-SPINGARN)

Having outlined the poor circumstances of women on black campuses, the conferees decided to meet annually under the sponsorship of the NACW, and for the next five years they assembled to discuss and examine mutual problems and concerns. These meetings were held at Fisk University, Nashville, Tennessee, 1930; Talladega College, Talladega, Alabama, 1931; Tuskegee Institute, Tuskegee, Alabama, and Virginia State College, Petersburg, Virginia, 1932; and Hampton Institute, Hampton, Virginia, 1934. No meeting was held in 1933.

A sixth conference was held at Howard University in March 1935; attending were twenty-eight women from eleven states and the District of Columbia. As with previous gatherings, this one was chaired by Slowe, but the conferees set an important new course by voting to establish an independent organization. Elected to office were Lucy Diggs Slowe of Howard University, president; Dorothy Hopson of Hampton Institute, first vice president; Georgia Myrtle Teale of Wilberforce University, Wilberforce, Ohio, second vice president; Eva Burrell Holmes of Howard University, secretary; and Tossie P. Whiting of Virginia State College, treasurer. A year later the seventh conference—the organization's first as an autonomous body—was held at Wilberforce University.

No meeting was held in 1937 because of the death of Slowe, and without her leadership the group nearly disintegrated. Fortunately, several members who had attended the 1929 conference urged a reconvening, and Georgia Myrtle Teale assumed the presidency. The dean of women at Tuskegee Institute hosted a conference in 1938, and at this, the ninth annual meeting, the first constitution was presented and adopted. The organization took as its name the Association of Deans of Women and Advisers to Girls in Negro Schools. Its threefold purpose was: to bolster a spirit of unity and cooperation among deans and advisers of Negro women and girls; to create a recognized professional status for deans, advisers, counselors, and others engaged in the building up of girls and young women physically, mentally, socially, and morally, both in the field of education and in civic and economic life; and to study the best methods of counseling girls and young women.

Also established were membership criteria as well as a dues and leadership structure. Elected as officers of this reconstituted organization were Hilda A. Davis of Talladega College, president; Mamie Mason Higgins of **Bethune-Cookman College**, Daytona Beach, Florida, vice president; Emma C. W. Gray of Paine College, Augusta, Georgia, secretary; Mary Turner of Shaw University, Raleigh, North Carolina, treasurer; and Hazel B. Williams, Louisville Municipal College, Louisville, Kentucky, membership committee chair.

For the next sixteen years, the association met annually on black college campuses: Louisville Municipal College, 1939; South Carolina State College, Orangeburg, South Carolina, 1940; Fisk University, 1941; Howard University, 1942; Florida Agricultural and Mechanical College, Tallahassee, Florida, 1943; North Carolina State College, Durham, North Carolina, 1944; Lincoln University, Jefferson City, Missouri, 1945; Dillard University, New Orleans, Louisiana, 1946; Tuskegee Institute, 1947; Howard University, 1948; Florida Agricultural and Mechanical College, 1949; Southern University, Baton Rouge, Louisiana, 1950; North Carolina Agricultural and Technical College, Greensboro, North Carolina, 1951; Morgan State University, Baltimore, Maryland,

1952; Virginia State College, 1953; and Howard University, 1954.

Succeeding Slowe (1929–37), Teale (1937–38), and Davis (1938–40) in the presidency were Ina A. Bolton, 1940–42; Flemmie P. Kittrell, 1942–44; Mayme U. Foster, 1944–46; T. Ruth Brett, 1946–48; Emma C. W. Gray, 1948–50; Virginia S. Nyabongo, 1950–52; and Louise Latham, 1952–54.

In 1946, the association held its first joint conference with the National Association of Personnel Deans and Advisers of Men in Negro Institutions. Seven years earlier the female deans had passed a recommendation that the deans of men be contacted "for the purpose of having joint annual meetings, since their problems are so closely woven." As these combined meetings became a tradition, which was especially beneficial to the male deans because their association was not as organized as the women's, many questioned the need for there to be two independent associations. Eight years later, at a joint meeting hosted by Howard University in 1954, both groups voted to merge. Some women were unhappy about merging their vibrant and growing association with the men's group, which was seen as moribund. The prevailing sentiment was for unification, however, and the two groups dissolved, later forming a new body known as the National Association of Personnel Workers (NAPW). The female deans contributed substantially to the NAPW's leadership. Among the founding officers were Sadie M. Yancey of Howard University, president; Arlynne Jones of Grambling State University, Grambling, Louisiana, recording secretary; Jean Spinner of North Carolina Agricultural and Technical College, assistant recording secretary; and Valleta H. Bell Linnette of Virginia State College, first regional vice president.

In its twenty-five-year history, the Association of Deans of Women and Advisers to Girls in Negro Schools played a critical role in the academy. First, it was a professional and social support network for female deans and related educators, many of whom felt discouraged and embattled. Second, it provided a comfortable setting where women could observe role models and discuss institutional politics. Third, its conferences represented one of the few training opportunities for black women, who were routinely denied full participation at meetings of white associations where similar activities took place. Fourth, it became a national voice for black women's educational concerns, as its members typically were the highest placed and most articulate women on the campus and in the nation.

In sum, the Association of Deans of Women and Advisers to Girls in Negro Schools laid the framework for a philosophy of higher education that was sensitive to the unique circumstance of black women and girls. This framework, and the issues articulated by the association, have influenced educational debate and practice throughout the twentieth century.

HILDA A. DAVIS
PATRICIA BELL-SCOTT

B

Baker, Gwendolyn (1931–)

When Gwendolyn Calvert Baker took the job of National Executive Director of the YWCA, she inherited a deficit of over half a million dollars and an organization that, despite a 135-year history, had lost its sense of purpose. She changed all that during the nine years of her watch, for six of them balancing YWCA's troubled books.

She has inherited a $50 million budget with her most recent job as president and chief executive officer of the U.S. Committee for UNICEF, the United Nations Children's Fund. The Committee is the oldest and largest of thirty-five committees that mobilize support for UNICEF, and among her goals is the doubling of its budget to $100 million. She seems to be the one to do it.

Baker was born in Ann Arbor, Michigan, on December 31, 1931, the daughter of Burgess Edward and Viola Lee Calvert. That city became the hub of much of her initial (though late-blooming) academic and professional life. At its University of Michigan campus she earned three education-related degrees: a B.S. in 1964, an M.A. in 1968, and a Ph.D. in 1972. She was an Ann Arbor schoolteacher between 1964 and 1969 and a University of Michigan assistant and then associate, professor of education between 1969 and 1976. For the next two years Baker directed the university's affirmative action program.

The year 1978 saw her divorce from James Grady Baker (after a marriage that

Among her many accomplishments, New Yorkers will remember Gwendolyn Calvert Baker best for holding "the hardest job in the world"—president of the New York Board of Education. (U.S. COMMITTEE FOR UNICEF)

produced two daughters and a son), as well as a move to Washington, D.C. There she became chief of the Minorities and Women's Research Program of the National Institute of Education, a post she held until 1981. For the next three years she was in New York City as vice president and dean of graduate and children's programs of Bank Street College. A member of the New York City Board of Education from 1986 to 1991, she served as its president in 1990 and 1991.

During her YWCA years (1984–1993), she found ways to cut costs, streamline and computerize the aged institution's stagnant procedures of operation, and refashion its image. She also reduced its staff by 50 percent, while creating retirement packages and helping to relocate those who were laid off. Many of her changes went under the heading of Project Redesign, which Baker launched in the late 1980s in the teeth of a severe national economic recession.

But perhaps her signal contribution was to reawaken YWCA's advocacy role in helping women and people of color by seeking social and legislative reforms. This in turn made the organization once again, as an admirer said, "a player on the national stage." In Baker's last YWCA year, *Working Woman* magazine named her one of its Ten Most Admired Women Managers of 1993.

That was the year she became the first African American and the second woman to be president of the U.S. Committee for UNICEF. As spokesperson, advocate, and fund-raiser, her stated intent is to broaden the Committee's mission as she did the YWCA's. She had desired the YWCA's meaning to extend beyond "a place to go swimming and make cookies." In the same way, she wants UNICEF volunteers to be placed in America's 16,000 school districts in order to teach U.S. youngsters about youngsters worldwide. That way, she has said, UNICEF will start to mean more than "just a group that hands out orange boxes for collections on Halloween."

GARY HOUSTON

Baldwin, Maria Louise (1856–1922)

"I dare not fail," said the distinguished educator Maria Louise Baldwin. She did not fail.

For four decades she dedicated her mind and her voice to education.

Maria Louise Baldwin was born on September 13, 1856, in Cambridge, Massachusetts, to Mary E. and Peter L. Baldwin, one year after the Massachusetts legislature passed the 1855 act desegregating all public schools in the state. Maria attended the Sargent Primary School, the Allston Grammar School, and the Cambridge High School, from which she graduated in June 1874. In June 1881, she graduated from the Cambridge Training School for Teachers. Almost immediately she taught for one or two terms in Chestertown, Maryland.

Several black citizens of Cambridge who knew of Baldwin's excellent scholastic record and her futile attempts to secure a teaching position in Cambridge formed a committee to urge the school board to appoint her to a teaching position. As a result, Baldwin was appointed in 1887 as an elementary school teacher of all seven grades in the interracial Agassiz Grammar School. A competent scholar and excellent disciplinarian, Baldwin was selected in 1889 as principal of the school, a position she held for over thirty years.

The deteriorating Agassiz school building was demolished in 1915, and a new $60,000 structure was built in its place. When the school reopened in the fall of 1916, the position of principal was elevated to that of master. Baldwin became one of only two female masters in Cambridge, and the only black master in New England. In this capacity she directed the work of a dozen white teachers who taught more than 500 students, most of whom were white and many of whose parents were on the faculty of Harvard University. Baldwin held this position with great distinction and efficiency for the remainder of her life.

Maria Louise Baldwin continued her education by enrolling in courses at Boston University and Harvard University. She also collected a large number of books. Her library was used by the many friends and literary associates who were frequent visitors to her home on Prospect Street in Cambridge. Among her many friends were Thomas Wentworth Higginson, a Harvard-trained Unitarian minister, and Edward Everett Hale, a writer of New England history and a chaplain of the U.S. Senate. Baldwin enjoyed the friendship and wise counsel of numerous black persons whose views she shared, such as William H. Lewis, once assistant attorney general of the United States; William Monroe Trotter, publisher and editor of the *Boston Guardian*; and the Honorable Archibald Grimké, a Harvard Law School graduate and editor of the *Hub* newspaper in Boston.

Baldwin frequently lectured, particularly to her own people. She opposed all forms of racial discrimination and praised the achievements of black Americans. One of her important addresses was delivered at the annual George Washington Birthday Memorial before the Brooklyn Institute in 1897. This was the first time in the fifty-year history of the New York Institute that a woman had given this address. Her speech was entitled "The Life and Services of the Late Harriet Beecher Stowe." The applause was so great she had to stand repeatedly to acknowledge it. As a result of this historic speech, Baldwin was offered another teaching position at twice her salary at Agassiz, and she was much sought after for speaking engagements.

On the evening of January 9, 1922, while Baldwin was addressing members of the Council of the Robert Gould Shaw House Association at the Copley-Plaza in Boston, she collapsed and died of a heart attack.

Many tributes were expressed to the life of this unique woman. Memorials were named for her—scholarships, libraries, halls—and in 1952, a new women's dormitory at **Howard University** in Washington, D.C., was named Maria Baldwin Hall.

Perhaps no teacher has inspired so many or been loved more. Funeral services were held on January 12, 1922, at the Arlington Street Church in Boston. Her ashes were buried in Forest Hill Cemetery. Baldwin was survived by a sister and a brother.

DOROTHY PORTER WESLEY

Little more than two decades after black Americans emerged from slavery, Maria Louise Baldwin was serving as principal of an interracial grammar school in Cambridge, Massachusetts, supervising the education of the children of Harvard faculty members. (MOORLAND-SPINGARN)

Barnett, Marguerite Ross   (1942–1992)

As a political scientist, Marguerite Ross Barnett had wide-ranging interests, and her writings covered issues from cultural nationalism in India to contemporary black politics in the United States. As a university administrator, Barnett became noted for the successful development of high school-to-college transition programs in New York, Missouri, and Houston. As both a scholar and an administrator, she made significant contributions to American education.

Born in Charlottesville, Virginia, on May 21, 1942, Marguerite Ross Barnett grew up in Buffalo, New York. She was an only child and her academic interests were encouraged from an early age. She went to Antioch College and then to the University of Chicago, where she received her M.S. and Ph.D. in political science. Her studies led her to do

Programs for disadvantaged students were the hallmark of Marguerite Ross Barnett's administration when she became the University of Houston's first woman president. (OFFICE OF MEDIA RELATIONS, UNIVERSITY OF HOUSTON)

research in several other countries, including Turkey, England, and India.

Barnett taught at Princeton, Howard, and Columbia, but her real calling was administration. Her first important position in that area was vice chancellor for academic affairs at the City University of New York (CUNY), a post she held from 1983 to 1986. During her time there she worked to establish a program for high school students from poor families. The purpose of the program was to smooth their transition to college and from college to worthwhile work.

After CUNY, Barnett moved to the University of Missouri–St. Louis. During her tenure there she established a number of new degree programs, doubled the amount of federal research and service grant dollars received, tripled the scholarship support, raised more than $9 million in new donations, and has been credited with the 18 percent increase in enrollment. She repeated her successful program for disadvantaged students at that school and, later, at the University of Houston. The Bridge Program, as it was called, was named the outstanding public school initiative in the country in 1991, receiving the Anderson Medal from the American Council on Education.

Her appointment as president at the University of Houston was groundbreaking in more than one way. She was the first woman to be president of that university, and one of the few to lead any school that was not historically a women's college. A parallel situation existed with regard to her race.

Barnett was at Houston for only two years before her death in 1992 of complications from cancer. During that time she earned a reputation for creative cooperation with the business community. She was both a successful fund-raiser and a proponent of the idea that universities should spur economic growth and solve social problems in their communities. In July of 1991 she was the only representative of a university who was named to the President's Commission on Environmental Quality. That commission was formed to explore ways to check environmental destruction without impairing economic development.

Barnett also was the author or editor of five books and forty articles. Her most acclaimed work was *The Politics of Cultural Nationalism in South India* (1976).

She died in Wailuku, Hawaii, of a blood disorder involving hypoglycemia with metastatic cancer in 1992.

IFE WILLIAMS-ANDOH

Bell-Scott, Patricia (1950–)

While peering through microfilm in search of Marion Cuthbert and stumbling over many of my sisters and mothers, the likes of Eva D. Bowles, Lucy Slowe, and Juliette Derricotte jump up at me. I only wish that I had twenty arms, fifty pairs of eyes, money and time to reconstruct their stories.

The daughter of Dorothy and Louis Wilbanks, Patricia Bell-Scott was born on December 20, 1950. She received her bachelor of science degree in 1972, her master's in 1973, and her Ph.D. in 1976, all from the University of Tennessee, Knoxville. Her fields of study were child and family development and black studies. From 1979 through 1980 she was a post-doctoral fellow at the John F. Kennedy School of Government at Harvard University.

Having mastered a broad range of fields and subjects, Bell-Scott became an associate professor at the University of Connecticut,

School of Family Studies. Later, she moved to Wellesley College Center for Research on Women. She also served as an assistant equal opportunity officer at MIT. Currently she is a professor of child and family development, psychology, and women's studies at the University of Georgia.

Bell-Scott has made enormous contributions to black women's studies. She coedited *Double Stitch: Black Women Write About Mothers and Daughters*, and *All the Women are White, All the Blacks Are Men, But Some of Us Are Brave: Black Women's Studies.* She is a cofounder of *SAGE: A Scholarly Journal on Black Women.*

Bell-Scott's most recent work is the beautiful and original volume, *Life Notes: Personal Writings by Contemporary Black Women.* She has one sister, Brenda Faye Bell, and is married to Arvin Scott. She currently lives in Athens, Georgia.

In the introduction to *Life Notes*, Bell-Scott says, "I wish to connect future generations of Black women and girls to our wonderful tradition of life-writing." We are very lucky that Patricia Bell-Scott is making her wish come true.

HILARY MAC AUSTIN

Bennett College

Bennett College, one of only two still existing historically black institutions of higher learning for women, was founded in 1873 as a coeducational school in the basement of Saint Matthew's Methodist Episcopal Church in Greensboro, North Carolina. It was named Bennett Seminary in honor of Lyman Bennett of Troy, New York, who was the school's first large donor. The Freedman's Aid Society took responsibility for the school in 1874, and Reverend Edward O. Thayer, a Wesleyan College alumnus, became its second principal.

Thayer left in 1881 to assume the presidency of Clark College in Atlanta. In 1886, an industrial work/domestic science program was begun and a home for women (later named Kent Hall) was built on the Bennett campus under the auspices of the Woman's Home Missionary Society of the Methodist Episcopal Church. In 1889, Reverend Charles N. Grandison became the first African-American president of Bennett and the first black president of any of the Freeman's Aid Society-funded schools.

In 1926, Bennett became a college for women primarily as a result of the Woman's Home Missionary Society's desire to enlarge its educational programs to include African-American women, a primary objective of the society. After 1926, the society assumed greater responsibility for Bennett College for Women. The retirement of Frank Trigg in 1926 ended the era of coeducation at the institution. David Dallas Jones, a white businessman living in Atlanta, became the first president of Bennett College for Women, where he remained for thirty years, until 1956.

Black women college presidents, even at black women's colleges, have been extraordinarily rare, which is a reflection of the persistent male control of historically black institutions in general. When **Willa Player** became president of Bennett College in 1955, after having served the college in various capacities for twenty-five years, she became the first African-American woman to head a college for black women.

Player, a native of Akron, Ohio, who had earned a Ph.D. from Columbia University, joined the Bennett faculty in 1930 as a teacher of French. In 1952, she became director of admissions and vice president in charge of instruction. During Player's presidency, Bennett gained membership, in 1957, to the Southern Association of Colleges and Schools.

Bennett resigned in March 1966 and assumed the position of director of the Division of College Support with the U.S. Office of Education, Department of Health, Education and Welfare. Isaac H. Miller, Jr., succeeded Player as president in September 1966; his father, Isaac H. Miller, Sr., had been dean of Bennett College beginning in 1923. Isaac H. Miller, Jr. was associate professor of biochemistry at Meharry Medical College prior to assuming the Bennett presidency. Following Miller's retirement, a second black woman, Gloria Randle Scott, then vice president of Clark College, assumed the presidency of Bennett College.

Although the majority of black women have been educated in coeducational institutions, single-sex colleges for black women, all of which have been located in the South, have provided unique educational experiences for generations of women who have chosen through the years to attend Bennett, Spelman, Barber-Scotia, Hartshorn, and Houston-Tillotson.

BEVERLY GUY-SHEFTALL

Bethune-Cookman College

Bethune-Cookman College, a living legacy of **Mary McLeod Bethune**, is the only historically black college founded by a black woman that continues to thrive today.

In 1904, Mary McLeod Bethune went to Daytona Beach, Florida, to respond to the black community's need for education. The Eastcoast Railway had attracted thousands of black workers to this coastal community, and their children needed to be educated. A

Bethune-Cookman College, a living legacy of Mary McLeod Bethune, is the only historically black college founded by a black woman that continues to thrive today. Bethune is shown here in front of a college building. Seen over her right shoulder is Dorothy Height.
(BETHUNE MUSEUM AND ARCHIVES)

daughter of ex-slaves in South Carolina, Mary Bethune was the answer to their prayers. Along with faith in God, this black woman had been educated in, and been a teacher at, girls' schools, and she had a missionary zeal to effect change among black people, especially black women.

The Daytona Normal and Industrial Institute for Negro Girls began with faith in God, $1.50, and five little girls. Although she was the mother of a son, Bethune had a challenging vision that included the education of female children. Influenced primarily by **Lucy Laney** of the **Haines Institute** and

Booker T. Washington of the Tuskegee Institute, Bethune's initial curriculum focused on religion and the three Rs. These primary skills were later complemented by vocational training in domestic work, sewing, and farming. Indeed, Bethune's school reflected the era, with its emphasis on traditional female vocational skills, and this emphasis endured throughout Bethune's tenure as president and president emeritus.

When the school merged with the all-male Cookman Institute in Jacksonville, Florida, in 1923, the curriculum broadened to include Cookman's mission of training women for the public school system while training men to preach the gospel. The new school was known as the Daytona Cookman Collegiate Institute until 1933, when it was renamed Bethune-Cookman College. It proved to be a beneficial merger, establishing a source of stable funding by the Methodist Episcopal Church, and providing an infusion of male students while allowing the continuity of traditional female education to remain intact. In fact, the first four-year degree program to be instituted, in 1943, was in teacher education. Thus, at the time of the historic 1954 U.S. Supreme Court decision *Brown* v. *Board of Education*, the primary contribution of Bethune-Cookman College was educating teachers for the mostly segregated public school systems of Florida.

By the time of the merger with Cookman in 1923, the original enrollment of five girls had increased to several hundred young women and men. The male population has increased gradually, but the majority of graduates have been female. During World War II, when a decline in enrollment was expected, enrollment actually increased because the number of female students increased. The college survived the war by

serving as a training center for women to participate in the wartime economy. In 1944, 111 women passed secretarial training and were placed in various government agencies in Washington, D.C., and other locations throughout the United States and Europe. That same year, sixty-five girls volunteered their services to the college in the production and harvest of food to aid in the war effort. This organization, called the Farmettes, was recognized by the Florida Education Department and touted as a model for other colleges in the state.

No doubt the college received attention and was awarded government contracts during the war because of its president emeritus, Mary McLeod Bethune, who capitalized on her prominence in order to draw public attention to the college. For instance, a forum called the Women for Peace Conference was held on the Bethune-Cookman College campus in 1952. Bethune and Mrs. Samuel Caverts, a theologian and member of the World Council of Churches, co-chaired this racially integrated forum on women's and minority rights. Academic freedom, fair employment, and equal political access and participation for women and minority groups in America were among the timeless issues discussed at this historic event, and the list of participants reads like a Who's Who among women. Representatives of the **Young Women's Christian Association** (YWCA), the League of Women Voters, the Republican National Committee, the National Council of Women, the National Council of Churches, the National Council of Jewish Women, the Democratic National Committee, and the Women's Bureau of the Department of Labor were among the more than 150 participants. This conference, occurring only three years before her death, demonstrated Bethune's unrelenting desire to achieve equality and sisterhood among women in America.

Today Bethune-Cookman College comprises approximately fifty-two acres and thirty-two buildings, and produces graduates in twenty-five major degree programs. Women hold high administrative positions, and female students continue to make up the greater percentage of the more than ten thousand graduates as well as a majority of the international student population, which numbers around twenty-five hundred. Female students are represented not only in the traditional fields of nursing and teaching. They also make up a large percentage of students in such nontraditional fields as business, engineering, and law. Mary McLeod Bethune's legacy, Bethune-Cookman College, continues to make a difference for women in the world.

SHEILA Y. FLEMMING

Boone, Sylvia A. (1941–1993)

The first black woman to be given tenure at Yale University, Sylvia Boone was a pioneer in Afro-American studies and a scholar of outstanding achievement.

Sylvia A. Boone was born in 1941 in Mount Vernon, New York. She received her bachelor's degree from Brooklyn College and then earned a master's degree from Columbia University. She then studied for a time at the University of Ghana, where she welcomed such visiting Americans as Malcolm X, **Maya Angelou**, and W. E. B. DuBois.

Going to Yale first, as a visiting lecturer in Afro-American studies in 1970, Boone soon became a student there, earning both her master's and her doctorate in art history.

During those years she organized one of the first conferences on black women, and founded a black film festival.

Boone became a member of the faculty at Yale in 1979. In 1988, she became the first black woman to be a tenured full professor at Yale. A fine scholar and teacher, she wrote *Radiance from the Waters: Ideals of Feminine Beauty in Mende Art* and *West African Travels: A Guide to People and Places*. She was scholarship chairperson of the Roothbert Fund, which gives aid to students studying for careers in education, and served on a committee that chose UNICEF's annual fund-raising greeting card.

Sylvia Boone died of heart failure in 1993 at the age of fifty-two. She was buried in the Grove Street Cemetery in New Haven, which is a burial ground reserved for presidents of Yale and other prominent University scholars and officials.

KATHLEEN THOMPSON

Brown, Charlotte Hawkins
(1883–1961)

Charlotte Hawkins Brown was committed to good manners, and she made sure that students at her school, Palmer Memorial Institute, were carefully drilled in the proper social graces. But her interest in manners and education was coupled with a fierce determination to fight for civil rights and not to accept injustice quietly. This, too, she conveyed both to her students and to clubwomen, black and white, throughout the South. Brown was a major force in the educational and club work of early twentieth-century African-American women. Born Lottie Hawkins on June 11, 1883, in Henderson, North Carolina, she was the daughter of Caroline Frances Hawkins and

Edmund H. Hight. Her grandmother, Rebecca, was a descendant of the English navigator John D. Hawkins and worked as a housemaid on the Hawkins plantation.

Caroline Hawkins, who had received an education in the elementary department of Shaw University, was determined that her daughter and her son, Mingo, should have opportunities for a better life. So when young Lottie was seven years old, the family moved to Cambridge, Massachusetts. The

Charlotte Hawkins Brown was only nineteen years old when she founded the Palmer Memorial Institute at the beginning of the twentieth century. She retired over fifty years later, with generations of students in her debt. She is shown here with a bust of Alice Freeman Palmer, her mentor, for whom the institute is named. (SOUTHERN EXPOSURE)

family, in this case, consisted of nineteen people, including cousins and aunts and Caroline's new husband, Nelson Willis.

In Cambridge, the Willises operated a hand laundry, boarded Harvard students, and took care of infants in their home. Lottie Hawkins went to the Allston Grammar School and became friends with the children of Henry Wadsworth Longfellow. At twelve, she organized a kindergarten in the Sunday school of the Union Baptist Church. She excelled in her schoolwork and, when she went on to Cambridge English High School, she cultivated a talent in art by sketching her classmates.

It was when she was about to graduate that fate stepped in for the first time. She decided that her white organdy graduation dress called for a silk slip, and took a job caring for two babies in order to pay for it. She was pushing a baby carriage and reading Virgil in her Latin book when she was spotted by Alice Freeman Palmer. Palmer, second president of Wellesley College, was impressed by the girl's intelligence and determination. She would enter Hawkins' life again shortly.

Besides the slip, Lottie Hawkins felt there was one other prerequisite for her graduation: a more dignified name. She became Charlotte Eugenia. She wanted very much to go to Radcliffe College, but her mother was firmly against it, insisting that she ought to go directly into teaching. They compromised, agreeing on the State Normal School at Salem. In the catalog for that institution, Hawkins saw that Alice Freeman Palmer was a member of the board that supervised normal schools for the state and she wrote to her asking for a recommendation. Palmer wrote back, offering to pay for the young woman's education.

Hawkins was in her second year at Salem when fate stepped in again. On her way home to visit, she met a stranger on a train, a field secretary of the American Missionary Association (AMA). The AMA was a group of white New Yorkers who provided schools for black children in the South. When the secretary straightaway offered Hawkins a job, she accepted immediately and left Salem before graduation. She had long believed that her purpose in life was to go back to the South and use her education to benefit her people.

When the AMA gave her a choice between a thriving school in Orlando, Florida, and a one-room school in rural North Carolina, Hawkins did not hesitate. Soon she was stepping off another train in McLeansville, North Carolina. The school was in Sedalia, four miles away. It was housed in a dilapidated country church. Hawkins' quarters were an attic room above the parsonage. If she had wanted a challenge, she had it. There were fifty children in Hawkins' first class. Most of them were so poor that she spent almost all of her salary buying them clothing and school supplies. Then the AMA informed her that they were closing the school, along with all the other schools in their network that were being operated by one or two teachers. The decision was a blow to the people of Sedalia, and one they were not willing to accept. They urged Hawkins to stay and open another school. Hawkins agreed. She was now nineteen years old.

The community gave her fifteen acres of land, and the minister of the Bethany Congregational Church donated an old building that had once housed a blacksmith shop. It was Hawkins' job, however, to find money. So she gave music recitals and recitations at New England resorts. She talked to Alice

Freeman Palmer—who died before she was able to help as she had promised—and to Palmer's friends, who gave her the money she needed to begin. Hawkins named the school the Alice Freeman Palmer Memorial Institute.

In the years that followed, Hawkins was administrator, teacher, and fund-raiser. She also continued her own education, taking classes in the summer at Harvard, where she met Edmund S. Brown. She and Brown were married in 1911, and he joined her in Sedalia. He taught and administered the boys' dormitory at Palmer Memorial for about a year before taking a teaching job in South Carolina. The marriage ended in 1915; but Charlotte Hawkins Brown was not alone. She reared her brother Mingo's three daughters, after their mother died, and the four children of her young aunt, Ella Brice, who was away from home a great deal pursuing her career in music. All seven children graduated from Palmer Memorial.

Brown continued to expand the school, initiated interracial cultural activities in the community, and became an active clubwoman. She was a founding member of the **National Council of Negro Women** and served as president of the North Carolina State Federation of Negro Women's Clubs and the North Carolina Teachers Association. She was the first African-American woman chosen for membership in the Twentieth Century Club of Boston. She also served on the national board of the YWCA. During all this, she took courses at a number of universities and had a modest career as an author.

In 1941, Brown's *The Correct Thing to Do, to Say, and to Wear* was published, and she became known as the "First Lady of Social Graces." Some, less charitably, called her a "social dictator." She wrote many articles and short stories as well, the most famous of which was "Mammy: An Appeal to the Heart of the South" (1919).

Brown was an impassioned advocate of civil rights. She was proud of the number of times she was ejected from Pullman berths and first-class railway seats in the South and she refused categorically to ride freight elevators in New York City buildings. Brown became a key figure in the Southern interracial women's movement as it developed in the 1920s. In fact, her speech at a 1920 interracial meeting in Memphis, in which she detailed the everyday examples of disrespect which black women regularly endured from Southern white men and women and challenged the Christian principles of the white female delegates, was one of the key moments in the difficult struggle to create a working relationship between black and white women. She spoke out against lynching, publicly stating that colored women were insulted by white men a thousand times more than the opposite.

Brown retired as president of Palmer in 1952. She remained an active member of the board of directors and director of finances, however, until 1955. She died in 1961, just a decade before Palmer was forced to close because of financial problems.

KATHLEEN THOMPSON

Roxbury Community College president Grace Carolyn Brown believes that community colleges provide culturally diverse students with opportunities to participate in the American Dream. (ROXBURY COMMUNITY COLLEGE)

Brown, Grace Carolyn (19??–)

Grace Carolyn Brown views community colleges as being so many opportunities for culturally diverse students to participate in the American Dream. Since 1992 she has been the President and Chief Executive Officer of Roxbury Community College near Boston, Massachusetts. Brown received B.S. and M.S. degrees in Nursing from Case Western Reserve University, then went on to obtain an Ed.D. in Community College Leadership at Nova University in Fort Lauderdale, Florida.

After spending a number of years at Cuyahoga Community College in Ohio, eventually becoming provost and vice president, Brown moved on to Roxbury. There she helped to revitalize that institution by, among other things, increasing the diversity and number of students, developing a second campus, increasing revenue, and building a new track and athletic center. One of her goals is to develop a core of talented, community-oriented teachers of color, who will in turn encourage their students to give back to their own urban or rural communities.

Brown, Letitia Woods (1915–1976)

As one of her colleagues once wrote, "Those who knew her soon learned never to name her to a committee unless one intended to take care of business. One learned never to engage her in conversation unless ready for real talk." Letitia Woods Brown was a historian committed to being an educator.

Born in Tuskegee, Alabama, in 1915, she received her B.S. in 1935 from the Tuskegee Institute, where both parents had been teachers. After receiving that degree, she taught in the segregated school system of Macon County, Alabama, and then went to Ohio State University, where she received an M.A. in 1937, after which she returned to teaching, accepting appointments at Tuskegee Institute and Lemoyne-Owen College in Memphis, Tennessee. She decided again to return to graduate school, at Harvard University, where she received her Ph.D. in 1966. While pursuing her doctorate, Brown taught at **Howard University** and later became a full professor of history in the American Studies Department at George Washington University, both in Washington, D.C. Her writings include *Free Negroes in the District of Columbia, 1790–1846*, published by Oxford University Press in 1972, and for the National Portrait Gallery she coauthored "Washington from Banneker to Douglass, 1791–1870" as well as other articles about the history of black Americans in Washington, D.C. Active in professional organizations, she served in 1971–73 on a restructuring committee formed to reorganize the American Historical Association, and her tenure as a senior Fulbright Lecturer in Australia led to collaborations with foreign scholars through the American Studies Association. Her commitment to school-age children was evidenced by her involvement in the National Assessment for Educational Progress.

Toward the end of her life, Brown became a prime advocate for the creation of an oral history project on black women, which was organized by the Schlesinger Library. Letitia Woods Brown died in August 1976, in Washington, D.C. Her memorial service was held at the National Cathedral.

In 1983, the Association of Black Women Historians established the Letitia Woods Brown Memorial Publication Prizes to honor excellence in scholarship by or about black women.

NORALEE FRANKEL

Butcher, Margaret Just (1913–)

When one hears the name Margaret Just Butcher, it is usually in conjunction with Alain Locke, for she completed what was to have been his "magnus opus." Before his death in 1954, Alain Locke turned over his research materials to Margaret, the brilliant daughter of one of his best friends. *The Negro in American Culture* (1956, 1971), which historically yet topically traces "the folk and formal contributions" of the Negro to American culture, is an important African-American reference text that is often cited in discussions of the artists Edward Bannister and Meta Warwick Fuller. Yet *The Negro in American Culture* is not Margaret Just Butcher's sole accomplishment; she also was an educational and political activist.

Born April 28, 1913, in Washington, D.C., Margaret was the oldest of the three children of Ernest Everett Just, the famed cell biologist and first recipient of the Spingarn Medal, and Ethel Highwarden, daughter of one of the first black female graduates of **Oberlin College**. Margaret's brilliance and preference for the humanities were recognized even in her early years. Her educational training included attending school in Naples, Italy, when she accompanied her father to Europe in 1927; Emerson College; and Boston University, where she received her Ph.D. in 1947.

The influence of her parents, both educators, is evident in Margaret Just Butcher's choice of a profession. As an English professor, she taught at Virginia Union University (1935–36), in the Washington, D.C., public schools (1937–41), at **Howard University** (1942–55), and at Federal City College (1971–82). Her interest in the humanities also took her abroad—as a Fulbright visiting professor in France (1949–50), as the director of the English Language Training Institute in Casablanca (1960–65), and as assistant cultural affairs officer of the U.S. Embassy in Paris (1968).

While teaching was her primary profession, Butcher made inroads as a reformer in education and politics. From 1953 to 1956, she served on the board of education for the Washington, D.C., schools during the time the school system was to be integrated, and was the only board member who fought for equality in integration.

Butcher became well known in the District for her scathing criticisms of the board, and her challenges often were reported in the newspapers. She was honored in 1955 by Lambda Kappa Mu "for her militant fight for integration of education."

Butcher also was active in the political arena: she served as a member of the National Civil Defense Advisory Council in 1952 (replacing **Mary McLeod Bethune**); she was a special educational consultant to the **National Association for the Advancement of Colored People** during 1954–55 (assisting Thurgood Marshall); and she was elected as the district's delegate to the Democratic Party's national convention in 1956 and 1960.

Margaret Just was married for a short time to Stanton L. Wormley (the precise dates are unknown); the couple had one daughter, Sheryl Everett. In 1949, she married James W. Butcher; they divorced ten years later. Margaret Just Butcher currently resides in Washington, D.C.

PAULA C. BARNES

Butler, Lauretta Green (1881–1952)

Lauretta Green Butler relinquished a professional music career to devote her life to training children to perform for the stage. Lauretta Green was born November 6, 1881, in Los Angeles, California. She was one of three children born to Joseph and Amanda Shelton Green. She married Charles Butler, of whom very little is known.

Butler began her musical career as a church pianist. For several years she performed with many of the best black orchestras in the country. Inspired by a children's production she saw in Chicago,

Butler returned to Los Angeles and opened the first black professional dance studio for children. A great lover of children, Butler realized that with the proper training she could develop the latent talent not only in precocious youngsters but also in those considered to be without ability or aptitude.

The Butler Dance Studio, for children from two years old to teenagers, opened in 1916. At the studio, the students learned dancing, singing, and mime along with strong discipline. In 1917, Butler presented her first Kiddie Minstrel Review, which established her as the foremost producer of children's acts. The Butler Studio became an established tradition and institution in Los Angeles until the late 1940s. Around 1923, the Kiddie Minstrel Review was renamed the Kiddie Review, and the use of blackface makeup was eliminated.

Butler trained many of the young people, directed productions, played piano, and conducted the orchestra for performances. The "Butler Kids" were in constant demand to perform for major social events, nightclubs, military bases, and the movie industry. The children were highlighted in numerous black films of the 1930s and 1940s. While the Butler Studio was established primarily for black children, many white children were trained by Butler, including cast members from *The Little Rascals* and *Our Gang*.

Butler also trained many legendary young black stars for the stage and screen, such as **Dorothy** and Vivian **Dandridge**, the great dancing team of Ananias and James Berry, and Jimmie and Freddy Moultrie.

Butler, who never had any children of her own, adopted several during her lifetime. She inspired other black professionals to open schools for young people, but none saw the success of the Butler Studio.

KATHY A. PERKINS

Byrd, Flossie M. (1927–)

Flossie M. Byrd's more than four decades of outstanding teaching and leadership in home economics led to her selection as recipient of the Distinguished Service Award from the American Home Economics Association in 1990, and to her induction into the Gallery of Distinction for Agricultural and Home Economics Graduates at Florida A & M University. She has taught at Florida A & M University, Oregon State University, and Prairie View A & M University, where she is now vice president for academic affairs. Byrd holds an M.Ed. from Pennsylvania State University and a Ph.D. from Cornell University. She also has studied at Trinity University, Pepperdine University, and the University of Southern California.

Born to John and Elizabeth Byrd in Sarasota, Florida, on August 8, 1927, she served as president of the National Council of Administrators of Home Economics, 1971–72; cochair of the Home Economics Commission of the National Association of State Universities and Land Grant Colleges, 1966–69; chair of the Southern Region of Home Economics Administrators, 1978–79; vice president of the American Home Economics Association, 1985–87; and president of the Association of Administrators of Home Economics, 1981–83. She has published articles in the *Journal of Home Economics* and contributed chapters to books and edited volumes. More than $800,000 of funding for home economics research was garnered by Byrd while she was professor and dean of home economics at Prairie View, 1964–87. Since 1987, she has received grants for more than $2 million for Title III projects.

JEWEL LIMAR PRESTAGE

C

Cable, Mary Ellen (1881–1944)

African-American educator, director of practice teaching, principal, supervising principal, clubwoman, and civil rights activist, Mary Ellen Cable was born and raised in Leavenworth, Kansas.

She graduated from Leavenworth Teachers' Normal School in the late 1890s. After graduation she taught elementary school for a brief time in Topeka, Kansas, where she met her husband, George Cable, at that time also a teacher. The couple had moved to Indianapolis by 1900, where George accepted a position at the post office and Mary began her forty years of service with the Indianapolis Public School System. Cable further enhanced her education skills and abilities through study at the University of Chicago, Columbia University in New York, and the Indiana University Extension at Indianapolis. In 1903–05, Cable successfully oversaw the black community's elementary school vegetable garden project, which ultimately prompted residents in surrounding neighborhoods to plant gardens and improve property upkeep.

In 1916–17, with the support of several black women's clubs, Cable instituted the first "fresh air" classroom for black children with tuberculous, at Public School 24. During Cable's tenure as director of practice teaching, the Indianapolis School Board certified sixty-one much-needed African-American teachers.

Mary Cable also was an active member of various social and civic groups, among them the Bethel African Methodist Episcopal Church, the Browning Literary Society, and the Sigma Gamma Rose sorority. In 1912, as president of the Colored Women's Civic Club, a local philanthropic group, Cable provided the impetus for organizing the local chapter of the **National Association for the Advancement of Colored People** (NAACP)—its westernmost branch at that time. She served as Indiana's first NAACP president, and for the first thirteen months all other officers and members of the executive board were clubwomen. In 1913, finding themselves overwhelmed by family, club, and NAACP responsibilities, the women petitioned the black community's men—"who have more time"—to shoulder the burden of leadership.

EARLINE RAE FERGUSON

Calloway, Bertha (1925–)

"We cannot direct the wind, but we can adjust the sails," Bertha Calloway has said. "The Museum moves on, and we know we are going in the right direction."

She was speaking of the Great Plains Black Museum, which she started in 1974 with her husband, J. T. Calloway, in Omaha, Nebraska. It is the largest such operation in the Midwest. Its goal is to address the longstanding, persistent ignorance of the African-American legacy in

Nebraska, the Great Plains, the western United States and even in all of global history.

Not long after her birth in 1925 in Denver, Colorado, Calloway began to hear tales of relatives who had been cowboys. Nearly as early, she met disbelief that such black cowboys as Nat Love could ever have existed. This spurred a lifelong search for proof, and an interest in knowing more of the entire black heritage.

Having studied at Langston University in Oklahoma and **Howard University** in Washington, D.C., she moved to Omaha, where, on the College of Saint Mary and Creighton University faculties, she became one of Nebraska's first teachers of black history.

The first step toward realizing the museum was taken in 1960, when with the help of friends and local and state agencies, Calloway launched the Negro Historical Society of Nebraska, the first of its kind in the Midwest. Culling artifacts and documents, often from newspaper archives, she and her husband held meetings with members of Omaha's northside black community to plan fund drives.

The building acquired for the museum was at 2213 Lake St., and had been erected in 1906 to house the Webster Telephone Exchange. It was a community center in 1933 and an apartment dwelling in 1952. In 1976, a federal Bicentennial commission grant of $101,000 and two others, plus $10,000 from Nebraska's bicentennial commission, enabled the Calloways to hire community employees and pay operating costs.

The museum's many exhibits highlight the Plains' black women, and African-American contributions to music, religion, politics, athletics, the military and, of course, the Old West. It houses vintage black publications (including a private rare-book collection), manuscripts, oral history recordings, and even some specimens of traditional African art.

The museum's multifaceted community involvement reflects Bertha Calloway's personal missions, and she has served a multitude of causes and organizations. These include Omaha's public schools, the Smithsonian Institution, the **National Association for the Advancement of Colored People** (NAACP), the Red Cross, and the **National Council of Negro Women**. There are many others, often with a focus on education, and in return she has received many plaudits and honors.

GARY HOUSTON

Campbell, Zerrie D. (1951–)

Zerrie D. Campbell is the seventh president of Malcolm X College, part of the City Colleges of Chicago (CCC) system. She is the first African-American woman to be permanently appointed to that position.

Campbell holds bachelor's and master's degrees from Northern Illinois University and a master's degree from Chicago State University. She began her career with CCC in 1974 as director of student supportive services at Malcolm X College, and she has served as a faculty member at Malcolm X and Harold Washington Colleges, acting associate vice chancellor for liberal arts and sciences at Central Administration, vice president for academic affairs, and interim president. She also served on the CCC's three-person Interim District Management Team, directing the day-to-day operations of the seven-college district for fifteen months, and is a member of the Consultant Evaluator Corps for the North Central Association of Colleges and Schools.

Under Campbell's leadership, Malcolm X College was awarded the Illinois Community College Board's 1994 Award for Excellence in Institutional Effectiveness and Strategic Planning, and its 1995 Award for Excellence in Teaching and Learning. Campbell herself has received numerous awards, including the National Association of University Women's Distinguished Imprint Award, the Orchid Award from the Top Ladies of Distinction, and President of the Year honors from the American Association for Women in Community Colleges.

Campbell has presented workshops on diversity, race, and women in higher education at regional, national, and international conferences, and she is in great demand as a commencement and youth-motivation speaker. She participated in workshops for the development of women in higher education sponsored by the National Institute for Leadership Development's Leaders Project for three years, then was named to the institute's advisory board.

A practitioner of "Empowerment through Education," Campbell believes she is in partnership with all segments of the Malcolm X College community to build the bridges that make educational opportunities available to the students it serves.

INDIA COOPER

Zerrie D. Campbell is the seventh president of Malcolm X College in Chicago and the first black woman to hold that position.
(MALCOLM X COLLEGE)

Cline, Eileen T. (1935–)

A passion for music and a zest for life inspired Eileen Tate Cline to a career in music education that ultimately took her to the position of dean of the prestigious Peabody Conservatory of Music at Johns Hopkins University. Along the way, as educator and role model, she influenced a generation of young musicians who came to know her as "Dean Mom."

Eileen Tate Cline was born in Chicago on June 15, 1935, to Herman Tate and Inez Duke Tate, well-educated people whose probing minds and hands-on community activism were an early influence. Raised in a middle-class black neighborhood in Chicago, Cline's view of the world was expanded, and challenged, when her family moved to a white-dominated suburb when she was six years old. The combination of the rejections she felt from the white com-

For thirteen years, Eileen Cline was "Dean Mom" to students at the Peabody Conservatory of Music.
(PEABODY CONSERVATORY OF MUSIC)

munity and the judgments she endured in her all-black school contributed to her own growing sense of character: "I was considered: too light-skinned, too smart, too square, too tall, feet too big, the wrong religion, four-eyed, ugly—you name it. But I was adventuresome—a sports nut, a tomboy, and a bookworm—and I had a good time anyway."

This bookworm took to academics with a relish that allowed her, at the age of fifteen, to undertake a liberal arts course of study at the University of Chicago. Her musical education took place at such institutions as the Geneva C. Robinson Chicago Musical College, where she studied piano from the ages of ten to seventeen, and the Oberlin Conservatory of Music, where in only four years' time she earned bachelor's degrees in both music education and in piano performance in 1956. She went on to graduate study at the University of Colorado at Boulder, where she received her master's degree in music in 1960. From the Indiana University School of Music she received her doctorate, with highest distinction, in 1985. Her dissertation on piano competitions is widely regarded as the first authoritative resource on this subject.

During her time in Boulder, Cline married linguist William Cline, began to raise two children, and also continued to expand the range of her activities as performer, teacher, conductor, and church organist. After her husband accepted a position as visiting scholar at Princeton in 1978, Cline (by now studying for her doctorate as a Danforth Fellow at Indiana University) and the children moved with him to the east coast.

His sudden death one month later presented Cline with perhaps the greatest challenge of her life. She had lost her partner, had no job, and had two children to support. By chance she happened on a radio broadcast in which Maya Angelou was being interviewed about pressures in her life. "Let me tell you about pressure," Angelou said. "Take a lesson from Mother Nature. When you have the greatest amount of pressure, what do you get? Diamonds! And when there is less pressure? Coal! And less pressure? Carbon! And when there is no pressure at all? Just plain dirt!" It was just the message that Cline needed to rally herself, and it became a significant turning point in her life.

Cline served a stint as executive director of the Neighborhood Music School in New Haven, Connecticut, after which she was appointed associate dean of the Peabody School in 1982. One year later she was promoted to dean, a position she held for thirteen years. As dean, she established a policy of openness and interaction between students, faculty, and staff. She raised both the enrollment and the quality of students at

Peabody and paid special attention to minority recruitment. According to Peabody Director Robert Pierce, Cline worked to "improve access and retention to the point where our African-American students became outstanding for their artistic achievements and leadership skills."

A recognized leader and influential voice in music education, Cline has served on the boards and committees of numerous institutions, including the Oberlin Conservatory of Music, the American Symphony Orchestra League, and the Van Cliburn International Piano Competition, among many others. She has done postdoctoral work at the Aspen Institute, Harvard University, and Johns Hopkins University.

In 1995, after thirteen influential years as dean, Cline was appointed a university fellow in arts policy at Johns Hopkins. Her new mission is to influence the growth and development of arts policy on a national scale—a fitting challenge for one who has met so many already in her remarkable life.

CHRISTINE SUMPTION
RICHARD E. T. WHITE

Cobb, Jewell Plummer (1924–)

Jewell Plummer Cobb has achieved an impressive record as educator, administrator, and author, and done it all with grace and style.

Born to an upper-middle-class family in Chicago in 1924, Jewell Plummer had parents who could scarcely have been better role models. Her father, Frank V. Plummer, one of the founders of Alpha Phi Alpha fraternity when he was at Cornell University, began practicing medicine in Chicago in 1923 and served that city's black population for many years. Her mother, Carriebel

Cole Plummer, was a teacher of dance who had studied at Sargeants, a physical education college affiliated with Harvard. Among her parents' friends were historian Carter G. Woodson, poet Arna Bontemps, and anthropologist Allison Davis.

Young Jewell Plummer attended Chicago's primarily segregated public schools, but her education was supplemented by her parents' remarkable library and trips to New York City for cultural events. She was an honor student throughout her elementary and high school years and became interested in biology when she was a sophomore. After graduation, she attended the University of Michigan.

In her second year at Michigan, she decided to transfer to Talladega College in Alabama. She graduated with a major in biology in 1941 and went on to New York University. In 1950, she completed work on her Ph.D. in cell physiology and began a career in research. Her primary area of concentration was pigment cell research, dealing especially with melanin. She did particularly important work investigating melanoma, tumors on the skin that usually are malignant. She did research at the Cancer Research Foundation with Dorothy Walker Jones that involved studying the effects of cancer chemotherapy drugs on human tumors that the two women grew in culture in the laboratory.

In 1954, Jewell Plummer married Roy Paul Cobb and, three years later the couple had a son, Roy Jonathan. After a time at the University of Illinois College of Medicine, she joined the faculty of Sarah Lawrence College in 1960. There she taught, carried on her research, and became dean of the college. She and Roy Cobb were divorced in 1967. In 1969, she became dean of Connecticut College and professor of zoology. It was not until she became dean of Douglass College in 1976 that she finally gave up her research.

While at Connecticut College, she founded a privately funded premedical and predental program for minority students. That program has served as a model for similar programs at twenty other colleges, but it was dropped by Connecticut College after Cobb left.

In 1981, Cobb became president of California State University at Fullerton. While she was there, she accomplished a great deal for the school and the community. She established, for example, the first privately funded gerontology center in Orange County. She created an opportunity program for ethnic students. She also built an apartment complex for students, transforming the former commuter campus into a residential school. That complex was named in her honor.

In 1990, at the age of sixty-six, Cobb became Trustee Professor at California State College in Los Angeles. She is working with a consortium of six colleges whose goal is to encourage minority students to enter the fields of science and engineering. The group hopes to get corporate funding to replace the federal grants and fellowships that are rapidly disappearing. They also are working on a more personal level with individual students, to remedy any deficiencies in their educational backgrounds.

The recipient of many honorary doctorates and other awards, Cobb has published extensively. The majority of her publications are scientific in nature, but several deal with issues concerning women and minorities. One of her best known is an article, "Filters for Women in Science," published in the *Annals of the New York Academy of Sciences* (1979). In it, she draws a parallel between the process of achieving success in the sciences and a filter, such as that used in a laboratory. For women, she says, the filter is much finer than for men. Fortunately for women and other minority members in the sciences, Jewell Plummer Cobb focuses on locating talent, not filtering it out.

KATHLEEN THOMPSON

Cole, Johnnetta Betsch (1936–)

Johnnetta Betsch Cole is the seventh president of **Spelman College,** the oldest college for black women in the United States; she is the first black woman to serve as president since the college's founding in 1881. She was born October 19, 1936, in Jacksonville, Florida. Her maternal great-grandfather, Abraham Lincoln Lewis, cofounded the Afro-American Life Insurance Company of Jacksonville in 1901. Her father, John Betsch, Sr., worked for Atlanta Life Insurance Company but later joined his wife's family's business. Her mother, Mary Frances Lewis Betsch, an educator and graduate of Wilberforce University in Ohio, taught English and was registrar at Edward Waters College in Jacksonville before joining the family insurance business after her husband's death.

When Cole was appointed president of Spelman on April 5, 1987, she was professor of anthropology and director of the Latin American and Caribbean Studies Program at Hunter College of the City University of New York; previously she had been associate provost for undergraduate education at the University of Massachusetts at Amherst.

In her acceptance statement, Cole said she envisioned Spelman under her leadership as a "renown[ed] center for scholarship by and about black women," as well as a place where "Black women leaders of the world are nurtured, trained, and developed." She indicated that "scholars, teachers, artists, policy analysts, and community leaders will turn to Spelman for comprehensive information on the rich and diverse history, struggles, conditions, and accomplishments of black women."

The historic appointment of Cole as the first African-American woman to head Spelman was significant also because for the first time in its history the college was to be headed by a president with an explicitly black feminist vision. In her first statement to the Spelman community, Cole alluded to the essence of her work prior to becoming president: "I have *consciously* lived and studied, taught and written, as an African-American woman. The issues of race and gender have been central in my life, in my work as an anthropologist, and in my community activities. There is a fundamental question at the base of the work that I do: how can people of color, poor people, and women become full, productive, and equal members of the society in which they live?"

Shortly after coming to the campus, Cole donned the affectionate title of "sister president," a label she gave herself in her first published interview as president, which was alluded to in the October 1987 issue of *Ms.* A year later, during her November 8, 1988, inauguration, Cole announced that a historic gift of $20 million had been made to the college by Bill and Camille Cosby.

Cole spent her formative years in Jacksonville and, in 1952, at age fifteen, entered Fisk University in Nashville, Tennessee, under its early admissions program. After only a year at Fisk, she left to join her older sister,

Marvyne Betsch, at **Oberlin College** in Oberlin, Ohio. During her first year at Oberlin (1953), Johnnetta Betsch took a class on racial and cultural minorities; taught by George Eaton Simpson, the class inspired her to major in sociology and to pursue a career in anthropology. After graduating from Oberlin in 1957, she went to Northwestern University to pursue a master's degree in anthropology, which she received in 1959. In 1967 she was awarded the Ph.D. in anthropology at Northwestern, after studying under noted anthropologists Melville J. Herskovits and Paul J. Bohannan.

Following appointments at the University of California at Los Angeles and at Washington State University in Pullman, Washington, Cole joined the faculty of the University of Massachusetts at Amherst, where she remained for thirteen years. She went to Hunter College in 1983, first as

In accepting her historic appointment as the first African-American woman to head Spelman College, Johnnetta Cole described her vision of Spelman as a place where "black women leaders of the world are nurtured, trained, and developed." Here she speaks with students on campus. (SPELMAN COLLEGE)

African-American Women Who Serve as College Presidents

Anderson, Del M.	San Jose City College
Baccus, Eileen	Northwest Connecticut Community Technical College
Belcher, Jacquelyn	Minneapolis Community College
Boyd-Scotland, Joann R.G.	Denmark Technical College
Brown, Grace Carolyn	Roxbury Community College
Campbell, Zerrie D.	Malcolm X. College
Carroll, Constance	San Diego Mesa College
Cole, Johnnetta	Spelman College
Cross, Delores E.	Chicago State University
Farris, Vera King	Stockton College of New Jersey
Harris, Marjorie	Lewis College of Business
Harris, Zelema M.	Parkland College
Hatton, Barbara R.	South Carolina State University
Horton, Joann	Texas Southern University
Hughes, Marvalene	California State University, Stanislaus
Jenkins, Sebetha	Jarvis Christian College
Johnston, Gladys Styles	University of Nebraska at Kearney
Jolly, Linda C.	Salem Community College
Keizs, Marcia V.	Borough of Manhattan Community College
Kennedy, Yvonne	Bishop State Community College
Ladner, Joyce	Howard University
Lewis, Shirley	Paine College
Mitchell, Katherine	Shorter College
Moses, Yolanda T.	City College, City University of New York
Pettigrew, L. Eudora	State University of New York at Old Westbury
Porche-Burke, Lisa	California School of Professional Psychology, Los Angeles
Rice, Constance W.	North Seattle Community College, Washington
Richards, Hilda	Indiana University Northwest
Scott, Gloria	Bennett College
Simmons, Ruth	Smith College
Smith, Eleanor J.	University of Wisconsin at Parkside
Smith, Mary L.	Kentucky State University
Sudarkasa, Niara	Lincoln University
Surles, Carol	Texas Woman's University
Thornton, Jerry Sue	Cuyahoga Community College
Ward, Arnette	Chandler-Gilbert Community College
Whelan, Belle S.	Central Virginia Commuity College
Williams, Lois Stovall	Knoxville College, Tennessee
Williams, Carolyn	Los Angeles Southwest College
Wilson, Blenda	California State University, Northridge
Yancy, Dorothy	Johnson C. Smith University

Russell Sage Visiting Professor and then as a tenured professor of anthropology. She also has held visiting appointments at Oberlin and Williams College in Williamstown, Massachusetts.

Cole's scholarly research and writing have been in the areas of cultural anthropology, African-American studies, and women's studies. She is especially interested in systems of inequality based on race, gender, and class, and in the Pan-African world of the United States, the Caribbean, and Africa. Her major publications include *All American Women: Lines That Divide, Ties That Bind* (1986), *Anthropology for the Eighties: Introductory Readings* (1982), and *Anthropology for the Nineties* (1988). She has researched female-headed households in New York City, the lives of Caribbean women, racial and gender inequality in Cuba, and economic issues in Liberia. She is former president of both the Association of Black Anthropologists and the International Women's Anthropology Conference.

During her first marriage to economist Robert Cole, she had three sons; currently she is married to Arthur Robinson III.

BEVERLY GUY-SHEFTALL

Collins, Marva N. (1936–)

"When we create a positive environment for our students, we can see some miraculous things happen." This is the view of Marva N. Collins, an innovative black educator of national reputation who concentrates her interests on teaching as well as on creating and implementing progressive educational concepts. After nineteen years of experience with the methods and policies of the Chicago public schools, Collins found herself openly challenging a system that failed to educate all children with equal vigor and reasonable success. By 1975, she had realized that her dissatisfaction could not be remedied through a large, impersonal, and politicized school system of nearly half a million children who were predominantly nonwhite. Consequently she established the Westside Preparatory School, an alternative educational institution for black children on Chicago's neglected and maligned West Side.

Marva Nettles Collins was born on August 31, 1936, in Monroeville, Alabama. She "grew up in a very nurtured background." She had much support for her own education: "If you went to college in Alabama, you were a celebrity. The minister had you stand in church and all the people would give you a quarter or fifty cents, what they could. You didn't get into trouble because in your mind's eye you could see all these people caring about you, depending on you." This was the same supportive and demanding environment that Collins sought to create for black children in Chicago.

Attaining her goal required traits that Collins possesses in abundance: a strong will, dedication to the highest principles of teaching, an abiding love for the young students whose future she embraced, and full confidence in her ability to move forward from critic to builder. Her greatest obstacle was financing, which she provided herself from personal funds and loans. Even today she disdains the receipt of any financing from federal or corporate sources that might inhibit her independence.

Collins has critics, but she also has legions of supporters whose recognition of her successes influenced Presidents Ronald Reagan and George Bush, successively, to offer her an appointment as U.S. Secretary of Education; she declined each time. Collins also received the attention of the national media when she was featured on *60 Minutes* and was the subject of a television movie.

In her role as builder, Collins refined, blended, and implemented traditional as well as progressive teaching concepts and methods at Westside Prep. National interest in her demonstrated success convinced some Ohio parents to seek her assistance in creating an alternative school in Cincinnati, which opened in 1990 as the Marva Collins Preparatory School. In 1991, the state of Oklahoma invited Collins to design a training program for its staff to show what can be accomplished academically with youngsters who often are written off by mainstream school systems as ineducable.

Collins' success at Westside Prep depended, first, on creating an environment that was conducive to learning and bringing out to the greatest measure every child's intellectual potential and, second, on assembling a teaching staff with broad liberal arts training, a dedication to teaching, and a love of children. Students are accepted from throughout Chicago, with the preponderance coming from the city's West Side black neighborhoods. Contrary to some of the criticism, there has never been an exclusionary admissions policy based on previous academic performance, economic status, or behavioral problems. The miracle of Westside Prep has rested on heavy doses of time-tested basics such as phonics, memorization, reading aloud, exposure to foreign languages, and exercises in critical thinking—all undergirded by the use of interdisciplinary materials that range from the classics to modern thought.

Further, Collins structured her school so that students attend four clusters of classes that are formed without regard to age differences, rather than in the standard nine grade levels (K–8) found in most elementary schools. At present, the miracle continues, as Collins encourages her pupils to say good-bye to failure.

CHRISTOPHER R. REED

Cooke, Anne (1907–)

In 1949, the Howard Players of **Howard University** became the first American undergraduate group to be invited by the U.S. State Department and a foreign government to perform abroad. This historic event was spearheaded by Dr. Anne Cooke. Anne Cooke was known for nearly four decades as an innovative director and educator in theater. Throughout her career, she developed and maintained professional standards in the theater programs on predominantly black campuses such as Howard University, **Spelman College**, and Atlanta University.

Cooke was born Anna Margaret on October 6, 1907, in Washington, D.C., but she spent her early years in the Midwest. She is the daughter of Mr. and Mrs. William W. Cooke. She received her A.B. from **Oberlin College** in 1928. Cooke also studied at Columbia University, the American Academy of Dramatic Arts, and the Chicago Art Theatre. Cooke was a recipient of Fulbright, Rosenwald, and Rockefeller Fellowships. She received her Ph.D. in theater from Yale University in 1944, making her possibly the first black American to receive such a degree. During her time at Yale, Cooke had an opportunity to work with film director Otto Preminger.

Through Preminger, Cooke was able to gain experience as a director during the early years of television.

In 1928, Cooke became director of dramatics at Spelman College. In 1934, she organized and directed the Atlanta University Summer Theatre, a dramatic organization comprised of Atlanta University, Morehouse College, and Spelman College students. This organization gained a reputation for excellence in dramatics. Cooke brought in the best and brightest black theater educators and professional actors to work with the students. Major white designers also would lend their expertise to the program. Students from around the country converged on Atlanta to work under Cooke. For many years, the summer theater was the only place in the country where black American students were afforded an opportunity to have a concentrated professional theater experience.

In 1942, Cooke left Spelman to become director of the Communications Center at Hampton Institute. From 1944 to 1958, she organized and chaired Howard University's first drama department, making it the premiere black institution for drama. Cooke brought international acclaim to the Howard Players when the group traveled to Norway and other Scandinavian countries.

In 1958, Cooke married sociologist and author Ira De A. Reid. While her husband was on the faculty of Haverford College, Cooke was active in campus and community drama in Haverford. After the death of her husband in 1968, Cooke became a professor of drama at the University of Maryland, from which she retired.

KATHY A. PERKINS

Cooper, Anna Julia (1858–1964)

"Not the boys less, but the girls more," wrote Anna J. Cooper in her collection of writings and essays, *A Voice from the South by a Black Woman of the South* (1892). Marked by an unusual maturity and mental aptitude, Cooper said that "not far from . . . kindergarten age" she had decided to be a teacher. Her early and unbridled passion for learning, and her belief that women were well equipped to follow intellectual pursuits, carried Cooper from the then-ungraded St. Augustine's Normal School and Collegiate Institute in Raleigh, North Carolina, to the Sorbonne in Paris.

During this more than fifty-year sojourn in pursuit of her dream, she also earned A.B. (1884) and M.A. (1887) degrees from **Oberlin College**, was principal of the M Street High School in Washington, D.C. (1902–06), and, in 1929, became the second president of Frelinghuysen University, in Washington, D.C. Best known as an educator, Cooper also was a feminist, human rights advocate, distinguished scholar, essayist, author, lecturer, and vital force in the late nineteenth-century black woman's club movement.

The daughter of a slave woman, Hannah Stanley, and her master, George Washington Haywood of Raleigh, Cooper was born Annie Julia Haywood on August 10, 1858. Hired out as a nursemaid for Charles Busbee (later a successful lawyer), Hannah named the infant girl for Charles' mother. No one in her own home was literate, so probably it was in the Busbee home that young Annie's love for books and learning blossomed. Years later, however, as president of Frelinghuysen, Cooper touchingly honored her mother by naming one small department

In 1901, Anna Julia Cooper became the second black female principal in the history of the famous M Street High School in Washington, D.C. She succeeded Robert H. Terrell. A lifelong educator and leader, she received her Ph.D. from the Sorbonne at the age of sixty-six. She is shown here on the veranda of her Washington, D.C., home. (SCURLOCK STUDIO)

of the struggling institution the Hannah Stanley Opportunity School. As Cooper wrote about her mother, "mother . . . sacrificed and toiled to give me advantages that she had never enjoyed herself." Of her father, Cooper later wrote that beyond the act of procreation she owed him nothing.

Cooper entered St. Augustine's in 1867. There she coached or tutored other students, some of whom were years beyond her tender age of nine. About a decade later, when she protested the exclusion of young women from higher courses scheduled only for min-

isterial studies and, therefore, only for men, Cooper met her future husband. From Nassau, British West Indies, George A. C. Cooper was an Episcopal theology student and St. Augustine's new Greek teacher. Although George was nearly fourteen years her senior, teacher and pupil developed a friendship, which later grew into love. They were married on June 21, 1877. With shared career goals, the couple worked tirelessly to achieve them during the two years they were married. George died on September 27, 1879, just two months after becoming the second black ordained clergyman in the Protestant Episcopal Church in North Carolina.

At the age of twenty-one, Cooper was alone. Not one to complain about adversities, the young widow stoically continued on in the pursuit of her goals. Denied a modest increase in her thirty-dollar-a-month teaching salary, she left St. Augustine's in the fall of 1881 to travel to Oberlin, Ohio. The previous summer she had written to James Harris Fairchild, president of Oberlin College, saying "for a long time, I earnestly desired to take an advanced course in some superior Northern college, but could not . . . for lack of means."

Given Oberlin's enviable reputation for liberal thought and superior scholarship, Cooper believed that admission to Oberlin would be an important step in her long quest for higher education. Unlike most young women students of the time, Cooper—along with **Mary Eliza Church (Terrell)** and Ida A. Gibbs (Hunt)—took the four-year "gentlemen's course." The trio graduated from Oberlin in 1884, following **Mary Jane Patterson** (1862) as the first black women to complete a four-year course of study from an accredited American college.

While at Oberlin, Cooper began to see herself as a defender of her race and an advocate for black women. Personal successes and achievements to one side, she remained sensitive to the plight and needs of oppressed peoples, and was encouraged to be a free thinker and the voice of unheard southern black women. Her interaction with faculty members and peers, whose sound scholarship and intelligence reinforced her own views, helped Cooper prepare for her lifelong work. The first member of her family to go beyond the primary grades, Cooper left Oberlin eager to serve those who were unserved. Confident, poised, self-assured, and armed with an A.B., she felt ready to address the inequities and indignities that black women like her mother had experienced in slavery and in the post–Civil War South.

Cooper postponed for a year her planned return to Raleigh in order to teach at Wilberforce College in Ohio. As a devout and lifelong Episcopalian, Cooper had many contacts in the national black church community. At Wilberforce she met Bishop Benjamin W. Arnett, a noted cleric of the African Methodist Episcopal (AME) Church. Cooper admired Arnett for his support of the cause of black women, and Arnett later wrote a favorable introduction to *A Voice from the South*.

Also among her supporters were clergymen Alexander Crummell, Francis J. Grimké, and Walter H. Brooks. Later she befriended Alexander Walters, a bishop in the AME Zion Church and head of the National Negro-American Political League. All social activists, these men worked to help those who, in Cooper's words, "were stuck at the bottom." In each of them she found a brother's sympathy for the difficult and adverse situation of black women.

As in her life experiences, Cooper forthrightly addressed critical issues in her writings. Not given to expediency or vagueness, she never avoided tough situations or difficult decisions. She used cogent arguments to persuade others of the importance and correctness of the causes she embraced. Although some people found her to be difficult, intractable, and blunt, St. Augustine's principal, John E. C. Smedes, described her in 1881 as "a woman of unusual culture and intelligence, and of unfeigned zeal and piety." Cooper, he said, had decided to "be better qualified to take part in the great work going forward in the South for the . . . education of its colored people."

After a year as head of the modern languages department at Wilberforce, Cooper returned to Raleigh to deal with urgent family matters. (In 1880–81, she had purchased a modest dwelling for her mother from Richard Battle, a member of the prominent Haywood clan.) For the next two years Cooper taught mathematics, Greek, and Latin at St. Augustine's, began outreach extension programs under the school's aegis, and helped found a Sunday school and a mission guild. As a member of the North Carolina Teacher's Association, she involved herself with critical education issues, and in signing the group's report to the state legislature, she was very outspoken about the failure of lawmakers to appropriate "reasonable and just provisions for the training of . . . colored youth."

In 1887, Washington, D.C.'s first black Superintendent of Colored Schools, inspired

Frelinghuysen University was dedicated to providing an education to adult "colored working people." Anna Julia Cooper was its second president and she fought valiantly for the school's survival. (SCURLOCK STUDIO)

by high praise from people at Oberlin, invited Cooper to join the faculty of M Street (now Paul Laurence Dunbar) High School. Not completely unknown in Washington, Cooper boarded with the Rev. Alexander Crummell and his wife. Already living with the Crummells were Oberlin graduates Mary Jane Patterson, also from Raleigh, and her sister Channie; Mary Eliza Church (Terrell); Ida Gibbs (Hunt); and, later, Gibbs's sister, Harriet Gibbs Marshall. Cooper quickly joined with them and others in order to work for social progress, allying herself with groups that addressed issues important to the national black community. Battles won in Washington often had broad implications for black Americans across the nation, and Cooper worked unstintingly to present a more positive image of her race.

The decade of the 1890s was an important period in the fostering of black intellectual and political thought. In the vanguard of the struggle for human rights, Cooper and the groups with whom she was associated promoted opportunities for academic excellence for black youth; built groups and clubs of learning and culture for black women; defended the honor of, and demanded respect for, the reputations and views of black people; and effectively articulated their needs, hopes, and aspirations. To these efforts Cooper and her colleagues brought more than a half-century of commitment to, and activism in, antislavery groups, abolitionist societies, women's rights groups, literary and self-improvement clubs, and benevolent organizations. Some, like Cooper, had published and lectured on circuits such as Chautauqua. Known for her learning, modesty, and culture, Cooper herself was recognized as an "inspiring lecturer and leader."

As spokeswomen for their race, Anna Cooper, **Fannie Barrier Williams**, and **Fanny Jackson Coppin** were invited in 1893 to address a special meeting of the Women's Congress in Chicago. This international gathering of women was held to coincide with the World's Columbian Exposition, in order to ensure a large audience and wide press coverage. A special session addressing the theme "The Intellectual Progress of Colored Women of the United States since Emancipation" was held to give black women a hearing before an international body of white women. Cooper's thesis was a subject she often addressed, "The Needs and Status of black Women." A platform guest who was deeply moved by what he had heard, Frederick Douglass, rose to make impromptu remarks. In closing he said: "When I hear such speeches . . . from our women—*our women*—I feel a sense of gratitude to Almighty God that I have lived to see what I now see."

Cooper was the only woman elected to membership in the esoteric American Negro Academy, founded in 1897 by Alexander Crummell. Among its select members were W. E. B. DuBois, Kelly Miller, Jesse E. Moorland, Arthur A. Schomburg, and Carter G. Woodson. This late nineteenth-century black think tank had among its objectives "the publication of scholarly work and the defense of the Negro against vicious assault."

At the first Pan-African Conference in London's Westminster Hall in 1900, Cooper and Anna H. Jones of Missouri were the only two black women to address the international gathering of African, Afro-Caribbean, and Afro-American descendants. Cooper's address, "The Negro Problem in America," was to have been published in the conference report, but has not been found. An official

U.S. delegate and elected member of the executive committee, Cooper also served on a committee that drafted a memorial to Queen Victoria, which also addressed the issue of apartheid. Concisely and poignantly, the conferees appealed for immediate relief from "acts of injustice directed against Her Majesty's subjects in South Africa."

Cooper followed this heady experience with a trip to France to tour the Paris Exposition. Among egalitarians and black expatriates, and accompanied by DuBois, Cooper visited the Social Economy Building's Negro Pavilion, which housed the Exposition des Nègres d'Amérique. Mounted by the Library of Congress and first displayed at M Street High School, the exhibit featured the black community of Washington, D.C.

Revitalized by her involvement in the Pan-African Conference, Cooper returned home to her teaching duties. Although she had been asked to serve on the planning committee for the next gathering, to be held in Boston in 1902, this conference did not materialize. The conference's cancellation may have been linked to monitoring by the U.S. State and War departments of black activists in Puerto Rico, the Philippines, and Cuba, where a Negro revolution was rumored to be under way in 1900–01. The Interior Department's Bureau of Insular Affairs compiled files (captioned "Negro") about the militancy of black islanders. These so-called investigations were followed by a second occupation of Cuba and American civil-military rule there from 1906 to 1909.

When Robert H. Terrell resigned as principal of M Street High School on December 31, 1901, to become the District of Columbia's first black municipal judge, Cooper, who had taught math and science at the school since 1887, succeeded him, becoming the second black female principal in the school's history. Others who had served in the post were Mary Jane Patterson, Richard T. Greener, Francis L. Cardozo, and Winfield Scott Montgomery.

Cooper began her new duties on January 2, 1902. At the time, M Street was the only high school in the nation to offer a diverse curriculum that prepared black students for either industry or college, including the Ivy League schools. Under Cooper's leadership the school became a showcase for the best and brightest, and Cooper and her faculty used their alumni contacts to get scholarships for worthy pupils. When Father Felix Klein of the Catholic Institute of Paris visited the school in 1903 and observed a Latin class being taught by Cooper herself, he found it incredible that a terrible race problem existed in the United States. However, Cooper's leadership and the school's college preparatory work were not to go unchallenged.

The 1904–05 school year was one of turmoil, as allegations of insubordination and personal impropriety by Cooper, and rumors of student misconduct, circulated around the city. Cooper was the fulcrum of what was called "the M Street High School controversy." Community opinion—whether for or against her—depended largely on so-called revelations in the local press. The *Washington Post* reported in 1905 that the controversy began with an address to M Street students by W. E. B. DuBois in the winter of 1902–03. His remark that there was "a tendency throughout the country to restrict the curriculum of colored schools" sent shock waves through the city school system. Cooper's chief antagonist was her supervisor, Percy M. Hughes, director of

Washington's high schools. Despite the school board's promise to conduct a speedy inquiry, it dragged through inconclusive evidence for months.

Finally, in October 1906, the board decided not to reappoint Cooper; school board member Mary Church Terrell, part of the Oberlin trio, and her husband, Judge Robert H. Terrell, were silent about the board's reasons and actions. The tendency of Congress to meddle in the affairs of the District of Columbia cannot be ignored as a factor in Cooper's dismissal, but some people suspected the influence of Booker T. Washington and the so-called Tuskegee machine. Amid the recurring debate over vocational training (Washington's position) versus classical education (the position of DuBois), Cooper left Washington, D.C., proud of M Street's record, now recognized as a creditable college preparatory high school whose students merited admission even into Ivy League colleges. Cooper taught at Lincoln University in Missouri for four years, then returned to Washington, D.C., to teach Latin again at the school she had formerly led.

Tough-minded and tenacious, Cooper would meet new and diverse challenges. She bought a home, made extensive repairs, and became guardian to five great-nieces and nephews, aged six months to twelve years. It was a strenuous challenge at any age, but Cooper, then in her fifties, persevered. In 1911, while pursuing a Ph.D., she attended summer sessions at "La Guilde" in Paris. From 1915 to 1917, she attended summer classes at Columbia University and later took extension courses there. Sponsored by Father Klein, she applied to the Sorbonne in 1923. When that school accepted her Co-lumbia credits, she studied for many hours at the Library of Congress and then traveled to France to meet dissertation requirements; this, of course, was before teachers were allowed sabbatical leave.

On March 23, 1925, Cooper became the fourth African-American woman to earn a Ph.D. (preceded by **Georgiana R. Simpson, Eva B. Dykes,** and **Sadie T. M. Alexander**). Cooper's dissertation, "The Attitude of France toward Slavery during the Revolution," was indicative of her broad knowledge, sound scholarship, and continued interest in pan-Africanism. At the age of sixty-six, she had completed her journey from slavery to the Sorbonne; her dream had become a reality. On December 29, 1925, William Tindall, a D.C. commissioner, awarded her the degree at **Howard University**'s Rankin Chapel in a ceremony sponsored by the Xi Omega chapter of the **Alpha Kappa Alpha Sorority**.

Frelinghuysen University was founded in Washington, D.C., in 1907 by Jesse Lawson. This nontraditional group of schools was to be a beacon of hope for "colored working people," and Cooper was installed as its second president on June 15, 1930. There were serious problems, however. Frelinghuysen had no permanent building or endowment; tuition alone paid teachers' stipends; and university trustees seemed unable to overcome old management disputes.

Recurring exigencies forced Cooper, at great sacrifice, to move some academic programs into her home at 201 T Street, N.W. She neither charged rent nor accepted a salary. Instead, she chartered the Hannah Stanley Opportunity School, which was annexed to the university but had a self-governing board of trustees charged to protect the school and Cooper's property from any threat of dissolution that the university might face. A 1933 codicil to Cooper's will devoted her property "in perpetuo to [the] Education of Colored Adults."

Frelinghuysen lost its charter in 1937 and no longer awarded degrees. The Washington, D.C., Board of Education, the only agency that could independently recognize it as a university, refused to do so. The university's trustees urged Cooper to make a public appeal for funds needed in order to upgrade Frelinghuysen and attract a stronger faculty. Feeling that such an appeal would be an unfair burden on the very community the institution was founded to serve, she refused. Instead, at age seventy-nine, Cooper sought a job with the Works Progress Administration's Office of Education, but she was not hired. She then tried to sell her property in Raleigh. The U.S. District Court upheld the school superintendent's decision not to accredit Frelinghuysen's law school, a disastrous ruling for the university. With just a few students enrolled, Cooper remained in a largely ceremonial role. In about 1940, the university became the Frelinghuysen Group of Schools for Colored Working People, and Cooper became its registrar.

The death of her great-niece and namesake, Annie Cooper Haywood Beckwith, of pneumonia in 1939 hastened Cooper's decline. Beckwith was six months old in 1915 when Anna Cooper became her guardian. After refusing to yield to most adversities, she had rested her hope for Frelinghuysen's future in Annie; now that hope was gone. Her post-Frelinghuysen endeavors were anticlimactic. In 1951, she privately published *Personal Recollections of the Grimké Family and the Life and Writings of Charlotte Forten Grimké.* In her book, Cooper told about the lives of the Grimkés, who were also slave descendants. She lived many more years—mostly with her memories—and spoke of other books she wished to write, but her failing health did not permit her to do so.

Anna J. Cooper was a versatile woman whose cogent ideas and diversity of thought are best demonstrated in her published works, lectures, poems, and miscellaneous writings. A consummate teacher, she ranked high among her peers. She was a feminist and a stoic activist in the struggle for the betterment of black people. A much sought-after speaker, she was outspoken on such subjects as racism, the status of black women, and educational systems that failed to consider the needs of black and female students. Continuing to seek solutions to vexing problems, she addressed diverse themes, including "College Extension for Working People," "Modern Education," "The Negro Dialect," "A Problem in American Education: Loss of Speech through Isolation," and "Legislative Measures Concerning Slavery in the U.S." Cooper's commitment to education and organizational work left scant time for her personal life. She did not retire from her active career as an educator until her eighty-fourth year.

At the age of 105, Cooper died peacefully at her Washington, D.C., home on Thursday, February 27, 1964. She asked only to be remembered as "somebody's teacher on vacation . . . resting for the Fall opening." After a simple service at St. Augustine's College Chapel, she was buried in Raleigh, North Carolina, on Wednesday, March 4, 1964.

LOUISE DANIEL HUTCHINSON

Cross, Delores E. (1938–)

Dr. Delores Cross describes her current success as the president of Chicago State University this way:

> We subscribe very much to the African tradition of "we." It looks at our inter-relatedness and inter-connectedness. We taught ourselves to read and write. We built our own schools and succeeded despite the odds.

Such a philosophy reflects Cross' life and work. Life did not start out easily for her. Born on August 29, 1938, in Newark, New Jersey, she was raised in public housing projects. Her mother was divorced and raised the family alone. When Cross was thirteen, the family was evicted for not paying the rent and moved in with relatives. At fifteen, she went to work in a factory to add to the family income. Graduating from high school at the age of sixteen, she married at eighteen and had two children by the age of twenty-one.

Yet despite all her responsibilities, Delores Cross never stopped educating herself. Commuting to school and supporting a family, it took her eight years to earn her bachelor's degree in elementary education at Seton Hall University. She graduated in 1963 and began teaching kindergarten in the New York public school system. Five years later she had a master's degree from Hofstra University. In the late 1960s she and her husband, from whom she was later divorced, moved to Michigan. By 1971, she had received her Ph.D. in higher education administration from the University of Michigan.

Cross has held a variety of jobs in the academic world since taking up her first teaching position in New York. She has been

At Chicago State University, says President Delores Cross, "we subscribe very much to the African tradition of 'we.' It looks at our interrelatedness and inter-connectedness." (CHICAGO STATE UNIVERSITY)

the director of teacher education at Claremont Graduate School, vice chancellor for student affairs and special programs at the City University of New York, director of the masters of arts in teaching and tutorial clinic programs at Northwestern University, and president of the New York State Higher Education Services Corporation (a state cabinet post). Prior to her move to Chicago State University, Dr. Cross held the position of senior provost and associate vice president for academic affairs at the University of Minnesota. She reaches out to both the local and educational communities by serving on the boards of many organizations.

A marathon runner who has competed in the Boston, Chicago, and New York marathons, Delores Cross never seems to stop. She credits her mother, a lifelong student, with teaching her "that as African Americans we can excel. . . . She taught me that despite distractions and setbacks you can still make it." Not only has Delores Cross made it; she is giving something back by helping others to make it too.

HILARY MAC AUSTIN

D

Davis, Hilda (1905–)

Accompanying the senior class photo and résumé of Hilda Andrea Davis in the 1925 **Howard University** yearbook is the caption "Prexy," a diminutive for president. This inscription, as well as the activities listed, prophetically capsulize the career of a distinguished educator and organizational leader. A dean of women, professor of English, mental health administrator, and leader of educational, women's, civic, and religious organizations, Davis has waged a struggle for race and sex equality throughout the twentieth century.

Born to Louis Alexander and Ruth Gertrude Cooke Davis on May 24, 1905, in Washington, D.C., Hilda Davis was the fourth child in a family of eight daughters—Ruth Olivette, Henrietta Josephine, Charlotte Isabelle, Rhoda Alexandra, Thalia Annazean, Norma Eugene, Jean-Marie—and one son, Louis Alexander. During her youth, the family household briefly included a white foster child, Virginia McKay. The extended family included two sets of grandparents, three aunts, and six uncles. Her paternal uncle, Benjamin Oliver Davis, Sr., became the nation's first black general of the regular army.

Davis attended public schools in the District of Columbia, graduating in 1921 from Dunbar High School at age sixteen. First in the family to enroll in a four-year university, she earned a bachelor's degree magna cum laude in English and Latin from Howard University in 1925. Always eager for more education, she later earned a master's degree in English from Radcliffe College in 1932 and a doctorate in Human Development from the University of Chicago in 1953.

For nearly twenty-six years, Davis was a teacher and advocate for women's concerns in historically black institutions. She was director of girls' activities, teacher of English and Latin, and registrar at Palmer Memorial Institute, Sedalia, North Carolina, from 1925 to 1931; dean of women and assistant professor of English at Shaw University, Raleigh, North Carolina, from 1932 to 1935; and dean of women and professor of English at Talladega College, Talladega, Alabama, from 1936 to 1952. Like most early deans of women, she was the principal guardian of women's interests and, at both Shaw and Talladega, the sole woman administrator in the president's cabinet.

In 1952, after sixteen years at Talladega, Davis left the field of higher education, resigning in protest when the college's first black president, Arthur Douglass Gray, tried to displace her through reassignment. She accepted an administrative post in the Delaware State Mental Health Department in Delaware City and remained there for eleven years. Returning to education in 1965, she broke the color barrier as the first black educator to be awarded a full-time faculty contract at the University of Delaware in Newark. Upon leaving the university in 1970, she accepted a faculty appointment at Wilmington College in New Castle, Delaware. She retired in 1977.

Coupled with Davis's lifetime of service to higher education has been a similar commitment to progressive organizations. Since her undergraduate days, Davis has nurtured and provided leadership to numerous groups. Among these are Delta Sigma Theta Sorority, Inc., for which she served as president of the Alpha Chapter during the 1924–25 term and as chair of the National Projects Committee from 1963 to 1967. In 1938, she became the second elected president of the Association of Deans of Women and Advisers to Girls in Negro Schools after the death of its founder, **Lucy Diggs Slowe**. By creating stability and engendering self-confidence, Davis rescued the organization from despair and dissolution. She provided similar leadership for the National Association of College Women as its acting president from 1939 to 1945 and from 1957 to 1961. She was the only person elected to the presidency for two non-consecutive terms.

An unwavering integrationist, Davis was among the earliest black members of the American Association of University Women, the National Association for Women in Education (formerly the National Association of Deans of Women), and the Society of Companions of the Holy Cross, an Episcopalian women's group. In addition to fighting racial barriers, she challenged sex prejudice and religious traditions to become the first woman senior warden of the Episcopalian Diocese of Delaware.

For her contributions to higher education and progressive organizations, Davis has garnered many honors, including induction into the Delaware Women's Hall of Fame, 1986; the Medal of Distinction from the University of Delaware, 1987; and an honorary doctor-

ate from Trinity College, Washington, D.C., 1989. In addition, she received citations for outstanding service from the Wilmington, Delaware, chapter of the Talladega College Alumni and the Wilmington Alumnae Chapter of Delta Sigma Theta Sorority, Inc., both in 1981. Scholarships and awards in her name have been established by the National Association for Women in Education, *Sage: A Scholarly Journal on Black Women*, Wilmington College, and the National Association of University Women (formerly the National Association of College Women). In 1988, the **Young Women's Christian Association** (YWCA) of New Castle County, Delaware, dedicated the new Hilda A. Davis Residence, designed to house women in need, as a public symbol of Davis's commitment and generosity.

Davis currently resides in Newark, Delaware, where she remains active in regional and national organizations.

PATRICIA BELL-SCOTT

Denning, Bernadine (1930–)

Bernadine Newsom Denning was born August 17, 1930, in Detroit, Michigan, one of three children of William Charles Newsom and Evelyn T. (Pembrook) Newsom. Her family lived in a low-income public housing project until after her graduation from college. She developed an interest in athletics at an early age, learning to swim at eight. She became a swimming instructor at sixteen at the black branch of the Detroit **Young Women's Christian Association** and later worked as a lifeguard and swimming instructor to help pay her college expenses.

After graduation from Northeastern High School in Detroit in 1947, she attended Michigan State Normal College in Ypsilanti, relying on scholarships and work to pay expenses. She graduated in 1951 with a B.S. in physical education and taught in the Detroit public schools from 1951 to 1959. In 1956, she married Blaine Denning, a professional athlete with the Harlem Globetrotters and the Baltimore Bullets who later worked as a businessman, youth counselor, and owner of rental homes. They had one son, Blaine Denning, Jr.

From 1959 to 1972, Denning was administrator of a variety of programs in the Detroit public schools. Starting her graduate study in the 1950s, she received the Ed.D. in curriculum development from Wayne State University in 1970. In the 1970s, she held administrative positions at the University of Michigan, and also was an assistant professor of education. In 1975, she was named director of the Civil Rights Office for the Detroit public school system. The quality of her work in this office brought her an appointment in 1977 as director of the Office of Revenue Sharing for the United States Department of the Treasury. Over 39,000 state and local governments relied on this office to receive a share of the federal taxes collected. As the third director of this office, she administered a fund of $9 billion and enforced civil rights laws prohibiting federal funds from going to any unit practicing racial discrimination. Denning received high praise in this position.

Returning to Detroit in 1979, she became executive director of the School-Community Relations department for the Detroit public schools until her retirement in 1985. She served as director of the Human Relations Department for the city of Detroit from 1986 to 1987, before becoming an educational consultant. By 1989, she had founded and become president of DMP Associates, an interracial consulting firm emphasizing education and leadership training. She has exercised leadership in a wide variety of civic and social affairs and received numerous awards.

DE WITT S. DYKES, JR.

Derricotte, Juliette (1897–1931)

Juliette Derricotte's sincere wish for all humankind was that everyone should be free of the debilitating effects of repression and discrimination. She knew that working together in harmony could be achieved despite differences and difficulties, and her career as a **Young Women's Christian Association** (YWCA) official, and later as a college dean of women, provided the means to work for the realization of this ideal.

Born in Athens, Georgia, on April 1, 1897, Juliette Derricotte was the fifth of nine children born to Isaac and Laura Hardwick Derricotte. She grew up in Athens and became aware at an early age of the racial conventions of a small Southern town in the early 1900s. This knowledge was crucial in forging her determination to fight discrimination.

After completing public schooling in Athens, Derricotte went to Talladega College in Alabama. Here she was a popular and active student, a member of the debating team, and president of the campus YWCA. As she planned student activities, made speeches, and mediated disputes, her leadership potential began to emerge. It was during these formative years that she came to believe she should work toward her ideals.

She graduated from Talladega in 1918 and enrolled in the national YWCA training school in New York City. That fall she was made secretary of the national student council of the YWCA, a post she held for eleven years. In this position she worked with student groups around the country, bringing ideas, building leadership, and pioneering the work methods and organizational structure that made the council an interracial fellowship. Through the warmth and forcefulness of her personality she succeeded in making people understand each other in the most practical manner.

In 1924, as a member of the general committee of the World's Student Christian Federation, she attended a meeting in England to discuss the responsibilities of Christian students in the world. Four years later she was one of the American delegates to the committee's Mysore, India, conference. She remained for seven weeks, living in student hostels, mission schools, and Indian homes, and she came to understand the worldwide extent of discrimination and its various and complex forms. She came to realize that the general committee, with over ninety delegates from around the world, was a microcosm of what was possible among people.

Coming home from the Mysore conference, she stopped in China and Japan for meetings with students. Summing it all up, she wrote: "My head whirls, but now and again I remember 'that there is so much more to know than I am accustomed to knowing, and so much more to love than I am accustomed to loving.'"

In 1927, she received a master's degree in religious education from Columbia University, and from 1929 to 1931 she was the only woman trustee of Talladega College, her alma mater. Feeling a special call to participate in the education of black Southerners, she resigned from the YWCA in 1927 and went to Fisk University as its dean of women.

In November 1931, she decided to drive to Athens to visit her mother. Making the trip with her were three Fisk students from Georgia. After stopping for lunch in Chattanooga, they headed south to Atlanta, with Derricotte driving. About a mile outside Dalton, Georgia, their car collided with that of a white couple. The details of the accident have never been known. Derricotte and one student were seriously injured, and the two other students were treated and released.

As the local tax-supported hospital did not admit black patients, Derricotte and the student were taken to the home of a black woman who had beds available for the care of black patients. The student died during the night, and Derricotte was driven by ambulance to Chattanooga's Walden Hospital, where she died the next day, November 7, 1931. Many in the black community attributed her death to the segregationist policies that kept her from getting immediate hospital care.

Perhaps Juliette Derricotte is best remembered for her death and the national outrage it caused. Nonetheless, her contributions remain. At a time when race relations in the United States were eroding, she maintained an uncompromised vision of the universality of human dignity and a just future for her own people. Memorial services were held all over the country. Her friend Howard Thurman delivered the eulogy at the service held in her hometown, reading her haunting words from the Mysore conference.

JEAN CAZORT

Dykes, Eva Beatrice (1893–1986)

Eva Beatrice Dykes devoted her early life to acquiring impeccable academic credentials. A pioneer and model of academic excellence, Dr. Dykes served the black community throughout her life, using her knowledge to educate thousands of young black people. Born in Washington, D.C., in 1893, Dykes was one of three black women to receive their Ph.D. degrees in 1921, the first black women to earn doctorates.

Dykes graduated from **Howard University** with a B.A. in English (summa cum laude) in 1914. She entered Radcliffe College in 1916, earning a second B.A. (magna cum laude) in 1917, and was elected to Phi Beta Kappa. She received her M.A. degree in English in 1918 and a Ph.D. in English philology in 1921.

In 1929, after teaching at Dunbar High School in Washington, D.C., for eight years, she became associate professor of English at Howard University. Dykes moved to Oakwood College in Huntsville, Alabama, in 1946 to head the English department, and in 1958 she chaired the accreditation quest committee. In 1978, in appreciation of her contributions, Oakwood College named its new library the Eva Beatrice Dykes Library.

A dedicated teacher, author, and scholar, Eva Beatrice Dykes held her students to the same standards of achievement she demanded of herself. When she died in 1986, Eva Dykes left an enduring legacy of excellence and service.

CATHERINE JOHNSON

Longtime head of the English Department at Oakwood College in Huntsville, Alabama, Eva Beatrice Dykes was one of the first three black women to earn a Ph.D. (MOORLAND-SPINGARN)

E

Edmonds, Helen Gray (1911–1995)

Helen Gray Edmonds was a distinguished historian, educator, political activist, and teacher whose contributions to the study of history have been recognized by numerous universities. Her philosophy of education

Distinguished historian Helen Gray Edmonds helped to make history herself when she seconded Dwight D. Eisenhower's nomination for reelection at the 1956 Republican National Convention. (NORTH CAROLINA CENTRAL UNIVERSITY)

was a traditional one. It sought to equip students with the essential tools of a holistic education, one that includes all areas of history, not just African-American history.

Helen Gray Edmonds was born in Lawrenceville, Virginia, on December 3, 1911, to John Edward Edmonds and Ann Williams. Her education began at St. Paul's High School and St. Paul's College. "My mother and father inspired us all," Edmonds once said in an interview. "There was never a moment in our family that higher education wasn't stressed." After attending the Lawrenceville schools, she entered Morgan State College and earned a B.A. in history in 1933. Edmonds furthered her education at Ohio State University, receiving an M.A. in history in 1938 and a Ph.D. in history in 1946. In 1954–55, she did postdoctoral research in modern European history at the University of Heidelberg, Germany.

Edmonds was associated with North Carolina College, now North Carolina Central University (NCCU), during most of her academic career. She served as chair of the history department and also as dean of the graduate school. In addition to these duties, she served as a visiting professor at more than 100 institutions of higher education in the United States and abroad, including Portland State University, the University of Rochester, Virginia State University, The Ohio State University, MIT, Harvard University, Radcliffe College, University of Stockholm, the Free University of Berlin, the

University of Liberia, and the University of Monrovia.

In recognition of her outstanding accomplishments in higher education, Edmonds received numerous honors and awards including The O. Max Gardner Award, The William Hugh McEntry Award, and the Award of Scholarly Distinction from the American Historical Association. Her books include *Black Faces in High Places* (1971) and *The Negro in Fusion Politics in North Carolina, 1894–1901* (1973). She published widely in professional journals.

Edmonds contributions were not limited to the university. She was actively involved at the local, national, and international levels in civic, governmental, and social organizations. At the Republican National Convention in 1956, Edmonds seconded the nomination of President Dwight David Eisenhower for reelection. She served as a special emissary for President Eisenhower in Liberia. In 1970 she chaired the United States delegation to the Third Committee of the United Nations. She was appointed by President Richard Nixon to serve on the National Advisory Council of the Peace Corps and as an alternate delegate to the United Nations in celebration of their twenty-fifth year. She served in appointed capacities for the Departments of State and Defense, and on the board of directors for the International Women's Year Conference in Mexico City. She received three citations from President Nixon in recognition of her government service. Edmonds also was active in the black community, serving as president of **The Links, Inc.,** a national service organization, from 1970 to 1974.

Helen Gray Edmonds was a giant in the field of history, who always sought to achieve a sense of balance in her teaching, writing, and public speaking. She died in Durham, North Carolina, on May 9, 1995.

BEVERLY JONES

F

Farris, Vera King (1940–)

Vera King Farris' career is marked by notable accomplishment not just in one field but in several: science, education, administration, and community service. President of Richard Stockton College of New Jersey, she was elected chairperson of the American Association of Colleges and Universities in 1995.

Farris was born July 18, 1940, in Atlantic City, New Jersey. She graduated magna cum laude with a B.A. in biology from Tuskegee Institute in 1959, receiving the Romm Award for the science student with the highest grade average, and the James Foundation Fellowship for being the outstanding senior in science. Her undergraduate career also was distinguished by a research assistantship at Oak Ridge National Laboratory. In her graduate studies at the University of Massachusetts, she specialized in zoology and parasitology, earning an M.S. in 1962 and a Ph.D. in 1965.

After three years at the University of Michigan as a research associate and instructor, she joined the faculty of the State University of New York at Stony Brook as a lecturer in biology in 1968, later moving to the Brockport campus and becoming a full professor in 1977. While teaching at SUNY, she also held significant administrative positions, culminating in her service as vice provost for academic affairs in 1979–80.

From 1980 to 1983, Farris was vice president for academic affairs at Kean College of New Jersey in Union, where she received an award from the student government for her outstanding achievement and service to students. In 1983, the year she became president of Stockton, she was honored by the New Jersey College and University Coalition on Women's Education as the state's outstanding woman college president. At both colleges, she also held a biology professorship.

She has published many articles in education and science journals and has received,

Vera King Farris, president of Richard Stockton College of New Jersey, was elected chairperson of the American Association of Colleges and Universities in 1995.
(STOCKTON STATE COLLEGE)

among other professional awards, honorary doctorates from seven schools, the University of Massachusetts Chancellor's Medal, and the New York University Presidential Medal.

Farris' accomplishments in civic and humanitarian service are perhaps even more impressive, and her awards for them are literally too numerous to list. She is very active in support of B'nai B'rith and the Anti-Defamation League and was appointed by the governor to the New Jersey-Israel Commission in 1989. When she was honored for leadership in Holocaust education by the U.S. Holocaust Memorial Council in October 1993, she became the first person to receive that award who was not the head of a government. Among other highlights are the Dr. Mary McLeod Bethune Achievement Award from the **National Council of Negro Women** in 1994, and the 1992 Woman of the Year Award from *New Jersey Woman* magazine.

INDIA COOPER

Forsythe, Ruby Middleton (1905–1992)

Ruby Middleton was born in 1905 in Charleston, South Carolina, the daughter of Lewis Burns Middleton and Marthenia E. Middleton. She received her earliest education from Mrs. Seward Montgomery. She attended Charleston's prominent black private school, Avery Normal Institute. After she received her licentiate of instruction certificate in 1921 from Avery, she embarked on a teaching career in South Carolina's low country that would span seven decades.

She taught for one year under the supervision of Charlotte Ross at Laing School in Mt. Pleasant, South Carolina. From 1924 until 1938, she taught in the North Charleston schools. In 1928, she married the Reverend William Essex Forsythe, an Episcopalian minister at Holy Cross–Faith Memorial Church and School on Pawley's Island and at St. Cyprian's Church in Georgetown, South Carolina. In 1938, at the age of thirty-four, Ruby Forsythe began teaching at the one-room private school on the island, the only educational facility available to black people on the island. Pawley's Island—like most of South Carolina's Sea Islands—was overwhelmingly black, largely isolated, impoverished, and neglected until a bridge was built in the relatively recent past. When Forsythe's one-room wooden school and adjacent church burned, they were rebuilt. When the bridge and a highway were built, the school was moved to make room for the road.

In the mid-1950s, Ruby Forsythe attended South Carolina State College, and by 1956, she had earned a bachelor's degree in education. In 1988, the historically black institution awarded her an honorary doctorate in education. The Forsythes had one son, Burns Maynard Forsythe, a **Howard University** graduate and school administrator in Mt. Pleasant, South Carolina, who is married and has five children. In 1974, the Reverend William Forsythe died.

Ruby Middleton Forsythe continued to teach at Holy Cross–Faith Memorial School until she retired in 1991. Never one to coddle her charges, she did not hesitate to resort to corporal punishment. She acknowledged that "I use the strap." In more eloquent words she summed up her legacy to education and to the people of the island where she labored for much of the twentieth century, by affirming that she sowed "the best seed into whatever soil we come into contact with, watching the growth, and the reproduction of the product sent forth." She died in Mt. Pleasant, South Carolina, on May 29, 1992.

WILLIAM C. HINE

G

Garnet, Sarah S. T. (1831–1911)

Sarah Smith Tompkins Garnet spent fifty-six years as an educator. She began as a teacher's assistant at the age of fourteen and by 1854 she was teaching in the African Free School in Williamsburgh, Brooklyn. In 1863, she was the first black woman appointed principal of a public school (Grammar School No. 80 and later No. 81) in the borough of Manhattan. She was a principal until 1900.

Born on July 31, 1831, Minsarah (known as Sarah) was the oldest of ten children of Sylvanus and Annie (Springstead) Smith. Both her father and her mother were descendants of Long Island Native Americans and black Americans. Sylvanus Smith was a landowner, successful farmer, and pork merchant in Weeksville, the oldest black community in Brooklyn.

Sarah was first married to Samuel Tompkins, an Episcopal minister, until his death in the late 1860s. Her second marriage, to Henry Highland Garnet in 1879, a Presbyterian minister, abolitionist, and diplomat, lasted only a few years. He died of an asthma attack in Liberia on February 13, 1882.

Principal Garnet devoted her life to the crusade against discrimination in education and civil rights. She was active in the National Vigilance Committee and the Women's Loyal Union Club, and she was a founder of the Equal Suffrage League, one of the earliest equal rights organizations in Brooklyn. A member of the **National Association of Colored Women**, she was superintendent of its suffrage department.

In July 1911, Garnet and her sister, Dr. **Susan Smith McKinney Steward**, were delegates to the first Universal Races Congress in London, England. Upon their return, the Equal Suffrage League held a reception in Garnet's honor that was attended by W. E. B. DuBois and other distinguished guests. Sarah S. T. Garnet died suddenly on September 17, 1911, of arteriosclerosis at her Brooklyn home at 748 Hancock Street. She is buried in Brooklyn's Greenwood Cemetery.

FLORIS BARNETT CASH

Garrison, Memphis Tennessee (1890–1988)

Born in McDowell County, West Virginia, on March 4, 1890, Garrison died in Huntington, West Virginia, on July 25, 1988. The youngest of two children of former slaves, Wesley Carter, a coal miner, and Cassie Thomas Carter, she grew up in the coalfields of southern West Virginia. After receiving her elementary education in the segregated public schools, she earned a B.A. with honors from Bluefield State College in West Virginia and pursued advanced study at Ohio State University in Columbus. Twenty-five years after the historic 1963 march on Washington, she received the governor's Living the Dream Award for distinguished service to West Virginia and the nation.

In 1908, she launched her public school teaching career in McDowell County, where she taught until her retirement in the early 1950s. She later recalled that she had wanted to be a lawyer, but her mother could not afford the required training. Memphis Carter married Melvin Garrison, a coal miner, but they had no children. If they had, it is likely that her teaching career would have been cut short because, as elsewhere, West Virginia openly discouraged the employment of married teachers with children.

Garrison not only completed a distinguished career as a public schoolteacher, she also influenced the political life of the region. As secretary of the Gary, McDowell County, branch of the **National Association for the Advancement of Colored People,** her activities covered a broad range of local, regional, and national projects. In addition to local campaigns against racial inequality before the law, she spearheaded the national Christmas seal campaign during the late 1920s and early 1930s. Under the motto, "Merry Christmas and Justice for All," the Christmas seal campaign generated widespread support for the NAACP and netted substantial sums for the national office.

Until her death in 1988, Garrison continued to serve the state and nation. She served as the first woman president of the West Virginia State Teachers' Association, 1929–30; treasurer of the NAACP West Virginia State Conference for twenty-two years; NAACP national field secretary, 1956–59; national vice president of the NAACP board of directors, 1964–66; member of the West Virginia Human Rights Commission, 1963–66; and member of President Lyndon B. Johnson's National Citizens Committee on Community Relations, 1964. For her distinguished public service, Garrison received numerous awards and

honors, including the NAACP's **Madam C. J. Walker** Gold Medal Award, 1929; the T. G. Nutter Award for outstanding achievement and service in the field of civil rights, 1959; the NAACP Distinguished Service Award, 1969; and an honorary doctorate of humanities, Marshall University in Huntington, West Virginia, 1970.

Although Garrison was recognized for fighting racial injustice, her activities demonstrated a keen interest in achieving equity across gender and class lines. Despite her professional training, Garrison retained close ties with the black coal-mining working class. In two very illuminating essays about black Americans in southern West Virginia, she exhibited an unusual sensitivity to the ideas, aspirations, and grievances of black voters.

During the 1920s, Garrison challenged the gender distribution of power within the McDowell County Colored Republican Organization, which often held the balance of power in West Virginia politics. The career of Memphis Tennessee Garrison takes on added significance because the southern Appalachian mountains often are perceived as being isolated from the main currents of American history. Her contributions deepen our understanding of life in the Mountain State, link black West Virginians to a national black community, and highlight the interplay of class, race, and gender in American society.

JOE W. TROTTER
H. LARUE TROTTER

Guy-Sheftall, Beverly (1946–)

Educator, author, and historian, Beverly Guy-Sheftall continues to mark out new paths, and to preserve the work of the pathfinders of the past. As head of the women's studies program at Spelman College and editor of several excellent compilations of current black feminist writers, Guy-Sheftall has been at the forefront of thought about what it means to be black, female, and politically aware.

Guy-Sheftall was born in Memphis, Tennessee on June 1, 1946, to a family of teachers. Her mother was Ernestine Varnado, and her father was Walter Peabody Guy, Jr. Her father taught, and her mother was a math teacher who went on to other lines of work. Guy-Sheftall attended Spelman College, where she majored in English and secondary education. She received a B.A., with honors, in 1966. She then went on to do a fifth year of study in English at Wellesley College in Massachusetts.

In 1968, after her studies at Wellesley, Guy-Sheftall went to Atlanta University to pursue graduate studies in English, receiving her M.A. in 1970. In 1969, she became a faculty member of Alabama State University at Montgomery, where she stayed until 1971. That year, Guy-Sheftall returned to Atlanta to join the faculty at her alma mater, **Spelman College**. There she became founding director of the Women's Research and Resource Center in 1981. In 1984, she received her Ph.D. from Emory University, in women's studies and African-American literature. She also became the Anna Julia Cooper Professor of Women's Studies.

Guy-Sheftall's teaching and research soon led her to write and edit several collections of black women's writing. In 1979, she co-edited (with Roseann P. Bell and Bettye J. Parker) *Sturdy Black Bridges: Visions of Black Women in Literature*. She also assembled, with Jo Moore Stewart, a pictorial history for Spelman University titled *Spelman: A Centennial Celebration*. Next, in 1990, her Ph.D.

dissertation was published by Carlson Publishing under the title of *Daughters of Sorrow: Attitudes Towards Black Women, 1880-1920*. She was also a co-editor of the collection *Double-Stitch: Black Mothers Write About Mothers and Daughters*, brought out by Beacon Press in Boston in 1991.

In 1995 Guy-Sheftall released her latest collection, *Words of Fire: An Anthology of African-American Feminist Thought*. In this collection she assembles essays, articles, and other original works dated from the 1830s to the present. These articles all discuss feminism, although many of them were written before the word became commonly used among black women.

Guy-Sheftall also is known as a founding editor of *SAGE: A Scholarly Journal on Black Women*. She cofounded the journal with Patricia Bell-Scott in 1983. The editorial board of this ongoing academic journal was responsible for co-editing *Double-Stitch*.

Guy-Sheftall has been a consultant to and public speaker at many universities. Her in-depth scholarship has won her fellowships from the Woodrow Wilson Fellowship for Dissertations in Women's Studies (1982) and W. K. Kellogg National Fellowship (1987–90). In 1989 she received a Candace Award in Education from the National Coalition of 100 Black Women.

A scholar and an analyst, Beverly Guy-Sheftall has been described as providing "a breath-taking sweep of African-American feminist thought." This tireless researcher helps to ensure that black women's words—and their ideas—will be seriously examined and preserved for generations to come.

ANDRA MEDEA

H

Hackley, Emma Azalia (1867–1922)

"The race needs daring, original people to think and speak"—these words were spoken by Azalia Hackley, concert soprano and pioneer music educator, during one of her inspirational lecture-recitals in the early decades of the twentieth century. Hackley believed that music could be a positive force in reclaiming black ethnic and cultural pride.

Emma Azalia Smith was born June 29, 1867, in Murfreesboro, Tennessee. In about 1870, she and a younger sister, Marietta, were taken to Detroit, Michigan, by their parents, Henry Smith and Corilla Beard Smith.

Azalia received her education in the Detroit public schools, where she graduated from Capital High School in 1886 and obtained a teaching certificate in 1887. She taught at the Clinton Elementary School from 1887 to 1894. Azalia was taught piano by her mother and took private lessons in voice and violin. She was a member of the Detroit Musical Society, played in a black orchestra, and performed vocal recitals in Detroit and nearby cities.

After her marriage around 1894 to Edwin H. Hackley, a newspaper editor, the couple moved to Denver, Colorado, where Azalia Hackley received a bachelor of music degree from the Denver College of Music. The Hackleys moved to Philadelphia, Pennsylvania, in 1901 to further her singing career. She studied in Paris with Jean De Reszke in 1905 and 1907 and made a trip to London in 1909.

From 1910 to 1920, Hackley funded a "foreign scholarship for black musicians," established the Normal Voice Culture Institute in Chicago, Illinois, and conducted mammoth folk festivals throughout the country in order to teach the Negro spiri-

Fervently believing that music can be a positive force in black life, folk festival organizer Emma Hackley has done much to awaken an awareness of the power of spirituals. (SCHOMBURG CENTER)

tual. Her name became synonymous with musical excellence and progress. She died in Detroit, Michigan, on December 13, 1922.

Her writings included *A Guide in Voice Culture* (1909); *Public School Lessons in Voice Culture* (n.d.); and *The Colored Girl Beautiful* (1916).

ELLISTINE P. LEWIS

Haines Normal and Industrial Institute

The history of Haines Normal and Industrial Institute began in 1886, when **Lucy Craft Laney** opened a grammar school in a rented lecture hall in the basement of Christ Presbyterian Church in Augusta, Georgia. Laney's short-term goal was to establish a boarding school for girls, but her long-range vision was to create a training school for teachers. The evolution of Haines Institute from a primary to a secondary and finally a normal and industrial school represented the fulfillment of Lucy C. Laney's dream.

Laney's goal and vision notwithstanding, when she welcomed her first pupils on January 6, 1886, the class was made up of four girls and two poor ragged boys whom she did not have the heart to turn away. Although boys were admitted to the school from its inception, the institution remained predominantly female throughout its history.

After the first month of operation the school was overcrowded; consequently, in February 1886, Laney rented a house from the president of the Augusta Board of Education and moved the school. Overcrowding remained a problem as the number of students in attendance went from 75 at the end of the 1886 school year to 362 in 1887, but in that year Laney was able to rent a two-

story frame house with a barn in the rear, and those two structures constituted the campus of Haines Institute until 1889.

Although the school was sanctioned by the Presbyterian board, Laney was left to her own devices and to what she could collect for its support. She received no salary and was forced to live on the food provided by the parents of her students and to maintain the school on the contributions from the community. During the school's first year, Laney was the only teacher, and she worked around the clock, personally overseeing each student as well as managing the affairs of the institution.

Despite numerous problems, by 1887 Lucy C. Laney's vision began to take shape, and by the end of that year the primary, grammar, and elementary normal departments had been established. In addition, an industrial course had begun, an effort was under way to secure a footpress, and plans for a class in printing had been finalized. Over the course of several years, Laney created a strong literary department and a well-planned, scientifically based normal program. She organized a well-equipped kindergarten at Haines in 1890. In conjunction with the city hospital she had helped to create, she began a training program for nurses in 1892.

Between 1886 and 1889, Haines Institute operated out of various rented buildings, and as enrollment increased it became increasingly difficult to find adequate space. The institution's lack of property lent an air of uncertainty to the school's existence. In 1889, the Presbyterian board purchased a permanent site for Haines and erected the institution's first building, Marshall Hall. In 1906, McGregor Hall was constructed. The last major new building on the Haines campus was Cauley-Wheeler Hall, constructed in 1924.

Lucy C. Laney died in 1933 and was buried on the campus. Owing to the Great Depression, the Presbyterian board withdrew support for the institution a few years thereafter. The school was able to continue for a while through the support of alumni and friends, but they were unable to keep the school going after 1949.

JUNE O. PATTON

Harris, Marjorie Lewis   (1924–)

In 1968, Dr. Marjorie Lewis Harris became president and CEO of Lewis College of Business in Detroit, Michigan, and the institution has benefited from her leadership. The college obtained a degree-granting charter, up to and including a master's degree. A ten-acre campus was purchased. Several million dollars in grants have been awarded to the school. And the U.S. Department of Education declared it an "Historical Black College," the only such designated institution in Michigan.

Harris earned a B.S. in business administration from West Virginia State College, then went on to the University of Michigan, where she received an M.A. in educational administration and a Ph.D. in higher education. She did postdoctoral study at Harvard University. Before assuming the presidency of Lewis, she served as registrar, instructor, and administrative director.

Harris' community involvement includes work with organizations such as the Detroit Council of Churches, the Michigan State Chamber of Commerce, the Detroit Library Commission, and the NAACP.

MICHAEL NOWAK

Marjorie Lewis Harris has been president and CEO of Lewis College of Business in Detroit since 1968. The college is the only one in Michigan to receive the U.S. Department of Education's "Historical Black College" designation. (LEWIS COLLEGE OF BUSINESS)

Hine, Darlene Clark   (1947–)

"Since black women entered the scholarly record, black and white women's historians have been responding to a different intellectual world," Darlene Clark Hine writes. Indeed, because of the efforts of historians such as Hine, **Jessie Carney Smith**, and **Paula Giddings**, American society itself is beginning to respond to a different world of ideas and perceptions.

Darlene Clark Hine was born on February 7, 1947, in Morley, Missouri, daughter of Levester and Lottie Mae Thompson Clark. Her father was a truck driver and her mother a homemaker. She received her bachelor's degree from Roosevelt University in Chicago in 1968 and her master's degree and doctorate at Kent State University.

To be in college in the late 1960s was to participate in a profoundly disturbing moment in history. Hine was, as she wrote in *Hine Sight*, ". . . very much caught up in the Black Arts and Consciousness, and Black Power movements, and was acutely aware that the gap between black and white Americans seemed to be growing. The decision to become a historian was driven not only by a desire to understand the origins of racism but also by a growing curiosity about the causes of white fear and black rage."

At first, Hine did not focus in on the situation of the black woman per se. Then, in 1980, a woman named Shirley Herd called her at Purdue University, where she was at that time an associate professor of history. Herd insisted that there should be a history of black women in Indiana and that Hine was the one to write it.

Hine resisted, relented, and wrote the book, *When the Truth Is Told: Black Women's Culture and Community in Indiana, 1875–1950*. It was published in 1981 by the **National Council of Negro Women**. As she was researching the book, Hine "experienced the beginning of my transformation into a historian of black women." Soon, she helped form the Black Women in the Middle West Project (BWMW) with historian Patrick Bidelman, Herd, and Virtea Downey. Together with 1,200 community black women—and with funds from the National Endowment for the Humanities—they gathered an abundance of primary materials.

In 1989, Hine published *Black Women in White: Racial Conflict and Cooperation in the Nursing Profession*. The following year, a sixteen-volume set of articles and monographs was published, under her editorship. It was entitled *Black Women in United States History: From Colonial Times to the Present*. In 1993, she published *Black Women in America: An Historical Encyclopedia*.

In 1994, Hine published a book of essays, *Hine Sight: Black Women and the Re-Construction of American History*, and in 1995, with Wilma King and Linda Reed, she edited *"We Specialize in the Wholly Impossible": A Reader in Black Women's History*. Her most recent publication is *Speak Truth to Power: Black Professional Class in United States History*. She is editing, with Evelyn Brooks Higginbotham and Leon Litwack, *The Harvard Guide to African-American History*.

She is the John A. Hannah Professor of American History at Michigan State University.

KATHLEEN THOMPSON

Darlene Clark Hine has written widely on the history of black women in the United States. She is the co-editor, with Elsa Barkley Brown and Rosalyn Terborg-Penn, of the award-winning Black Women in America: An Historical Encyclopedia. *(CARLSON PUBLISHING, INC.)*

Holland, Annie (1865–1934)

"Please do not mention to any one that I may get any publicity from friend or foe," wrote

Annie Holland to **Charlotte Hawkins Brown,** December 31, 1920, in support of Brown's fund-raising campaign to build the Alice Freeman Palmer building. Annie Welthy Daughtry Holland, Jeanes Fund teacher and supervisor, first black female supervisor of Negro elementary education in North Carolina, and the founder of North Carolina's Colored Parent Teachers' Association, was driven by a commitment to improve public education for black Americans rather than a desire for recognition for herself. This commitment and philosophy enabled her to influence black and white Southerners during the Jim Crow era.

Although other sources list Holland as the oldest of seven children of John and Margaret Daughtry, a death certificate completed by her son-in-law, Dr. F. N. Harris, lists her mother's name as Sarah Daughtry and her father's as J. W. Barnes. She was born in 1865 in Isle of Wight County, Virginia. After her mother and father separated, she lived with her grandparents, Friday and Lucinda Daughtry, until she completed her education at the county school. In 1881, at the age of sixteen, she entered Hampton Institute in Hampton, Virginia, where she stayed for a year and a half. Due to financial difficulties and a bout with malaria, she never graduated from Hampton.

Around 1886, she took the teacher's examination in Isle of Wight County and received a second-grade certificate. In 1888, she married Willis Bird Holland, an 1884 Hampton graduate. Their marriage was nontraditional. From 1897 to his death in 1925, they kept dual residences, allowing each other to pursue individual careers—even in separate states. Between 1886 and 1900, she organzied a temperance association and a Christian Endeavor Society. From 1892 to 1897, she worked as an assistant to her husband at

For more than two decades, Annie Holland was in charge of black elementary education in North Carolina. She influenced a white school administration, as well as teachers, future teachers, students, and parents. (VALINDA LITTLEFIELD)

Franklin Public School. After her fifth year, the school board honored her request to teach at a school in the country because she felt that it would be better for her health. In 1905 she succeeded her husband as principal when he went into the insurance and real estate business—a position she held for at least five years.

She became the Jeanes Fund state supervisor in Gates County, North Carolina, in 1911, and by 1915 she was the North Carolina State Home Demonstration Agent, responsible for supervising forty-four county supervisors. In 1921, she was appointed North Carolina State Supervisor for Negro Elementary Education, a position she held until her death. In 1927, she founded North Carolina's Colored Parent-Teachers' Association. In its first year, 784 local associations were established, and 15,770 people became members. In two years, the association raised $116,115. Monies were used to purchase such items as pianos, sewing machines, stoves, tables, chairs, shoes and clothing for children, as well as to support health clinics and school lunch rooms.

Holland died suddenly on January 6, 1934, while addressing a countywide meeting of black teachers in Louisburg, North Carolina. Over 800 people attended a memorial for her in Raleigh, North Carolina. She was buried in Franklin, Virginia.

Her influence on the education of black North Carolinians reached a white administration, teachers, future teachers, students, and parents. As State Supervisor of Negro Elementary Education, she was responsible for visiting and assisting nineteen county training schools, ten city schools, and three state normal schools. As founder of the Colored Parent-Teachers' Association, she was responsible for creating a climate in which parents and teachers worked to raise money, improve child health care, and improve the quality of life for black children in rural homes. Her ability as a peacemaker and her organizational skills allowed her to forge a cooperative arrangement between the Colored Parent-Teachers' Association and the white Parent-Teachers' Association decades before the 1969 unification of these groups. She used her resources to improve

education for black North Carolinians when funding for and attention to the problems of educating black Americans in the South were overlooked or blatantly ignored by many educational boards.

Remembered by her colleagues as a vibrant, practical, cultured, and capable organizer and peacemaker, Holland was able to achieve many of her accomplishments because she never sought publicity from either friend or foe.

VALINDA W. LITTLEFIELD

Howard University

Established by an act of the U.S. Congress in 1867, Howard University, located in Washington, D.C., was designated as "a university for the education of youth in the liberal arts and sciences." Consisting of four principal campuses totaling 241 acres, Howard is a comprehensive, research-oriented institution. Women comprise approximately 37 percent of the more than 2,000 faculty members, and represent 57 percent of employed staff members.

Howard University has, since its founding in 1867, been open to women, both as students and as faculty members. This 1893 portrait shows students posing on the steps of Miner Hall. (MOORLAND-SPINGARN)

The only constraint on female participation in Howard's administrative and educational systems, from the beginning until the present, has had to do with the availability of qualified women candidates. This photograph of a women's tennis team dates from the early 1930s.
(SCURLOCK STUDIO)

Founded primarily to provide postsecondary education to the newly emancipated slaves and free persons of color, Howard University serves the educational needs of students without regard to race, sex, creed, or nationality. Setting out in 1867 with an initial enrollment of four white female students, the university today enrolls a multiracial female population of over 7,000, representing more than 57 percent of the total student body. Women students enroll in the university's seventeen schools and colleges, selecting courses from a diverse curriculum offering degree programs in more than two hundred specialized subjects.

Howard University's women students, coming from various states and foreign nations, participate in undergraduate, graduate, and professional programs. Preparing female educators, lawyers, doctors, dentists, and other educated women, especially to work within the black community, has been a Howard tradition since the late nineteenth century. In contrast to many other postsecondary institutions during that period, Howard not only included women as students but also included them as faculty members. Beginning in the late 1860s and early 1870s, female faculty members taught in the fine arts and medical fields. During the 1880s a woman served as the administrator of the university's normal department.

Howard's first graduates from its normal and collegiate departments in the early 1870s were women. The university graduated a female doctor in 1872 and 1874, a female lawyer in 1872, a female pharmacist in 1887, and a female dentist in 1896 and 1900. The only constraint on female participation in the university's administrative and educational systems, from this early period until the present, related to the availability of qualified women candidates.

Howard University's historic mission symbolizes its ongoing adherence to the belief in female inclusion in the postsecondary educational process. Howard alumnae serving worldwide are living testimonies to the university's incalculable contribution to both the American and world communities. Individuals such as **Debbie Allen, Mary Frances Berry, Sharon Pratt Dixon**, Frankie M. Freeman, **Lois Mailou Jones, Toni Morrison, Jessye Norman, Eleanor Holmes Norton, Dorothy Porter Wesley**, and Jeanne C. Sinkford reflect the high caliber of women graduates from Howard, a university forever mindful of its female tradition and its commitment to educating this important component of its student constituency.

CLIFFORD MUSE

Hughes, Marvalene (1947–)

When Dr. Marvalene Hughes was appointed president of California State University

Marvalene Hughes was appointed president of California State University's Stanislaus campus in 1994. (CALIFORNIA STATE UNIVERSITY STANISLAUS)

(CSU)–Stanislaus in 1994, she already had a wealth of experience as an administrator and educator. She arrived from the University of Minnesota, Twin Cities, where she served as vice president for student affairs and vice provost for academic affairs. Before that she was vice president for student affairs at the University of Toledo and associate vice president for student affairs at Arizona State University, and also had held positions at San Diego State University, Eckerd College, and Florida A & M University.

Hughes received a B.S. in English and history and an M.S. in counseling and administration from Tuskegee University, before being awarded a Ph.D. in counseling from Florida State University. A prolific lecturer and writer, Hughes also has been involved with numerous academic, civic, and social organizations.

At CSU Stanislaus, Hughes presides over a student body of 6,000. She also is a professor in the department of psychology.

MICHAEL NOWAK

I

Institute for Colored Youth, Philadelphia

The Institute for Colored Youth, the oldest private high school established for African Americans, was founded in 1832 through a $10,000 bequest made by Richard Humphreys, a Philadelphia goldsmith. A thirteen-member Quaker board was established to carry out the terms of Humphreys's will, and in early 1840 a 136-acre farm was purchased seven miles from Philadelphia by the trustees of the school. Five boys from the Shelter for Colored Orphans in Philadelphia were enrolled in this farm school. The stringent rules and regulations resulted in a series of runaways, and by 1846 the unsuccessful farm school had closed.

In 1848, a group of African-American mechanics in Philadelphia approached the Quaker board with a proposal to establish an educational institution in Philadelphia where black students could be apprenticed to them to learn various trades and also to gain an opportunity to study the literary and "higher branches" of learning. The board agreed to the proposal, and by 1849 a black man, Ishmael Locke, was hired as a teacher for the evening school that opened in South Philadelphia. Within a month, thirty pupils were enrolled, and by the end of the 1850 term, forty-three boys had attended.

With the success of this venture, the black tradesmen were able to convince the Quaker managers to establish a day school that would be available to both boys and girls. In 1852, a building was erected at Sixth and Lombard streets in the heart of the Philadelphia black community and named the Institute for Colored Youth (ICY). Charles A. Reason, a distinguished African-American educator from New York, was named principal, and Grace A. Mapps, also of New York, was named head of the female department.

Under Reason's principalship the institute developed into a strong academic institution. Reason was succeeded as principal in 1856 by Ebenezer Bassett, a graduate of Connecticut State Normal School and a former student at Yale College. Bassett maintained the high academic standards of the school. Because the institution offered a classical college preparatory curriculum, it drew attention from persons throughout the nation, and visitors to Philadelphia frequently stopped by to observe the students.

In 1869, Bassett was appointed U.S. minister to Haiti, and he was replaced by Fanny Jackson, an 1865 **Oberlin College** graduate. **Fanny Jackson [Coppin]** joined the faculty of the institute in 1865 as principal of the female department. Her skills as a teacher were quickly recognized, and her appointment as principal of the entire school resulted in her heading the school for thirty-two years, until she retired in 1901.

During Coppin's direction the institute grew to attract a national and international student body and always had a long waiting list of applicants. The all-black faculty represented some of the best-educated black Americans of the time, including **Mary Jane Patterson**, the first black woman college graduate (Oberlin 1862); Richard T. Greener, the first black graduate of Harvard University (1870); and Edward Bouchet, the first black person to earn a Ph.D. (Yale 1876, physics). As a result of the institute's strong science faculty, numerous male and female students became physicians. In addition, the strong teacher-training program of the institute contributed to the making of most of the black teachers in the Philadelphia and New Jersey areas.

When Coppin retired as principal in 1901, the Quaker managers were persuaded by Booker T. Washington to change the classical thrust of the institution and replace it with a more industrial curriculum. Consequently, ICY closed its doors in Philadelphia in 1902 and moved to Cheyney, Pennsylvania, where it subsequently became Cheyney State College.

LINDA M. PERKINS

J

Jeanes Fund and Jeanes Teachers

The Negro Rural School Fund was established in 1907 by Quaker heiress Anna Jeanes, to improve small rural schools for southern African Americans. Commonly known as the Jeanes Fund, its trustees included Booker T. Washington, Andrew Carnegie, Robert Moton, and James Dillard. With the financial support of the fund, hundreds of blacks became Jeanes teachers in the first decades of the twentieth century and significantly improved the quality of education available to black children throughout the rural South.

Jackson Davis, school superintendent of Henrico County, Virginia, requested and received a Jeanes Fund grant after being denied county funds to implement new teaching methods in black schools. The methods were those of **Virginia Randolph,**

Quaker heiress Anna Jeanes established the Negro Rural School Fund in the hope of improving small rural schools for Southern blacks. With financial support from the fund, hundreds of blacks in the early twentieth century became Jeanes teachers. Of these teachers, 45 percent had bachelor's degrees, earned primarily through the taking of summer courses at Hampton Institute, where this group photograph was taken. (DONNA HOLLIE)

a daughter of ex-slaves who had graduated from high school and was teaching by age sixteen. In addition to academic subjects, she taught gardening, cooking, laundering, and sewing so as to encourage students to value labor and to maximize their meager resources. She urged community members of both races to support the students' activities, and she visited community members' homes, teaching health care, nutrition, homemaking, and needlework. In 1908, Randolph became the first Jeanes Supervising Industrial Teacher, with the responsibility of assisting and directing county teachers in their efforts to improve black communities.

Other Jeanes teachers were employed, and their success led to the receipt of increased financial support from local governments, resulting in the hiring of more teachers throughout the South. By 1936, 426 Jeanes teachers in fourteen Southern states were earning an average annual salary of $850. Although normal school degrees were not required, 45 percent of teachers had bachelor's degrees, earned primarily through summer courses at Hampton Institute and paid for by the fund. Teachers were required to file annual reports of school activities and to present public exhibits of students' projects.

In 1937, the Jeanes Fund merged with others. It is currently known as the Southern Educational Foundation, Incorporated, and is headquartered in Atlanta, Georgia.

DONNA TYLER HOLLIE

Johnston, Gladys (1943–)

When Gladys Styles Johnston became the chancellor of the University of Nebraska at Kearney in 1993, she brought with her a wide range of experience in education and

Chancellor of the University of Nebraska at Kearney since 1993, Gladys Johnston also is vice president of the University of Nebraska System. (JOHN REILLY PHOTOGRAPHY)

administration. She has needed them, as she has worked to improve undergraduate recruitment, student academic advising, and facilities. She also serves as vice president of the University of Nebraska System.

Johnston received a B.S. in Social Science from Cheyney University of Pennsylvania, an M.Ed. in educational administration from Temple University, and a Ph.D. in educational administration and organizational theory and behavior from Cornell University. She went from the public schools of New Jersey to administrative and teaching positions at Rutgers, Arizona State, and DePaul University in Chicago, where she was provost and then executive vice president before moving on to Nebraska.

In addition to publishing two books and numerous research articles, Johnston was appointed Distinguished Commonwealth Visiting Professor in the School of Education at William and Mary College in 1983. She currently serves as a national adviser for the Kellogg Foundation National Fellowship Program.

MICHAEL NOWAK

K

Kennedy, Yvonne (1945–)

Dr. Yvonne Kennedy made Alabama history in 1981 when she became president of Bishop State Community College in Mobile. At this point in time, she is the only black woman in Alabama ever to be appointed president of a state college.

Born in 1945 in Mobile, Yvonne Kennedy is the daughter of Leroy and Thelma McMillian Kennedy. A product of the Mo-

Yvonne Kennedy is not only the first black woman president of an Alabama state college, but also the first black woman to be elected to the Alabama House of Representatives from Mobile County.
(BISHOP STATE COMMUNITY COLLEGE)

bile County public school system, Kennedy received a B.S. in English and social science from Alabama State University, an M.A. in English from Morgan State University in Baltimore, and a Ph.D. in administration/higher education from the University of Alabama. At Bishop State, she established the first-ever capital campaign for any Alabama public two-year college, and she succeeded in raising over $1 million, which allowed her to consolidate three two-year colleges into a comprehensive Bishop State Community College.

This distinguished educator, also active in civic and religious organizations, has made her mark in government as the only black woman from Mobile County to be elected to the Alabama House of Representatives. In the Alabama legislature she was elected majority floor leader, as well as party leader by the Alabama Caucus of House Democrats and chairman of the Alabama Legislative Black Caucus. Her legislative peers presented her with an Outstanding Legislator Award, and she was named one of *Ebony* magazine's 100 most influential black Americans from 1989 to 1992.

MICHAEL NOWAK

Koontz, Elizabeth Duncan (1919–1989)

Elizabeth Duncan Koontz served as president of the National Education Association (NEA) in 1968–69 and set as her theme, "A Time for Educational Statesmanship." She called on teachers "to make use of their united power to bring about change." In her acceptance speech in Dallas, Texas, she further emphasized "that educators . . . men and women . . . young and old . . . black and white . . . stand together."

Born in Salisbury, North Carolina, on June 3, 1919, to Samuel and Lean Duncan, Elizabeth Duncan attended the Salisbury public schools and Livingstone College. She received a bachelor's degree in English and elementary education in 1938, a master's degree in elementary education from Atlanta University in 1941, and did further study at both Columbia University and Indiana University. She pursued additional training in education for the mentally retarded at North Carolina College in Durham, now North Carolina Central University (NCCU). On November 26, 1947, she married Harry Lee Koontz.

Devoting her entire life to the field of education, Koontz taught in the following North Carolina schools: Harnett County Training School, 1938–40; Aggrey Memorial School, Landis, 1940–41; Fourteenth Street School, Winston-Salem, 1941–1945; Price High School, Salisbury, 1945–49; Monroe School, Salisbury, 1949–65; and Price Junior-Senior High School, Salisbury, 1965–68.

Her involvement in teaching led her to become active in the local and state teachers' organizations for African Americans, and the North Carolina Teachers Association. Koontz served as president of the North Carolina Association of Classroom Teachers (NCACT) from 1959 to 1963. Under her leadership NCACT published its first edition of *Guidelines for Local Associations of Classroom Teachers* in 1961. Other accomplishments during her tenure included passage of a resolution against segregated accommodations at

NEA-DCT (Department of Classroom Teachers) regional meetings of the Southeastern Region; the resolution was cosponsored by the Florida Teachers Association. Other firsts for this African-American woman included being the first North Carolina Teachers Association member appointed to the NEA Commission. Her participation at NEA-DCT meetings led to her appointment to the advisory committee by Margaret Stevenson, executive secretary of NEA-DCT.

In 1960, she was elected secretary of the NEA-DCT, a position she held for two years. Then, after serving one year as vice president and one year as president-elect,

A lifelong educator, Elizabeth Koontz headed the Women's Bureau of the Department of Labor during the Nixon administration, and in 1970 she served as a delegate to the United Nations Commission on the Status of Women. (SCHOMBURG CENTER)

Koontz served as president of NEA-DCT from 1965 to 1966. She represented 825,000 teachers nationwide. She was the first African American to serve in each of these national offices.

In 1968, she was elected president of the NEA, another first for her and for African Americans. As NEA president, she outlined a nine-point program for her tenure in which she called for a unified, secure, respected, informed, and socially aware profession; a profession that also ensured adequate income after retirement, protected against unjust attacks, had teacher-leaders, and was undivided by artificial differences.

A statesperson for education, Koontz was one of sixteen Americans who visited the Soviet Union at the request of *Saturday Review* in 1964. She held membership in the North Carolina Council of Human Relations and the North Carolina Governor's Commission on the Status of Women, and in 1965 was a member of the President's Advisory Council on Education of Disadvantaged Children.

During the presidential administration of Richard M. Nixon, Koontz headed the Women's Bureau of the Department of Labor and served as a delegate to the United Nations Commission on the Status of Women in 1970. Her last career appointment was as assistant superintendent for the Department of Public Instruction. She retired from this position in 1982. Koontz served not only the educational system of North Carolina, but the nation and the world. She received many awards, citations, honors, and honorary degrees that eloquently testify to the esteem and appreciation felt for her by those she served. Elizabeth Duncan Koontz died in 1989 of a heart attack.

PERCY E. MURRAY

L

Ladner, Joyce A. (1943–)

Since the early 1970s, sociologist Joyce A. Ladner's writings have exposed the profound misunderstandings of black life that are kept alive by certain white academics. It is a preoccupation more than strongly implied in the title of the 1973 book of essays she edited, *The Death of White Sociology*.

It is also central to her important study of urban black teenaged women, *Tomorrow's Tomorrow: The Black Woman*, published in 1971 and reissued, with new reflections, nearly a quarter century later. It revealed that the young urban black woman is not—contrary to stereotype—lacking in self-esteem, hope, or ambition. In fact, the opposite is true.

Joyce Ann Ladner was born in Waynesboro, Mississippi, on October 12, 1943. From that state's Tougaloo College she received her B.A. in 1964. In St. Louis, Missouri, the city in which she would in a few years survey her *Tomorrow's Tomorrow* subjects, she earned her Ph.D. at Washington University in 1968.

Her subsequent academic career brought Ladner to far-flung places. Postdoctoral research took her to Africa and the University of Dar es Salaam in Tanzania. She was assistant professor and curriculum specialist at Southern Illinois University in Edwardsville, Illinois (1968–69) and an affiliate with Wesleyan University in Middletown, Connecticut (1969–70).

Ladner returned to Dar es Salaam for the 1970–71 academic year as a research associate. Her study "Involvement of Tanzanian Women in Nation Building" won her the first fellowship given by the Black Women's Community Development Foundation. Two years later she would win grants from the Russell Sage and Cummins Engine foundations.

Ladner was associate professor of sociology between 1971 and 1976 at **Howard University**, in Washington, D.C., of which in 1995 she would become interim president. During this and her ensuing job on the Hunter College sociology faculty in New York, Ladner researched her book *Mixed Families: Adopting Across Racial Boundaries*.

Published in 1977, *Mixed Families* presented both sides of the controversy as to whether white couples should adopt black children. Ladner found that some adoptors and adoptees, looking back, felt that black parentage might have been better for the children. Though Ladner concurred for reasons more practical than ideological, she wrote also that a child's having white parents was preferable to being raised under institutional or foster care.

Ladner is a member of the board of directors of the American Sociological Association, and she has written for many periodicals and anthologies. She has been contributing editor to *Black Scholar* and *Journal of Black Studies and Research*. With Peter Edelman she edited the volume, *Adolescence and Poverty: Challenge for the '90s*.

In June 1995, President Clinton appointed Ladner to a three-year term on a

Joyce A. Ladner's research and writings challenge many white sociologists' assumptions about black life. Pictured here on the left, she served as interim president of Howard University in 1995. (HOWARD UNIVERSITY)

five-member panel with the huge task of ending the District of Columbia's fiscal crisis, including a budget deficit of over $700 million. Called the District of Columbia Financial Responsibility and Management Assistance Authority, the panel has power viewed as greater than that of all the elected officials of Washington, D.C., and of any comparable panel in any American city.

Lyle, Ethel Hedgeman (1887–1950)

"As long as life lasts and beyond, I shall see the beautiful deeds done to help others less fortunate and the lovely hands of all the women of **Alpha Kappa Alpha** outstretched to the aid of others who, mentally, morally, and physically, are still poor and needy; and I will always thank God that I had some small part in it," Ethel Hedgeman Lyle once said. Although she would never say so herself, playing a role was something Ethel Hedgeman Lyle did well and often.

Far from making a cameo appearance, however, Lyle was the leading lady, and her most memorable performance was as the founder of Alpha Kappa Alpha (AKA) Sorority, the first Greek-letter organization for black women. Lyle believed that women united by a common bond could organize their talents and strengths for the betterment of themselves and humankind. It was this philosophy that led the honor student to establish AKA at **Howard University** in 1908, and the debut brought rave reviews.

Her performance in the educational arena also brought critical acclaim. After receiving her A.B. in English from Howard in 1909, she became the first college-trained black woman to teach in a normal school in Oklahoma and to receive Oklahoma's Teacher's Life Certificate. Yet Lyle's longest-running appearances came in Philadelphia. She taught in the public schools from 1921 to 1948, and seeing her students achieve and garner honors gave Lyle "the greatest happiness and thrill of my life!" Her civic performances brought additional plaudits, including a mayoral appointment as chair of the committee of 100 women charged with planning the 150th anniversary of the Constitution. At home, she played the traditional roles of wife and mother to her husband, George Lyle, a Philadelphia school principal, and son, George Hedgeman Lyle.

The daughter of Albert Hedgeman and Marie Hubbard Hedgeman of St. Louis, Missouri, Lyle grew up in a family that actively worked through their church and community to improve conditions for their children and those who were less fortunate. She spent her life maintaining that commitment. She died on November 28, 1950.

EARNESTINE GREEN McNEALEY

M

Marshall, Harriet Gibbs (1868–1941)

Educator, concert pianist, and author Harriet Gibbs was born in Vancouver, British Columbia, Canada, on February 18, 1868. The daughter of Marie A. Alexander and Judge Miflin Wistar Gibbs, she grew up in Oberlin, Ohio, where she attended Oberlin Conservatory of Music and became the first African-American woman to complete the course in piano (1889). She concertized early in her career and, after serving as the first director of music at Eckstein-Norton College (Cane Springs, Kentucky), she supervised music activities for students of color in Washington, D.C.'s public schools (1900–1903). Her official title, however, was assistant director of music for the District of Columbia public schools. In 1903, she founded the Washington Conservatory of Music and School of Expression. On June 3, 1906, she married Napoleon B. Marshall.

The Washington Conservatory was important to the city not only because it offered opportunity for college-level instruction in music but also because it provided cultural programs for the city from 1910 to its closing in 1960. Harriet Marshall had conceived of the school as part of a National Center of Negro Music, which she opened in 1936. From 1922 to 1928 she lived in Haiti, where her husband had been appointed a member of the American legation.

While there, Harriet Marshall became interested in the country and its culture, cofounding the industrial school l'Oeuvre des Femmes Haitienne pour l'Organization de Labour and researching the achievements of Haitian women. She later wrote *The Story of Haiti* (1930). Another literary effort was an unpublished drama titled *Last Concerto*, based on the life, love, and music of Samuel Coleridge-Taylor. Harriet Gibbs Marshall died in Washington, D.C., on February 25, 1941.

DORIS EVANS McGINTY

Maultsby, Portia (1947–)

If you want to see African America, try looking through the eyes of ethnomusicologist Dr. Portia Maultsby. Her work is a composite of African-American culture, history, and music (jazz, blues, gospel, spirituals, soul, funk, hip-hop, rap, and art music). She brings to it a wide-ranging knowledge of the philosophy, sociology, and language of African Americans.

Portia Maultsby was born on June 11, 1947, in Orlando. Her passion for music was cultivated early in her life. When she was five, her day began with 5:30 A.M. piano practice, her mother always at her side. She studied piano and theory with Leslie B. Weaver and Harold Lewis.

By the age of thirteen, Maultsby was Jones High School Choir accompanist and featured soloist. On Sundays, she played piano and organ for a Methodist Sunday school, for afternoon Presbyterian services, and for evening Pentecostal services. She also played

French horn in marching band and symphony, under James Wilson's direction.

In 1968, Maultsby received a B.Mus. with a double major in piano and theory/composition from Mount St. Scholastica College in Atchison, Kansas, where she studied under Sister Joachim Holthaus. A year later she was awarded an M.M. in musicology from the University of Wisconsin at Madison, where she also received a Ph.D. in ethnomusicology in 1974. Her doctoral studies included African-American and Japanese music, and African and African-American history.

Since 1971, Maultsby has taught at Indiana University, Colorado College, Seattle Pacific University, and Swarthmore College. She has developed courses in the art music of composers; popular and religious music; the music industry; and ethnomusicology.

Maultsby has traveled extensively in pursuit of her music—to Africa for research (Nigeria and Ghana in 1977 and Zimbabwe in 1988), to Austria in 1967 to study piano and German, to the Netherlands in 1994 to deliver a keynote address at a GATT conference on cultural exchanges through music and also to lecture on soul and rap music, and to Russia in 1988. No matter where she is, Maultsby is at home when she is teaching, learning about, or performing African-American music.

Currently, Maultsby is professor/ethnomusicologist and director of the archives of African-American Music and Culture at Indiana University. She is also—quite remarkably—founder of the I. U. Soul Revue, a music group modeled upon James Brown's.

There can't be many ethnomusicologists who would put together a group to sing soul music, but Maultsby is no ordinary academic. She has composed and arranged music for Soul Revue, which she also has directed. They recorded Maultsby's *Tell Me About It and Music Is Just a Party*, co-written by Marcellus Lawrence, which garnered a 1977 *Billboard* citation.

Maultsby has won grants from the Ford Foundation, the President's Council on International Programs, and the Indiana Committee for the Humanities. She is the subject of articles in the *New York Times*, *Rolling Stone* magazine, and the *Biographical Dictionary of Afro-American and African Musicians*.

Ethnomusicologist Portia Maultsby explores and expresses African-American culture, history, and music in her work. There probably aren't many academics who could put together a performing group like the Soul Revue *she founded at Indiana University.*
(INDIANA UNIVERSITY)

Maultsby has lectured in the Netherlands, at the Smithsonian Institution, the **Zora Neale Hurston** Festival in Eatonville, Florida, and other places worldwide. She is a board member of the Rhythm and Blues Foundation, which is housed in the Smithsonian Institution. Her impressive list of credentials as an editor includes work on hymnals, textbooks, museum exhibitions, movies, videos, and such television shows as *Eyes on the Prize II, That Rhythm . . . Those Blues, Record Row: The Cradle of Rhythm and Blues*, and the radio programs *Wade in the Water* and *Black Radio: Telling It Like It Was*.

In addition to articles and book reviews, Maultsby is in the process of writing *From Backwoods to City Street: Black Popular Music* and *The Evolution of African American Music*.

The rhythm of Maultsby's music is drawn from her personal, social, and scholarly lives. Above all, Maultsby presents to the world African-American vernacular music that can stand on its own merits as art.

REGINA HARRIS BAIOCCHI

Mable Parker McLean, the first woman to chair the Presidents of United Negro College Fund Member Institutions, received the Candace Award in Education in 1986. (BARBER-SCOTIA COLLEGE)

McLean, Mable Parker (1922–)

Dr. Mable Parker McLean was the ninth president of Barber-Scotia College in Concord, North Carolina. She was the first woman to lead the school. Upon her retirement in 1988, she became President-Emerita. She was the first woman chair of the Presidents of United Negro College Fund (UNCF) Member Institutions.

A native of Moore County, North Carolina, Parker was educated in the public schools of Virginia and North Carolina, did her undergraduate work at Barber-Scotia College and Johnson C. Smith University in North Carolina, her graduate studies at **Howard University** in Washington, D.C., and her postgraduate work at Northwestern University in Illinois and The Catholic University of America in Washington, D.C. Beginning her career as an educator in the North Carolina public schools, she went from being a classroom teacher to an academic dean and then a college president.

McLean has traveled widely speaking in support of black higher education and the UNCF. In 1986, she received the Candace Award in Education from the National Coalition of 100 Black Women.

MICHAEL NOWAK

Mitchell, Katherine (1943–)

Katherine Phillips Mitchell is the first woman president in the 109-year history of Shorter College in North Little Rock, Arkansas. During her tenure there, she has increased the enrollment 300 percent, and greatly reduced the college's indebtedness.

Mitchell was born in President Bill Clinton's hometown of Hope, Arkansas, but she grew up in Little Rock, where her parents moved when she was still an infant. A product of the Little Rock Public Schools, she received a B.A. in English from Philander Smith College in Little Rock, an M.A. in education from Cleveland State University, and a Ed.D. in higher education with an emphasis in reading from the University of Arkansas.

Katherine Mitchell is the first woman president in the 109-year history of Shorter College. (SHORTER COLLEGE)

While most of her work experience has been in the field of education, she served as the first coordinator of Storer Cable's Channel 14, the only black-access television channel in the nation. She left that position to accept the presidency of Shorter.

MICHAEL NOWAK

Moses, Yolanda T. (1946–)

Dr. Yolanda T. Moses is a nationally prominent cultural anthropologist. Adding honor upon honor, on August 1, 1993, Dr. Moses became the tenth president of City College of New York (CCNY). The oldest of the City University's colleges, City College boasts an enrollment of approximately 15,000 students and is one of the nation's leading sources of black and Hispanic engineers. Eight City College alumni have won Nobel Prizes, and CCNY is ranked sixth nationally in the number of Ph.D. recipients.

Although a native Californian, Moses is the child of working-class parents who migrated from rural Louisiana to the North in search of greater economic opportunity. The first in her family to receive a college degree, Moses discovered a world of opportunity all of her own within the public education system, having received her associate of arts degree from a community college, her B.A. in sociology with summa cum laude honors from California State College, San Bernardino, in 1968, and her master's degree and doctorate from the University of California at Riverside in 1976, also with highest honors.

Prior to her installation at CCNY, Moses served as vice president for academic affairs and professor of anthropology at California State University, Dominguez Hills, from 1988 to 1993. From 1993 to 1995, she was president-elect of the American Anthropological Association (AAA), which boasts over 11,000 members. In November 1995, she became the seventy-fourth president of the AAA.

Nationally prominent, Dr. Moses is also the former president of the AAA's Council on Anthropology and Education. Dedicated to the inclusion of more minorities in the field of anthropology, Dr. Moses co-chaired the AAA's task force developed to address that very issue. She was also one of an elect group of national experts on

Yolanda T. Moses, a noted cultural anthropologist, became president of the City College of New York in 1993. In a convocation speech, she urged her CCNY colleagues to "commit yourselves to building bridges of understanding." (CITY COLLEGE, CUNY)

cultural diversity selected by the Ford Foundation to review and evaluate diversity in all programs throughout the nation funded by the Foundation.

With her more than twenty years of involvement within the American Anthropological Association, Moses has served in many capacities, including that of board member of the Association of Black Anthropologists (ABA) and chair of the finance committee of that organization.

Moses also enjoyed a long association with California State Polytechnic University, Pomona, from 1975 to 1988, chairing the Ethnic and Women's Studies Department and moving from Acting Dean to Dean of the School of Arts from 1983 to 1988. She was a Visiting Professor at SUNY–Plattsburg, and a Distinguished Visiting Professor at the University of Tennessee, Knoxville. Committed to seeing that high school students learn those fundamentals that ensure collegiate success, Dr. Moses also has served as chair of the Operations Board for the California Academy for Mathematics and Science, a four-year comprehensive high school located at CSU, Dominguez Hills.

Actively involved in maintaining standards of excellence in higher education, Dr. Moses has served as leader of the Western Association of Schools and Colleges Accreditation Team since 1991. She also is a member of the Western College Association Executive Committee, a policy-making organization.

Moses is a prolific writer and has contributed to numerous scholarly publications. From the vantage point of consultant and researcher for the Association of American Colleges, Dr. Moses developed her pioneering monograph, *Black Women in Academe.*

Dr. Moses has produced a rich and varied body of anthropological field work, covering, among other topics, the impact of the Trans-Alaska pipeline on Alaskans and their environment in Valdez, Alaska, and a study of immigration and the roles of working women in Monserrat and Antigua, British West Indies. She has traveled extensively, gathering data from field visits to Kenya, Trinidad, and Jamaica, to name just a few of the more exotic locations. Dr. Moses is married to James F. Bawek. They have two daughters, Shana and Antonia.

On September 9, 1993, during a convocation in which she addressed the CCNY community, Dr. Moses had this to say: "Pluralism and diversity are among our greatest strengths as a College and as a nation. Each one of us has the opportunity—and the responsibility—to show that pluralism is a valued, unique, and productive characteristic of educational life. I urge you to commit yourselves to building bridges of understanding." Dr. Yolanda T. Moses, anthropologist and college president, is a most remarkable engineer of humanity's bridges.

ROSE WOODSON

Moten, Lucy Ella (1851–1933)

Born in Farquier County, Virginia, near White Sulphur Springs, Lucy Moten was the daughter of free African Americans, Benjamin and Julia (Witchers) Moten. Young Lucy's parents were so impressed with her early intellectual development that they relocated to Washington, D.C., so that she could attend a school for free African Americans conducted by John F. Cook, Sr. When public schools for African Americans opened in the District of Columbia in 1862, the Motens saw to it that their daughter was enrolled. It was probably this early thrust into the world of academia that resulted in Moten's lifetime commitment to education.

After graduating from **Howard University** in 1870, Moten began her teaching career in the primary division of the O Street School in Washington, D.C. As a teacher she continued to pursue her academic and professional training, graduating from the Normal School at Salem, Massachusetts, in 1876. In addition, she graduated with honors from the Spencerian Business College in 1883 and took classes in public speaking with Alfred Townsend, a respected Washington, D.C., teacher of the period.

Armed with an excellent academic record and a recommendation from Frederick Douglass, Moten was appointed and served as principal of Miner Normal School in Washington, D.C., from 1883 to 1920. For twenty-five years Miner Normal School was recognized as one of the top teacher-training institutions in America. Under Moten's leadership, the school's faculty and admission standards were raised and the curriculum was extended to a two-year program. Also during her tenure, a new Miner facility was built in 1914. Moten helped plan the design, securing well-lighted and well-ventilated stairs and corridors inside the structure.

According to official documents and correspondence dating to her tenure at Miner Normal School, Moten had strong opinions about teacher qualifications: "The teacher must be first class in every particular, a professionally trained person whose personality will impress itself on . . . pupils always for their best good. The aesthetic must be looked after as well as the moral and the physical." Moten trained meticulous, punctual, accurate, and thorough teachers who were recruited by state superintendents throughout the country.

After Moten received a medical degree from Howard Medical School in 1897, she was able to treat the medical needs of her students and establish a course in physical hygiene. By linking her professional advancement with that of the school, Moten became an inspiration to her students, instilling cultural pride, dedication, and discipline as well as developing their intelligence. Her emphasis on personal morals also influenced her students, provoking them to reach for higher goals.

For four decades, Miner trained the majority of teachers employed in Washington's African-American schools. Moten's teaching was not limited to Miner, however. She spent many summers training teachers in the South, which led to further graduate work at New York University in the field of education. Her commitment to education also led her to Europe, where she broadened her educational perspective and came upon the architectural style that she decided would be used in building the new Miner Normal School, a replica of Christ's College in Cambridge, England.

Lucy Ella Moten was struck and killed by a taxi in New York's Times Square on August 24, 1933. A pioneer in education even in death, she bequeathed more than $51,000 to **Howard University**. Ironically, given her cause of death, the money was to be used to fund student travel regardless of the recipient's sex, color, or creed. In 1954, a Washington, D.C., elementary school was named in her honor.

TOMIKA DePRIEST

N

National Training School for Women and Girls

The National Training School for Women and Girls, a boarding school that opened in 1909 and trained students in domestic science, business, and sewing in the first half of the twentieth century, prepared young black women both to "uplift" the race and earn a living. School founder **Nannie Helen Burroughs** (1879–1961) first presented the idea of a training school for young black women in her role as corresponding secretary for the women's auxiliary of the National Baptist Convention at the turn of the century. She found a receptive audience among Baptist women, who declared in a 1908 meeting: "We are not here to discuss the necessity of the institution. The preparation of our women for domestic and professional service, in the home and communities, ranks next in importance to preparation of their souls for the world to come." In 1907, Burroughs worked with a committee of the National Baptist Convention to purchase a site for a school in Lincoln Heights in Washington, D.C., and two years later the school enrolled its first thirty-one students.

The school was chartered independently of the National Baptist Convention, and Burroughs deliberately excluded the word "Baptist" from the school's name to emphasize its openness to students of all denominations. This original charter incited a debate in the 1920s and 1930s within the black Baptist community about who had control over the school's operations and finances.

Burroughs, however, maintained control over the school and ensured that nearly all of the members of the board of trustees were black women. Funding was drawn primarily from individual contributions within the black community, in contrast to many other private black schools that were dependent on support from white foundations. Fund-raising projects carried out by the students and staff of the National Training School included recitations, plays, and concerts. These performances raised money, advertised the school, and gave students practice in public speaking and performance. Other revenue was raised through operating a laundry, which also served as a training

The motto of the National Training School was the three B's: Bible, bath, and broom. The founder, Nannie Helen Burroughs, placed particular stress on training in domestic science. This card advertises services for which the students are being trained.
(LIBRARY OF CONGRESS)

center; selling student-made goods; and running a summer school for adult women offering courses in social service and community organizing.

The school's motto was the three B's—Bible, bath, and broom. The bath and broom symbolized training in cleanliness and housekeeping skills as part of racial advancement. Burroughs placed particular stress on the need for young black women to be trained in domestic science, a skill they could use in the workplace and the home. The central tenet of the school was the Bible, which emphasized spirituality and moral conduct.

The students of the National Training School lived in the campus dormitories, and they came from different regions of the United States as well as Africa and the Caribbean. They took courses in missionary work, domestic science, social work, clerical work, printing, sewing, music, beauty culture, and agriculture. This training was aimed at providing the skills needed for black women to become simultaneously wage workers, housewives, and community activists.

The National Training School also emphasized "race pride" through its required courses in "Negro history." Burroughs was a friend of Carter G. Woodson and a strong advocate of the teaching of black history. Every student was required to complete the course and pass a written and oral examination. In their 1929 yearbook, the students wrote of their appreciation for the opportunity to study the history of their race: "This school teaches History and Negro History and the students are tremendously inspired by learning the truth about their own race. We know now that our race has been a valuable part of all that has been going on in the building of world civilizations. Dr. Carter G. Woodson's books are used as the text here and we have a room, a real library—if you please—set apart for the study of Negro life and history."

After 1953 the school, then called the National Trade and Professional School for Women and Girls, narrowed its training solely to the field of missionary service, and Burroughs continued as the school's president until her death in 1961. For the first half of the twentieth century the National Training School prepared young black women for their dual roles as wage workers and "uplifters" of the race, and served as a model institution for the black community.

VICTORIA WOLCOTT

Nickerson, Camille Lucie (1887–1982)

Camille Lucie Nickerson was born in New Orleans, Louisiana, in 1887. She attended Xavier Preparatory School in New Orleans and did her undergraduate and graduate work at Oberlin Conservatory of Music in Oberlin, Ohio, where she received both a bachelor's and a master's degree in music and was elected to Pi Kappa Lambda National Music Honor Society. She wrote her master's thesis on Creole music. Later known as Miss NAACP, Nickerson became a nationally recognized authority on Creole music.

Camille Nickerson founded the Nickerson School of Music, and many of her students became teachers of music. One of them, Beryl Thornhill Richardson, remembers her "as an excellent teacher, demonstrating correct piano playing positions, technique of wrist control and all fundamentals. She played and sang for the class and clapped the rhythm. She was kind, thorough, impeccably dressed, and loved her students." In 1917, Nickerson founded the B Sharp Music Club, consisting of her piano pupils, in New Orleans. Two of the original members were Lucille Levy Hutton, who was the first black music consultant in the New Orleans public schools, and Charles B. Rousseve, pianist, organist, author, and public school principal.

Nickerson also served as president of the National Association of Negro Musicians (1935–37). The B Sharp Music Club became affiliated with the national association in 1921 and continues to be an important cultural organization in New Orleans, having celebrated its seventy-fifth anniversary in 1992. Nickerson appeared in many concerts with the B Sharp Music Club, and she represented Louisiana as a composer on stage at the Kennedy Center in Washington, D.C.

In 1926, Nickerson joined the faculty of **Howard University** in Washington, D.C., where she was professor of piano and an authority on Creole music. She established the Junior Department of the Howard University School of Music.

Her music lives on in the hearts of her music club and the extended community. The Robert Perry Singers of the B Sharp Music Club continue to sing her Creole songs. Five of her arrangements have been published by the Boston Music Company: "Chere, Mo Lemmé, Toi" (Dear, I Love You So) (1942); "Lizette, To Quitté la Plaine" (Lizette, My Dearest One); "Danse, Conni, Conné" (Dance, Baby, Dance) (1942); "Fais Do Do" (Go to Sleep) (1948); and "Michieu Banjo" (Mister Banjo) (1942). Her arrangement of "Oh, Susanna" was published in the Silver Burdett music textbooks.

Camille Lucie Nickerson died on April 27, 1982, in Washington, D.C. The B Sharp Music Club paid tribute to her on June 27 of that year. When the National Association of Negro Musicians met in New Orleans in 1987, members of the B Sharp Music Club highlighted the convention with their dramatic performance of Nickerson's arrangements of Creole folk songs.

LILLIAN DUNN PERRY

Camille Lucie Nickerson, a noted music educator and authority on Creole music, established the Junior Department of the Howard University School of Music.
(MOORLAND-SPINGARN)

O

Oberlin College

Trustees at American colleges and universities are not known for making radical pronouncements. Yet in 1835, the trustees of the Oberlin Collegiate Institute, sparked by an evangelical commitment to abolitionism, declared: "the education of people of color is a matter of great interest and should be encouraged and sustained at this institution."

As the first coeducational college in America, the school had been on the cutting edge of educational reform ever since its founding two years earlier. At a time when other college doors were closed to black students, or, in a few instances, open to only a single black male student, Oberlin's com-mitment had a profound impact on the educational aspirations and achievements of free black women. Aside from the short-lived New York Central College in McGrawville, New York (1848–58), Oberlin was the only college in America open to black women until after the Civil War. Over 140 black women had enrolled at Oberlin by 1865.

The school included a Preparatory Department (PD) that became especially important to black students and women who had received inadequate or discriminatory public secondary education. Oberlin was best known, however, for its two college-level courses: a Young Ladies' Course (LC), com-

One of the many distinguished graduates of Oberlin College is Virginia Florence, the first black woman to receive a degree in library science. She is shown here (far left, second row) in the formal photograph of the 1919 Women's Literary Society. (OBERLIN COLLEGE)

parable to the curriculum at women's seminaries; and a more rigorous College Course (sometimes called the "gentlemen's course") leading to a baccalaureate degree. The highest enrollments were in the school's preparatory department, but by 1865, sixty-one black women had enrolled in either the Ladies' or the College Course. Twelve completed the Ladies' Course, and three earned the A.B. degree.

These Oberlin-educated black women went on to become leading educators and social activists in emerging black institutions across the country. Among them were **Mary Jane Patterson** (A.B. 1862) and **Fanny Jackson Coppin** (A.B. 1865), who became principals at historic black high schools. **Sarah Woodson Early** (LC 1856) probably became the first black woman on a college faculty when, in 1866, she began to teach at Wilberforce University.

Black Oberlin women served with the American Missionary Association (AMA) as teachers in Southern black schools after the Civil War; they included Louisa Alexander (LC 1856), Emma Brown (LC), Clara Duncan (PD), Blanche Harris (LC 1860), and **Sarah Stanley** (LC). Mahala McGuire (LC) became an AMA missionary teacher in Africa, as did African-born Margru, known in America as Sarah Kinson (LC). Others, like Lucy Stanton Day (LC 1850), taught in the South without organizational support.

A few women achieved prominence outside the field of education: **Edmonia Lewis,** a student in the Ladies' Course in the 1860s, became a well-known sculptor; and Frances Norris (AB 1865) became a businesswoman in Atlanta after the war, specializing in real estate and catering.

Many of these women remembered Oberlin as an interracial utopia, recalling that

In 1835, the trustees of Oberlin College initiated a strong commitment to the education of people of color. However, when Mary Church Terrell (class of 1884) arrived at the school in 1913 to enroll her two daughters, she discovered that the segregationist practices of the society at large had eroded some of that commitment. She lashed out at the administration in a letter, suggesting that "if colored students are to be segregated at Oberlin . . . it seems to me it would be wiser and kinder to exclude them altogether." (MOORLAND-SPINGARN)

they had been members and officers of the literary society, and had roomed and eaten along with their white classmates in college dormitories and dining halls. Although Fanny Jackson realized that Oberlin was not the "pool of Bethesda for the sin of prejudice," she always maintained that it "came nearer to it than any other place in the United States." Bigotry, she explained, was not to be found in the Oberlin administration or faculty; indeed, "prejudice at Oberlin is preached against, prayed against, sung against, and lived against."

After the Civil War, Oberlin's black graduates played an important role in establishing the first black colleges and serving on their faculties. As these colleges grew and other white colleges began to admit black students, Oberlin began to lose some of its distinctiveness. However, in the 1880s, **Mary Church Terrell, Anna Julia Cooper,** and Ida Wells Gibbs Hunt (all A.B. 1884) still found Oberlin a comfortable and inspiring place to be. Terrell valued both her black and white friends, as well as the opportunity for social integration afforded by the dormitories and campus organizations. Less is known about the Oberlin experiences of two women who became early black physicians, Matilda Evans (PD) and Caroline Still Anderson (LC 1880).

Unfortunately, as segregationist practices grew in American society so they did at Oberlin, especially after 1900. In 1913, when Mary Church Terrell came to Oberlin to enroll her two daughters, she learned that only two college dormitories were open to black women and that literary societies were no longer admitting black students. She lashed out at the administration, writing: "If colored students are to be segregated at Oberlin with such a wonderful record as it once made for itself even in the dark days of slavery, it seems to me it would be wiser and kinder to exclude them altogether."

To counteract growing social segregation, black students began to establish organizations of their own, and newly integrated liberal associations, such as the **Young Women's Christian Association** and the **National Association for the Advancement of Colored People,** provided forums where race-related issues could be discussed and addressed. After World War II, special programs were offered to expose students to black culture, including exchange programs with historic black colleges.

During the civil rights and Black Power movements, renewed pride in Oberlin's early commitment to racial justice resurfaced. Compelled by this tradition, new and successful efforts were made to increase black enrollment and retention. Yet unlike Mary Church Terrell and earlier generations of black students, many black students now did not wish to be assimilated into white society. Their outspoken presence required the college to reassess what it was offering in the way of academic and social support. The result was that, among many changes, Oberlin stepped up its black recruitment through a special nondiscriminatory program for disadvantaged youths, added a black studies program (now a department), established an African Heritage House, and formed a black alumni group within the Alumni Association.

Oberlin's twentieth-century black women continue to be very much a part of the Oberlin experience and to play important roles in American society. Most would agree with **Johnnetta Betsch Cole** (A.B. 1957), president of **Spelman College,** that their Oberlin experience has greatly influenced their lives by its "staunch commitment to a liberal arts curriculum [and] emphasis on taking responsibility for oneself and the world."

MARLENE DEAHL MERRILL

P

Pettigrew, L. Eudora (19?? –)

Dr. Eudora Pettigrew, president of the State University of New York (SUNY) College at Old Westbury, has been blazing trails in the field of higher education her entire adult life. She attended West Virginia State College and graduated with a bachelor of music degree in 1950. She then moved on to Southern Illinois University, where she earned her master of arts degree in rehabilitation counseling in 1964 and a Ph.D in educational psychology in 1966. While at Southern Illinois she became the first African-American resident counselor.

After leaving Southern Illinois, Pettigrew became the first African American to join the department of psychology at the University of Bridgeport, where she served first as assistant professor and then as associate professor. In 1974, Dr. Pettigrew became chairperson of the department of urban and metropolitan studies at Michigan State University. In 1981, she moved to the University of Delaware, where she served as assistant provost for instruction.

She assumed her present position at SUNY Old Westbury in 1986. When she became president, she was the first black woman to hold that position in the entire SUNY system.

An educator with a wide range of interests and expertise, Dr. Pettigrew has recently led a delegation of presidents of public institutions to China, and she is the chair of the SUNY commission on Africa.

HILARY MAC AUSTIN

Throughout her career, L. Eudora Pettigrew has been blazing trails in the field of higher education. She is the first black woman president in the State University of New York system. (STATE COLLEGE OF NEW YORK AT OLD WESTBURY)

Player, Willa B. (1909–)

Willa B. Player is counted as a rare figure within education, not only for the historic place she holds as the first black woman president of a four-year women's college, but also for her commitment to the civil rights movement and equal opportunity for women. Her achievements reflect her enlightened beliefs and her dedication to increased opportunity for young Americans.

The youngest child of Clarence E. and Beatrice D. Player, Willa Player was born on

August 9, 1909, in Jackson, Mississippi. When she was seven, the family moved to Akron, Ohio, where she completed her elementary and high school education. Brought up in a devout Methodist family, Player decided to attend a Methodist college, Ohio Wesleyan University, in Delaware, Ohio. She graduated with a B.A. in 1929, and in 1930 she received an M.A. from **Oberlin College**, Ohio. Player continued to study French at the University of Grenoble, France, where she was awarded the Certificat d'Etudes in 1935. She earned a Ph.D. in 1948 from Columbia University in New York City.

In 1930, Player became an instructor of French and Latin at **Bennett College**, a historically black college in Greensboro, North Carolina. For the next fifteen years she worked her way up the academic career ladder, eventually becoming vice president. In 1955, Bennett College made history when Player was appointed university president, a position she held for the next ten years. Not only was Player the first black woman to preside over Bennett College; she also was the first black woman nationwide to be named to such a position at a four-year women's college. As college president during the years of the civil rights movement, Player looked upon student participation in sit-ins and other nonviolent protests as being entirely reasonable forms of dissent. Indeed, she said she was proud of the Bennett students who attempted to desegregate Greensboro during the 1960s.

After she retired from Bennett College in 1966, Player became director of the Division of Institutional Development in the Bureau of Postsecondary Education in Washington, D.C. During her tenure there, Player distinguished herself by establishing Title III as a major source of categorical support for historically black and other minority institutions of higher education. In an era marked by the neglect of those categorical programs that had been won through the civil rights movement, Player succeeded not only in maintaining but in further developing funding for Title III programs, often in the face of reactionary opinion. She retired from the bureau in April 1977.

Willa Player has served on many boards, committees, and organizations. Some, such as the United Negro College Fund, reflect her dedication to improving educational opportunities for black students, whereas others, such as the United Methodist Women (whom she assisted in establishing a charter for racial policy), testify to her lifelong involvement in the church. In addition to several honorary doctorates, Player has been the recipient of the Stepping Stone to Freedom Award for her contribution to the civil rights movement. In 1972, she was awarded both the Superior Service Award and the Distinguished Service Award from the U.S. Department of Health, Education and Welfare. In 1984, she was inducted into the Ohio Women's Hall of Fame in Columbus.

FENELLA MACFARLANE

Presley, Vivian   (1952–   )

In 1992, Vivian Mathews Presley became president of Coahoma Community College in Clarksdale, Mississippi, following a seventeen-year association with that institution.

She received M.Ed., Ed.S., and Ed.D. degrees in counselor education from Mississippi State University before going on to counsel and design counseling programs for economically and academically disadvantaged and so called "high-risk" students.

Community college president Vivian Presley (far left) still has plenty of opportunities to draw upon her counseling background, as she helps economically and academically disadvantaged students to achieve their educational goals. (COAHOMA COMMUNITY COLLEGE)

From 1988 until 1992, she taught graduate courses in counseling at Trevecca Nazarene College. During that time she was named one of the Outstanding Female Executives of America.

Presley first came to Coahoma as vice president in 1983. She was in charge of planning, development, and institutional relations. In January of 1992, she became interim president, a position she held until June of that year. In July, she was named president of the college, bringing to the job her extensive experience in helping students who have faced obstacles make the most of their education.

MICHAEL NOWAK

Prestage, Jewel Limar (1931–)

Jewel Limar Prestage is a pioneer with a long list of firsts, the most prominent being that she was the first American black woman to secure a Ph.D. in political science. A major highlight of her academic career was the founding of the School of Public Policy and Urban Affairs at Southern University, where she served as its first dean—a position from which she retired in 1989 after a thirty-three-year association with that university.

Jewel Limar, born in 1931 into a large family in Hutton, rural Louisiana, grew up in nearby Alexandria. During the height of segregation, she earned a B.A. summa cum laude in 1951 and a Ph.D. from the University of Iowa in 1954. Limar married James J. Prestage, a biologist and former university chancellor; they are the parents of five children.

Since 1954, Prestage has held directorships, memberships, and offices in major scholarly organizations, including the vice presidency of the American Political Science Association and the presidency of both the Southern Political Science Association and the Southwestern Social Science Association. Her initiative led to the founding of the National Conference of Black Political Scientists in 1969, and later she served as its president. She has served on editorial boards of six scholarly journals, contributed articles to the *Journal of Politics*, *Social Science Quarterly*, and other journals, and coauthored a textbook on women in politics.

Appointed to the National Advisory Council on Women's Educational Programs by President Jimmy Carter, she became the first minority person to chair that body. Prestage served as chair of the Louisiana State Advisory Committee to the U.S. Commission on Civil Rights and served on the Judicial Council of the Democratic party. As a result of her scholarship, her advocacy of women and minorities, and her leadership in higher education, Prestage was the recipient of Distinguished Alumni Achievement awards from both Southern University and the University of Iowa, as well as the Fannie Lou Hamer Award. She also was inducted into the Women's Pavilion at the 1984 World's Fair in New Orleans. In 1991, the Policy Studies Organization established the Jewel L. Prestage Award for the Study of Minorities and Public Policy. The American Political Science Association presented awards to her in 1984 and 1989 for contributions to the development of the profession.

Now dean of the Benjamin Banneker Honors College at Prairie View A & M University, the nation's first full-honors college at a historically black institution, Prestage plans to maintain her academic affiliations, work toward the development of honors education in the nation, and do research on women in politics.

IFE WILLIAMS-ANDOH

R

Randolph, Virginia (1874–1958)

Virginia Estelle Randolph was born June 8, 1874, to former slaves Sarah Elizabeth Carter and Edward Nelson Randolph, in Richmond, Virginia. The former owner of Randolph's mother, a professor at Old Richmond College, witnessed the parents' marriage and was responsible for naming each of the four children.

Virginia's mother, widowed when her youngest child was only one month old, worked day and night so that she could afford the rent on their one-room dwelling. According to Randolph, other necessities were provided by white friends and those who employed her mother as a domestic.

The second oldest of the four children, Randolph attributed her discipline, self-reliance, creativity, and belief in God to her mother. She was reared in Virginia during the turbulent Reconstruction period and began her teaching career just six years prior to *Plessy* v. *Ferguson* (1896), which endorsed "separate but equal" facilities and privileges for black and white Americans. Thus, times were socially, economically, and politically difficult.

In 1880, at age six, Randolph enrolled in the Baker School in Richmond. She was an excellent student and received a medal for highest honors at the end of her first term. At sixteen, in 1890, she passed her teaching examination, but she was too young to qualify for a school. Because an uncle assumed full responsibility for her, she was given a job teaching in Goochland County. Two years later, she passed another exam, this one for a more challenging position at the one-room Mountain Road School in Henrico County.

Randolph enrolled fourteen boys and girls on her first day at the Mountain Road School. She immediately improved the condition of the school building and the grounds. To support structural repairs and educational services, Randolph organized a Willing Workers Club and a Patrons Improvement League. With the support of the league, she purchased twelve sycamore trees for the school grounds. Each tree was named for a disciple. As a result of the tree-planting campaign, Randolph was the first individual in the state of Virginia to celebrate Arbor Day.

Jackson T. Davis, the first appointed superintendent of Negro instruction in Henrico County, Virginia, was impressed with Virginia Estelle Randolph and the Mountain Road School when he inspected the black schools in the county in 1902. Davis' educational beliefs came to include industrial education for black Americans, which he observed while visiting Hampton Institute. Convinced that Randolph's teaching methods should be communicated to other black teachers in one-room rural schools throughout the state, Davis sought funds from the Anna Thomas **Jeanes Fund**, which had been established in the name of a Philadelphia Quaker for the purpose of providing financial assistance to black rural schools. Davis's request was approved on October 26, 1908, and Randolph became the first Jeanes Supervising Industrial Teacher.

As a Jeanes teacher, Randolph administered, supported, and/or coordinated activities that ensured professional growth for rural teachers and, at the same time, provided resources and information to meet community needs. Teacher training and supervision were acute problems; adults needed literacy training and self-help projects in order to improve nutrition, health care, and hygiene. Randolph provided the needed link between the schools and the communities.

Randolph's ideas were practical, simple, and reflective of the needs of an agrarian rural community. She believed in the all-around development of the child. She taught girls to cook and sew and boys to make useful handicrafts from honeysuckle vines and hickory. In addition, Randolph believed in the industrial training philosophy that taught manual skills as well as religious and moral precepts. She argued that a mind is of little value if one has not learned to use one's hands. She was undoubtedly influenced by Booker T. Washington, a graduate of Hampton Institute. In addition to reading, writing, and arithmetic, Hampton's industrial education program taught gardening, woodworking, serving, and cooking. Most of all, students were trained to be resourceful, self-reliant, obedient, and docile.

The emphasis on manual labor and docility caused grave concerns, and at times Randolph met resistance. All parents were not interested in having their children taught industrial skills; rather, they wanted their children to learn the "classical or liberal arts." Some teachers were unaccepting of

Randolph's industrial training, too. However, possessed of an indomitable spirit, Randolph eventually secured the support of her opponents.

Randolph received the William E. Harmon Award for Distinguished Achievement in 1926; she was the first black American to receive this award. That year she also was honored by the Richmond Community Fund and the black teachers of Henrico County. As a further testament to her work, a Virginia Estelle Randolph Fund was established to assist boys and girls in southern rural schools.

Although she never married, Randolph usually had at least a dozen children living in her home. She owned a private bus that transported them to and from school, and over her lifetime she gave shelter to approximately fifty-nine children. Randolph was not selective in her support; she assisted delinquent youth, the handicapped, and the rural poor.

Randolph retired in 1949, after a long and productive career as an educator, social worker, and humanitarian. As the first Jeanes Supervisor, she provided the first formal in-service teacher training for rural black teachers, which led eventually to improved educational preparation and certification. She introduced supervision for black teachers and organized community development through adult education activities. Her work improved dramatically the educational practices of the rural one-room Southern schools. The school term was lengthened, attendance was improved, school buildings were maintained, and county training schools for teacher training were introduced. The county training schools later developed into secondary schools. Moreover, Randolph accomplished these changes during an era that supported a "separate and unequal" public school system.

Virginia Estelle Randolph died on March 16, 1958. In 1970, the old Mountain Road School was dedicated as a museum in her honor. It is one of the few in the South to honor a black female educator. In 1976, the Virginia Historic Landmarks Commission dedicated the Virginia E. Randolph Museum and the ten remaining original sycamore trees as a National and State Historic Landmark.

BERNADINE S. CHAPMAN

Reagon, Bernice Johnson (1942–)

Bernice Johnson Reagon not only researches African-American music and oral traditions, she brings it alive for modern audiences. She divides her time between projects at the Smithsonian Institution, where she is a curator, and concerts with her singing group, Sweet Honey in the Rock. Reagon is proof that the old traditions of transmitting strength and wisdom through song and story are not lost arts, but still very much welcome today.

Born on October 4, 1942, in Albany, Georgia, Bernice Johnson Reagon is the daughter of the Reverend Jessie Johnson and Bernice Wise Johnson. Reagon's father was a carpenter who served as pastor at four different Baptist churches. Her mother was a housekeeper, who also worked in the cotton fields. The music of southwest Georgia has influenced Reagon throughout her career.

In 1960, Reagon enrolled as a music major at all-black Albany State College, studying Italian arias and German lieder. Soon she became caught up in the civil rights movement. By 1962 she was the school's highest-ranking student, but she was expelled for taking part in demonstrations, which later also cost her two weeks in jail. She and the other demonstrators sang in jail, in order to hold themselves together.

It was in jail that Reagon discovered the power of the music she had grown up with. "I was moved by hearing songs," she says, "and after hearing them all my life, for the first time, I understood what they meant. . . . Somehow, it felt like all those words that Black people had been praying and saying was a language for us, a language we could not understand unless we were involved in practical, everyday struggle."

Reagon joined the **Student Nonviolent Coordinating Committee** (SNCC), the younger, more radical arm of the civil rights movement. She and her future husband, along with two other singers, formed the SNCC Freedom Singers. They traveled around the country, giving concerts and raising money for the cause.

In 1964, Reagon left the Freedom Singers and went back to school at **Spelman College**. She earned her B.A. in nonwestern history in 1970. Her marriage broke up in 1967, and in 1971 she moved with her two children to Washington, D.C. There she began working at the Smithsonian Institution and entered a Ph.D. program at **Howard University**. Her work in both places involved oral histories. She received her Ph.D. in 1975.

Meanwhile, Reagon had been hired as vocal director by the D.C. Black Repertory Company. In 1973 she formed the group, Sweet Honey in the Rock. The name comes from their signature song. Sweet Honey in the Rock is an all-women's group who sing a capella. While the songs are powerful contemporary political statements, the style taps the rich harmonies of African and African-

American traditions. In concert they are stunning. They usually perform to sold-out audiences. They have refused many mainstream recording offers and instead have issued twelve albums on labels where they have full artistic control. For their work they have won a Grammy.

While the membership of the group has changed over the years, other members of Sweet Honey in the Rock include Ysaye Maria Barnwell, Nitanju Bolade Casel, Aisha Kahil, and Carol Maillard. Reagon has written much of their material, although Evelyn Harris, a former member, also has written a number of pieces. Shirley Childress Johnson provides signing for the hearing impaired and is an integral part of the performance.

Sweet Honey in the Rock has appeared throughout the nation, with repeat engagements at festivals such as Sisterfire in the Washington, D.C., area, the Michigan's Women's Music Festival in northern Michigan, and New York's Caribbean Cultural Center's "Tribute to Women of Color."

Internationally the group has performed at festivals in Ecuador and Mexico and has toured Germany, Japan, England, Canada, Australia, the Caribbean, and many of the nations of Africa. They served as coordinators for the closing festivals of the U.N. Women's Conference in Nairobi, Kenya.

Reagon's work in musical scholarship has kept pace with her work in concert. She played an important role in the creation of the Smithsonian's three-record collection titled *Voices of the Civil Rights Movement: Black American Freedom Songs 1960–66*. She wrote the program notes for "A Program of Spirituals," offered by opera stars Kathleen Battle and Jessye Norman at Carnegie Hall in 1990. She also contributed music to Ken Burns' historic television series *The Civil War*. She has been a director of the Smithsonian's program on black culture, and is now a curator at the Smithsonian.

Reagon produced a remarkable twenty-six-part series on black sacred music for National Public Radio, entitled *Wade in the Water*. She curated an exhibit at the Smithsonian based on the series. Reagon was awarded a "genius grant" from the MacArthur Foundation in 1989.

One writer has noted, "on stage, Dr. Reagon appears majestic, a matriarchal figure rooted in black American tradition and steeped in African lore." Reagon has become a living testament to the power of traditional music and its relevance to modern life.

ANDRA MEDEA

Rice, Condoleeza (1955–)

Condoleeza Rice, the first African American and the first woman to serve as provost of Stanford University, was told by her high school counselor that she was "not college material." Those words obviously fell on deaf ears. Rice earned a B.A. (*magna cum laude*) in 1974, at the age of nineteen, and her Ph.D. in 1981 from the University of Denver. She received her M.A. from the University of Notre Dame in 1975.

Born on November 14, 1954, to John and Angelena Rice in Birmingham, Alabama, Condoleeza Rice has had a remarkable career. Her accomplishments in the area of foreign policy are as unusual for a woman and for an African American as are her achievements in education. She has advised generals and counseled presidents. She has sat at negotiating tables of international importance.

A leading Soviet scholar, Rice started teaching political science at Stanford University in 1981. In 1984, Stanford honored her with the Award for Excellence in Teaching. The Hoover Institute, an internationally recognized think tank at Stanford, accepted Rice as a fellow during the 1985–86 academic year.

In 1987, she served as adviser to the Joint Chiefs of Staff on strategic nuclear policy, briefing air force generals on strategy regarding the Soviet military. She traveled to Bulgaria in 1988, invited by the U.S. ambassador to the Soviet Union. There, she addressed Soviet officials on arms control policy.

Appointed director of Soviet and East European affairs on the National Security Council from 1989 to 1991, Rice helped then-president George Bush prepare for the summit meetings with Soviet president Mikhail Gorbachev. In Malta, Rice sat at the conference table with President Bush and Secretary of State James Baker. In 1990, leaders once again turned to Rice to provide background and analysis for the Washington, D.C., summit.

Rice returned to Stanford University as an associate professor in 1991. That same year, the governor of California, Pete Wilson, appointed Rice to a bipartisan committee to draw new state legislative and congressional districts in California. At thirty-seven, she was the youngest member.

Chevron elected Rice to its board of directors in May, 1991; Transamerica Corporation followed suit in October of that same year.

Rice contributes to numerous periodicals, including *Current History, World Politics,* and *Time.* She is the author of *The Soviet Union and the Czechoslovak Army: 1948–1983,* published in 1985, and *The Gorbachev Era,* published in 1986.

In her capacity as provost of Stanford University, Rice serves as the chief academic and budget officer, a rank second to that of president. Condoleeza Rice has traveled light years since her high school counselor's erroneous assessment of her abilities.

ROSE WOODSON

Condoleeza Rice's high school counselor told her that she was "not college material." Fortunately, Rice paid no attention and went on to unique achievements in the fields of education and American foreign policy. (RICE UNIVERSITY)

Constance Rice, who became president of North Seattle Community College in 1995, is not only a respected educator and administrator but also a dedicated civic activist. (NORTH SEATTLE COMMUNITY

Rice, Constance W. (1945–)

Constance Rice, the president of North Seattle Community College, is both an educator and a dedicated civic activist. Rice was born in Brooklyn, New York, on June 23, 1945. She studied anthropology and sociology at Queens College in nearby Flushing, graduating with a B.A. in 1966. She then relocated to the West Coast, receiving a master's degree in public administration in 1970 and a Ph.D. in higher education administration in 1975, both from the University of Washington.

Rice's career has included not only administrative and faculty positions in several sectors of higher education in Washington State but a stint as president of a public relations/management firm and membership on several corporate boards. She developed an undergraduate degree program for urban residents as director of the Seattle branch of the Western Washington University Center for Urban Studies, worked with Microsoft Corporation to establish an innovative computer-integrated curriculum program at the Seattle Community College District, and was instrumental in establishing the Martin Luther King, Jr., Math-Science Celebration, which has exposed more than 1,500 Seattle youngsters to opportunities for careers in science and technology.

In 1990, Rice founded the Seattle Health and Nutrition Education Project, which offers low-income families information about nutrition and serves meals to more than ten thousand students and their families at local schools. She is a board member of several nonprofit organizations concerned with health and civic improvement.

Rice has received numerous awards for her achievements and service, both as a businessperson and as a citizen. In 1995, she chaired the Northwest International Women's Conference.

INDIA COOPER

S

Scotia Seminary

For more than sixty years after its founding in 1867, this rigidly strait-laced Presbyterian girls' school, located about fifteen miles north of Charlotte in the old cotton-mill town of Concord, North Carolina, existed as Scotia Seminary. On November 22, 1870, the state of North Carolina had chartered it as such. In 1932, as the junior college movement swept the United States and Southern public authorities assumed greater responsibility for black secondary education, this elementary-secondary-normal institution, through a merger with Barber College for Women in Anniston, Alabama, became the nineteenth recognized black junior college in the country.

The transformed school, Barber-Scotia College, typified the black junior college in its private sponsorship, state accreditation, small enrollment, low tuition—$50 for nine months—and its combination of secondary and collegiate programs. The college was atypical, however, in that more than 50 percent of its faculty—seven out of twelve—held the master's rather than just the bachelor's degree. Moreover, most of its students—fifty-nine out of ninety-five—were enrolled in the collegiate curriculum, and, as previously, all of the students were women.

In the evolving pattern of other postsecondary black schools, the institution awarded its first four-year, state-approved college degrees in 1945; as earlier, it contin-

ued to enroll relatively small numbers. In 1947, it counted 157 students; in 1954, 191. That changed in 1955 when, shattering an eighty-seven-year tradition, it registered a white male. This was the result of a 1954 amended charter that permitted acceptance of students regardless of gender and race.

In 1958, again in keeping with contemporary currents in black higher education, Barber-Scotia College became a member of the regional accrediting agency, the Southern Association of Colleges and Schools. This occurred under the administration of Leland Stanford Cozart, who had been president since 1932. The institution continues under Presbyterian auspices to be a vital educational force in the Carolinas.

Just as the evolution of the Concord institution into a reputable senior college commands attention and respect, so should its extended phase as Scotia Seminary. Scotia enjoyed the distinction of becoming the first major boarding school for black girls in the vanquished Confederacy, and thus of being a prototype for other schools in the region. Existing in an era of virulent racial segregation, discrimination, and repression, it and kindred subcollegiate institutions before World War I offered the highest leadership training available in the South to a majority of upwardly mobile black women who lacked access to the college education available not only to white men and women but also to black men.

On behalf of the freedman's committee of the Northern Presbyterian Church, Scotia's founder, Reverend Luke Dorland of Toledo, Ohio, cast it in the mold of antebellum girls' seminaries. Specifically, Scotia modeled itself after Mount Holyoke Female Seminary in South Hadley, Massachusetts, which opened in 1837 and was noted for its independence, permanency, and intellectual rigor. Scotia was always an under-financed missionary enterprise—by 1894 it still had only a paltry endowment of $1,000. It could not match its mentor, but nevertheless it aimed high. Its purpose was "to educate colored girls in religion, and in the Arts and Science usually taught in seminaries of a high order; and in those domestic duties which belong to the highest type of wife, mother, and teacher."

Clearly, students were being trained to occupy a woman's place in a segregated society. Scotia's leadership believed that no higher place existed for its graduates in this society than the home, because it accepted the late nineteenth-century notion of women as civilizers; women were to instill higher virtues in family members.

Although this was the most prominent raison d'être for Scotia, a close second was to educate teachers. "Especially does it [the Seminary] aim to raise up effective teachers," Scotia announced in the mid-1870s, "now so much needed and sought by freed people." It was the teachers, not the homemakers—though often they were one and the same—about whom Scotia characteristically boasted. In 1894, roughly seven-eighths of its alumnae were teachers.

In 1891, under the leadership of President David Satterfield, it erected a new dormitory, Faith Hall, the second major building on campus. The new dormitory facilities meant that annual enrollments could expand, but had to be capped at a little below 300 students. In addition, the school found accommodations for twice the number of teachers, increasing its staff from eleven to twenty-two.

The growth never threatened the seminary's commitment to certain continuities. All of the presidents were well-credentialed white males. Most teachers were white women. Probably stemming most from a perceived need to shield students from deleterious influences, the institution isolated itself both physically and psychologically from Concord's black and white communities. Students submitted to school authority in all aspects of their lives, including what they wrote in personal letters.

Moreover, the seminary subscribed completely to the era's popular "head-hand-heart" approach to educating black youth. It fostered logical thinking and encouraged the acquisition of useful information, particularly through drill for mental development. It offered two curricula: a four-year grammar program of English, arithmetic, algebra, geography, science, history, and literature; and a three-year normal and scientific course that included geometry, astronomy, physics, chemistry, history, Latin, and rhetoric. The industrial department taught courses in sewing and cooking, and the students participated in a housekeeping program so as to minimize operating expenses.

Consequently, the girls washed, ironed, set tables, scrubbed floors, and dusted furniture. The seminary's curriculum also embraced training in refinement, teaching qualities such as a gently modulated voice, quiet dignity, and conservative dress. Most of all, it centered on promoting Christianity as "an intelligent faith." Students participated in worship services and studied the Bible daily. Most saw, for the first time, Christianity reflected in the egalitarian relationships between white and black faculty members. When, through merger, the seminary became a junior college, a liberalizing wind blew away some traditions, but others remained to anchor the school in a new era.

ELAINE M. SMITH

Scott, Gloria (1938–)

Recognized in the exhibit, *I Dream a World: Seventy-five Black Women Who Changed America*, Gloria Dean Randle Scott has played, and continues to play, an outstanding role in American higher education. As college president and member of numerous professional and voluntary organizations, Scott is also a strong proponent of women's rights. She describes herself as a "race woman," saying, "Giving something back, influencing what happens to black people has always been important. . . . I suppose I'm one of the vestiges of what you call 'race women,' people who really believe in African Americans."

Daughter of Randle Scott and Juanita (Bell) Randle, Gloria Dean Randle Scott was born on April 14, 1938, in Houston, Texas. She graduated from Jack Yates High School in 1955 as salutatorian. Her B.A. (1959), M.A. (1960), and Ph.D. in higher education, zoology, and botany (1965) were earned at Indiana University. In 1959, she married Will Braxton Scott, now a professor of sociology and social work at **Bennett College** in Greensboro, North Carolina. Scott's career reflects her special interest in educational research and planning, as well as her ongoing dedication to the needs of women and black youth.

In 1967, after holding teaching positions at Marian College in Indianapolis, Indiana, and Knoxville College in Tennessee, Scott went to North Carolina Agricultural and Technical State University in Greensboro, where she developed long-range institutional planning and set up the Office of Institutional Research and Planning. Between 1968 and 1973, she served as director of that office and also worked as a teaching faculty member.

In 1977, Scott served as assistant to the president for educational planning and evaluation at Texas Southern University in Houston. She then moved to Atlanta, where she served as vice president of Clark College for nine years. From 1978 to 1987, she returned to teaching, holding positions at several colleges, including Bryn Mawr in Pennsylvania, Atlanta University, and Grambling State University in Louisiana. In 1987, Scott was elected president of Bennett College, a historically black liberal arts college that enrolls more than 600 women students. Scott is the second woman president in the history of the college.

Scott has said she views the black college not only as the provider of education for economic, social, and intellectual betterment but also potentially as a "corporate citizen" representing the interests of black students. Scott has worked hard, both within her institution and in the larger community, to develop leadership qualities in young black women and to broaden access to higher education for black students. She has served since 1990 on the President's Board of Advisors on Historically Black Colleges, and the board successfully petitioned President George Bush in 1991 to overturn a Department of Education ruling that stated it was unlawful to provide minority-only scholarships for college students.

Scott has maintained a long association with the Girl Scouts (USA) and has been a member of its board of directors since 1969. In 1975, she became the organization's first black president. Scott views scouting both as an opportunity for personal growth and a means of enhancing the lives of poor and minority children. The nature trips that Scott experienced as a teenager were instrumental in generating her lifelong interest in the outdoors. As Girl Scouts president, Scott worked vigorously to update the concerns and issues being addressed by the organization, including women's issues, attitudes toward the natural environment, and justice for juveniles. She oversaw programs designed to increase participation by black and Puerto Rican youths and adults in the organization, particularly in its leadership, as well as programs aimed at mentally handicapped youth. Classes on venereal disease also were developed during Scott's tenure as president.

Scott's activities in national and regional organizations have been both varied and numerous. Between 1973 and 1976, she was active in dismantling dual systems in higher education, and she conducted program review and evaluation for the U.S. Office of Education in states where the dual system still operated. Currently she holds a position on the external review board for minority participation at Stanford University. From 1966 to 1982, she was a founding member and secretary of Persons Responsive to Educational Problems, and from 1976 to 1983, she served as vice chair of the National Advisory Committee on Black Higher Education and Black Colleges and Universities.

Both President Gerald Ford and President Jimmy Carter appointed Scott to the National Commission on International Women's Year between 1976 and 1978. President Carter also appointed her to the National Commission on International Year of the Child, a position she held from 1978 to 1980. In 1985, Scott convened Clark College's Conference on American Black Women, entitled "Have We Come a Long Way, Baby?," and she led a delegation to the International Women's Decade meeting in Nairobi, Kenya. She has been a member and chairperson of SERO (Service Employment Redevelopment Operation)/National Scholarship for Negro Students, 1982–85; a member of InRoads Atlanta, 1986–88; and a member of the board of directors and co-chairperson of the minority task force, National Association of Independent Colleges and Universities, 1989–92.

She also has been the recipient of numerous awards, including the Indiana Governor's Award, and was named Outstanding Negro Student in Indiana in 1964. She was selected as a Legendary Woman, Birmingham Southern College, in 1977; received a citation from the Texas House of Representatives for outstanding leadership and contribution through services in 1978; and was inducted into the Academy of Women Achievers, the **Young Women's Christian Association** (YWCA) of Atlanta, in 1986. In 1977, Scott was awarded an LL.D. from Indiana University, and in 1978 Fairleigh Dickinson University honored her with an honorary doctor of humane letters degree.

Gloria Scott is remarkable not merely for her spectacular achievements as a dynamic and determined leader within the field of education but also for her dedicated service to the needs and aspirations of women, black communities, and young people all across America.

FENELLA MACFARLANE

Sheen, Dolores (1938–)

Dolores Sheen has kept alive the Sheenway School and Culture Center in Los Angeles' Watts district since 1976, when her father, the school's founder, died. She has managed this despite having to battle against adversity of all kinds. Gang brutality, police hostility, her own ill health, but most of all dogged financial difficulties, have beset the educator, who helped her father Dr. Herbert A. Sheen to found Sheenway in 1971. What

was then a preschool for youngsters from low-income families came in time to be an inner-city private school, bringing with it all of the educational advantages that phrase usually implies.

She was born in 1939 in St. Louis but raised in Tyler, Texas, where Dr. Sheen, himself a minister's son from Decatur, Illinois, had his first medical practice. Third of six children, Dolores attended Catholic schools. In 1945, Dr. Sheen set up practice in Watts, where for office visits he charged $6, or nothing if the patient simply couldn't pay.

When Dolores was sixteen, her parents divorced. Later she was to learn, by chance, that in the 1920s her father had briefly been married to writer **Zora Neale Hurston**,

Dolores Sheen has kept alive the Sheenway School and Culture Center in Los Angeles' Watts district since 1976. (SHEENEY SCHOOL AND CULTURE CENTER)

whose letters to Dr. Sheen were found by Dolores after his death. A playwright, actor, and singer, as well as an educator, Sheen herself married and divorced actor Augie Blunt. One of her five children, Erin Blunt, acted in the *Bad News Bears* films. Two of her children she adopted when they were enrolled at Sheenway. She has eleven grandchildren and one great-grandchild.

In Los Angeles, Sheen interned as a nurse at the Julia Ann Singer Psychiatric Preschool at Cedars-Sinai Hospital and managed four clinics. In the wake of the 1965 Watts riots, her father used his own money to help rebuild the community. He at first tried to bolster small neighborhood businesses with interest-free loans, but these businesses flagged anyway. Deciding that a school was his best investment, he bought up houses in a new freeway's path and had them moved beside his office at 101st St. and Broadway.

Dr. Sheen was the school's primary benefactor when he was alive. After her father's death, Dolores put up her furniture as collateral on a loan to cover the school's utilities costs. Ever since, it has been an uphill struggle to find funding. About 70 percent of Sheenway's $250,000 annual budget comes from donations; past donors include son Erin, Richard Pryor, the cast of TV's *Beverly Hills 90210* and U.S. Representative **Maxine Waters**. Even so, utility cutoffs often have been threatened, insurance payments always are due, and one year Sheen nearly lost her Carson, California, home, which she had refinanced to raise money for Sheenway.

Sheen serves as executive director without pay, her work ranging from teaching to janitoring, her talents including karate and proficiency at playing seven musical instru-

ments. Formally accredited by the Montessori Institute of America, she has led Sheenway, a nonprofit, privately-funded, small-staffed, multi-program center, along Montessori lines. This entails self-learning and free exploration among varied subjects, and it means discipline (such as mandatory uniforms) yet wide leeway as to students' ages in forming classes. Studies include art, agriculture, literature, math, philosophy, science, history, and Japanese culture.

Sheenway has altered not only its pupils' paths of life but also those of their parents. More than 80 percent of the former, described almost without exception as having had a "troubled past," are said to go on to college. An important factor may be parental participation. Sheenway requires that parents work at the school seven hours monthly in exchange for lowered tuition; a sliding scale allows them to work for even longer hours for yet lower tuition.

The financial burden Sheen must carry has not stopped her from realizing her dream of setting up a school similar to Sheenway in Ghana. This was accomplished in early 1995. Back home, she wants to find funds for and to build a $15 million "urban village" in Los Angeles. The plan includes the hiring of gang members and the unemployed to do the construction work.

"My father was a visionary," she has said. "I'm just a dreamer."

GARY HOUSTON

Simmons, Ruth J. (1945–)

In December 1994, Ruth Simmons was named the ninth president of Smith College, in Northampton, Massachusetts, widely regarded as a conservative institution. In July 1995, she assumed that office.

Though this is in itself newsworthy, what is more so is that she became the first African American to preside over any of the northeastern institutions of higher learning that comprise both the Ivy League and the group of prestigious women's colleges sometimes called the Seven Sisters: Smith, Barnard, Bryn Mawr, Mt. Holyoke, Radcliffe, Vassar, and Wellesley.

Simmons did not step into this lofty arena as a newcomer. It is true that she was the youngest of twelve children born into poverty in Grapeland, Texas, where both her parents were sharecroppers. Yet long before her Smith appointment, she had studied at both Wellesley College and Harvard University, and at Princeton University she was both a faculty member and administrator.

Born in 1945, Simmons graduated summa cum laude from New Orleans' Dillard College, having spent her junior year at Wellesley. Her interest lay in the area of romance languages, and a Fulbright grant made possible a year's study in France, after which she attended George Washington University in Washington, D.C. She then earned her M.A. and Ph.D. in romance languages at Harvard.

A professor of French at the University of New Orleans in the mid-1970s, Simmons then became assistant dean of the college of liberal arts. At California State University in Northridge, she was serving by 1979 in the posts of administrative coordinator of the NEH Liberal Studies Project, acting director of international programs, and visiting associate professor of Pan-African studies.

Focussing on Caribbean and African literature in French, Simmons went to Princeton in 1983 as director of studies of the university's Butler College and became acting director of Princeton's Afro-Ameri-

In July 1995, Ruth Simmons became the first black woman president of Smith College. Simmons believes in treating students with "tough love." (EVAN RICHMAN)

can studies program. She was named assistant dean of faculty in 1986 and, in 1990, associate dean.

For the next two years she was in Atlanta, Georgia, as provost of America's oldest black women's college, **Spelman College**. It has been said that there, and through President **Johnnetta Cole**'s example, Simmons learned how to practice "tough love—nurturing students with a realistic view of the problems that confront the black community."

Back at Princeton in 1992, she was the university's vice provost and a trustee of the Woodrow Wilson National Fellowship Foundation until her Smith appointment.

Smith had admitted black enrollees since the 1920s, but as of 1994 there were only 86 African Americans in a student body of 2,700. Some parties, including Simmons herself, wondered whether staid Smith was ready for a black president. Its trustees assured her that it was.

Her life undeniably affected by the realities of race and gender, Simmons has expressed concern about the growing separation of racial groups into enclaves on America's campuses. At the same time she accepts, at least for the present, the value of non-coed institutions — "to separate women so that they can achieve." Her own achievements surely are of great value, both in themselves and as models for young women to follow.

GARY HOUSTON

Sizemore, Barbara (1927–)

The accomplishments of black women in education have been formidable, but seldom have these women reached the appropriate positions of responsibility and authority. Barbara Ann Laffoon Sizemore is one educator who has achieved eminence as the first black woman to head the public school system of a major city.

Barbara Laffoon was born in Chicago, Illinois, on December 17, 1927, the only child of Sylvester Walter Laffoon and Delila Alexander Laffoon. She grew up in Terre Haute, Indiana, where she attended Booker T. Washington Elementary School. Her father died when she was eight years old, and her mother later married Aldwin E. Stewart.

After graduating from Wiley High School, she went to Northwestern University in Evanston, Illinois, earning a B.A. in classical languages in 1947 and an M.A. in elementary education in 1954.

From 1947 until 1963, Sizemore was a teacher in the Chicago public schools. Her special subjects were Latin, English, and English for Spanish speakers. In 1963, she became one of the first black women to be appointed principal of a Chicago school when she went to Anton Dvorak Elementary School. She remained there for two years

Upon her election to the position of superintendent of schools for the District of Columbia public school system, Barbara Sizemore became the first black woman to head the public school system of a major city. (MOORLAND-SPINGARN)

before becoming principal of Forrestville High School. After two years at Forrestville, Sizemore became involved in an important attempt to improve the education of black children in the city. She was appointed director of the Woodlawn Experimental Schools Project, which was a joint effort of the public schools, the University of Chicago, and the Woodlawn Organization, a powerful community action group. Funds for the project were provided by the federal government through Title IV of the Elementary and Secondary Education Act (1965), but the program was controlled by the Woodlawn community.

The experience of these years in public education, from the late 1940s to the early 1970s, gave Sizemore tremendous insight into the problems of education in modern urban areas. While she worked with the Woodlawn project, she also shared that insight as a teacher at the Center for Inner City Studies at Northeastern Illinois State University.

In 1972, Sizemore moved to the Washington, D.C., area and became the first woman and the first black associate secretary of the American Association of School Administrators in Arlington, Virginia. The next year, her growing reputation led to her election as superintendent of schools for the District of Columbia public school system. The first black woman to head the public schools in a major city, she was committed to involving parents in the creation of quality education for students. That commitment led to controversy, and a difficult political situation. In 1975, her tenure in the position was terminated.

After two years as an educational consultant, Sizemore moved to Pittsburgh to become associate professor in the Department of Black Community Education and Development at the University of Pittsburgh. In 1989, she became full professor.

Since the late 1960s, Sizemore has published widely. Her first book, *The Ruptured Diamond*, appeared in 1981. It was a study of the politics of decentralization in the District of Columbia public schools. A second book, *An Abashing Anomaly*, was scheduled for publication in 1992. Sizemore is also active in local and national political movements. In the 1970s and early 1980s, she was a key figure in the Black Political Assembly and the National Black Independent political party.

Barbara Sizemore has been married twice, the second time to Jake Milliones, Jr. She has two children from her first marriage and three stepchildren.

KATHLEEN THOMPSON

Slowe, Lucy Diggs (1885–1936)

That deans of women at black colleges are no longer matrons, responsible only for the morals and physical well-being of their charges, is largely thanks to Lucy Diggs Slowe. Slowe's work at **Howard University** changed forever the role of deans in black schools.

Born on July 4, 1885, Slowe was the youngest child of Henry and Fannie Slowe. She lost both of her parents at an early age, her father when she was nine months old and her mother when she was six. After her mother's death, she went to live with her aunt, Martha Slowe Price, in Lexington, Virginia. When she was thirteen, the family moved to Baltimore, Maryland. She graduated from the black high school in Baltimore as salutatorian in 1904 and entered Howard University.

It was during her college years that Slowe's talents as an innovator came to the fore. She was one of the founders of the first black college sorority. It was not to be her last first. After graduation, she began teaching English in the Baltimore and Washington, D.C., public high schools. At the same time she completed a master's degree in English from Columbia University.

In 1919, the first black junior high school was established in the Washington, D.C., school system. Slowe became its principal. During her time at Shaw Junior High School, she developed an in-service training system for her teachers. She induced Columbia University to offer an extension course in education for teachers at the junior high level. The course was so successful that it was attended not only by her teachers but also by the faculty of the white junior high as well.

Three years later, Slowe was hired by Howard University as dean of women; she also taught English and education. There was a new movement afoot in college administration at that time. Such women as Sarah Sturtevant, Harriet Hayes, Esther Lloyd-Jones, and Thyrsa Amo had begun to redefine the role of the women's dean. Slowe began working to do the same at Howard. It was her idea that the dean of women should be a specialist in women's education. Eventually she was very successful, and her work inspired a similar change in black colleges around the country.

While working as a college administrator, Slowe also was active beyond the campus. In 1935, she helped to organize the **National Council of Negro Women** and became its first secretary. She also helped to found the National Association of College Women and became its first president. She worked with a number of other national organizations, such as the **Young Women's Christian Association** (YWCA) and the Women's International League for Peace and Freedom. The YWCA was problematic for her because, while theoretically in favor of black participation in policymaking, it maintained separate black branches. However, when Eva Bowles resigned in 1932 from the staff of the national YWCA because of a reorganization that she believed was a step backward, Slowe remained and kept up the struggle.

Slowe was also a competitive tennis player, winning seventeen cups, and she sang contralto in her church choir.

Slowe's health began to suffer from her intense schedule, and in 1936, she came down with a severe case of influenza. Weakened by that illness, she died of kidney disease. Four years after her death, the women of Howard University donated a stained glass window in her honor to the University Chapel.

KATHLEEN THOMPSON

Smith, Eleanor Jane (1933–)

Eleanor Jane Smith was born in Circleville, Ohio, on January 10, 1933, to John A. Lewis and Eleanor J. Dade Lewis. She began her career in education in 1956 as a public school teacher in Worthington and Columbus, Ohio, after receiving her bachelor's degree from Capital University in music education. At the same time she took courses in education at the graduate school of Ohio State University. She received her Ph.D., in 1972, from The Union Institute in Cincinnati, Ohio. That same year she married Paul M. Smith, Jr.

After receiving her doctorate, Smith became assistant professor of Afro-American studies at the University of Cincinnati. In 1977, she moved up to associate professor and became history coordinator and coordinator of the undergraduate program. She became full professor in 1982. At the same time, she became assistant senior vice president and assistant provost of the university.

During the 1970s and 1980s, Smith also traveled to the far reaches of the world, studying and researching in such places as Ghana, Surinam, China, Kenya, and India. In 1980, she became founder and codirector of the **Association of Black Women Historians**.

One of the founders of the Association of Black Women Historians, Eleanor Jane Smith has proven herself to be an effective and inspiring university administrator. (UNIVERSITY OF WISCONSIN-PARKSIDE)

Smith's remarkable effectiveness as an administrator led to her promotion to associate senior vice president, then to acting vice provost and, in 1985, to vice provost. She left the University of Cincinnati in 1988 to take the position of dean of institutional affairs at Smith College. Overseeing a budget of $14 million, she was responsible for enrollment management, planning, space utilization, campus computing and communications, the architecture and building committee, and long- and short-range planning for special needs.

Two years later, Smith moved to the William Paterson College of New Jersey as vice president of academic affairs and provost, as well as professor of Afro-American studies. There, her responsibilities were even wider and more varied than at Smith. Again she proved herself to be an effective and inspiring leader.

In 1994, Smith accepted her present position, as chancellor of the University of Wisconsin–Parkside.

KATHLEEN THOMPSON

Smith, Mary Levi (1936–)

"I think that education is and should be a lifelong process," says Mary Levi Smith. "What we are doing at the University is helping prepare students for life, which means preparing them for learning throughout their lifetimes."

Smith is president of Kentucky State University in Frankfort, Kentucky. The University, which was founded in 1889, was the only public institution of higher learning for black students in the state for the first seventy-five years of its existence.

Smith was born on January 30, 1936, in Hazelhurst, Mississippi, and received her

Mary Levi Smith, president of Kentucky State University, is shown here (right) at the Lexington Black Achievers Banquet. Kentucky governor Brereton C. Jones is second from left.
(KENTUCKY STATE UNIVERSITY)

bachelor's degree from Jackson State University. She earned both her master's and doctor's degrees from the University of Kentucky. She began her career in teaching in the public schools of Tennessee, Mississippi, and Kentucky. She went on to become assistant director of the reading clinic and reading instructor at Tuskegee University.

Smith joined Kentucky State University as assistant coordinator of their in-service reading program for classroom teachers and, in 1974, became an assistant professor of education. Then, in 1981, she became acting chair of the division of education, human services, and technology, and an associate professor of education. Two years later, she moved up to dean of the college of applied sciences and full professor of education.

Before becoming president, Smith was special assistant to the president and vice president for academic affairs. Then, beginning in April of 1989, she was interim president for fourteen months. She became president of the university in 1990.

KATHLEEN THOMPSON

Southern, Eileen (1920–)

"It has given me a real feeling of accomplishment. I always had the feeling that I was not really making a contribution to the history of my people. Now I feel that I have done something worthwhile. It's really the one thing I have ever done that I have not felt frustrated about." Eileen Southern, pianist, musicologist, educator, and author, is speaking of her landmark work, *The Music of Black Americans*, published in 1971. After a long and distinguished career, this book, in Southern's own estimation, is her crowning achievement.

Eileen Stanza Jackson was born on February 19, 1920, in Minneapolis, Minnesota, to Lilla and Walter Jackson. Her father, although a college graduate and university professor, worked on the railroad or in steel foundries in between teaching positions. When she was eight years old, Southern and her two younger sisters, Elizabeth and Estella, went to live with their father in Minneapolis and Sioux Falls, after their parents' divorce. All three girls later joined their mother in Chicago.

Whatever their differences, both parents agreed that Southern and her sisters would have music lessons. Consequently, Eileen Southern was only seven when she played her first concert. Music was indeed a family affair. Of the time she lived with her father, Southern recalls: "He was a violinist and every night he would play and I would play and my two sisters, Libby and Stella, would sing. It seemed natural at the time; I thought everybody lived that way."

Southern attended public schools in Chicago, then enrolled in the music department at the University of Chicago, earning her B.A. in 1940 and an M.A. in 1941. Since black colleges offered the only viable employment opportunities, Southern began to teach in 1941 at Prairie View Agricultural and Mechanical College in Texas. Joseph Southern worked in the business office at Prairie View.

The two were married in 1942. Over the next nine years, both Joseph and Eileen taught at several colleges in the South. In 1946, their daughter, April Myra, was born. Edward Joseph Southern was adopted by the couple in 1955.

Southern has appeared in numerous concerts throughout the United States and Haiti, including those at Carnegie Hall in New York and Orchestra Hall in Chicago, Illinois. In 1951, she began work on her doctorate at New York University, writing her dissertation on Renaissance music. She became a full, tenured professor of music at York College. In 1976, Eileen Southern went to Harvard when the Afro-American Studies and Music departments offered her a joint professorship.

The foremost authority on black American music, Southern outlined the course of black music from slavery to popular movements, covering the last 450 years in *The Music of Black Americans: A History*, released in 1971. She is also the author of *Source Readings In Black American Music*, published that same year. In 1973, Southern and her husband created *The Black Perspective In Music*, the first musicological journal devoted to the study of black music. In 1982, the *Biographical Dictionary of Afro-American and African Musicians* appeared, Southern's fourth major analysis of Afro-American music.

In 1985, Southern received an honorary degree of Doctor of Arts from Columbia College of Chicago. Over the years she has been the recipient of many awards and honors, including the Founders Day Award, New York University, 1961; the **Sojourner Truth** Award, National Association of Negro Business and Professional Women's Clubs, 1969; honorary M.A., Harvard University, 1976; and the Distinguished Achievement Award, National Black Music Caucus,

1986. A National Endowment of the Humanities grant was awarded to Southern from 1979 to 1983.

Eileen Southern has dedicated her life to the analysis and documentation of black American music. Her efforts have ensured that the richness of the African-American musical experience will be preserved for future generations.

ROSE WOODSON

Spelman College

On April 11, 1881, Sophia B. Packard and Harriet E. Giles, white missionaries from New England to the war-torn South, started a school for black females, later called Spelman College, in the basement of Atlanta's Friendship Baptist Church. Eleven black girls, just out of slavery and eager to acquire basic educational skills, made up the first student body of what was then called Atlanta Baptist Female Seminary.

The Spelman story began in February 1880, when Packard went to the South as a representative of the Woman's American Baptist Home Mission Society (WABHMS) of New England so that she might gain a better understanding of the plight of freedpersons. During her travels she was

This photograph of Spelman Seminary students, taken in the 1890s, gives a good indication of the school's appeal to students of varying ages, including older and even pregnant women. (SPELMAN COLLEGE ARCHIVES, ATLANTA, GEORGIA)

Clenched fists reflect the assertive mood among African-American college students of the 1960s. Sisters in Blackness, a Spelman College student organization, was formed in the late 1960s. (SPELMAN COLLEGE ARCHIVES, ATLANTA, GEORGIA)

disturbed by the extremely difficult conditions under which black Southerners were living, particularly black women. Educated in female seminaries, and a former teacher and administrator of several outstanding New England academies, she was particularly sensitive to the lack of educational opportunities for black girls.

When Packard became ill after reaching New Orleans, an urgent call went out to her longtime friend, Harriet Giles, a teacher in Boston, who joined her. They returned to Boston in late April, determined to start a school in the South for black females.

Packard and Giles solicited aid from WABHMS, but their request fell on deaf ears because of the riskiness of such a venture. Persistent in their efforts, however, the women took their plan in March 1881 to the First Baptist Church of Medford, Massachusetts, where they received a pledge of $100. Encouraged, they returned to the WABHMS and solicited support, eventually receiving it, and in March 1881 they left for Georgia.

After arriving in Atlanta on April 1, 1881, they contacted Dr. Shaver, a teacher at Atlanta Baptist Seminary (later Morehouse College), who took them the next day to visit Reverend Quarles, pastor of Friendship Baptist Church and the most influential black Baptist in Georgia. On April 4, Quarles convened a meeting of local black ministers, introducing them to Packard and Giles and encouraging them to help the women in any way that they could. Classes began a week later. The need for such a school was immediately evident; within

three months the school had grown from its original eleven pupils to eighty, and within a year enrollment was at two hundred students, ranging in age from fifteen to fifty-two.

In the summer of 1882, Packard and Giles went north, and at the invitation of Reverend King of Cleveland, Ohio, they visited his Wilson Avenue Church. King had promised the women that if they would discuss their school he would invite John D. Rockefeller, a member, to hear them. When the collection plate was passed, Rockefeller emptied his pockets and later pledged $250 for the building fund. This was Rockefeller's first gift to black education, a philanthropy that would continue for many years. In 1883, the seminary moved to its new site on property

Trustees walk through protesting students after the 1976 lock-in to protest the board's failure to appoint a black woman to the presidency of Spelman College. Eleven years later, in 1987, Johnnetta Betsch Cole became the first black woman to head the school.
(SPELMAN COLLEGE ARCHIVES, ATLANTA, GEORGIA)

known as "the Barracks" because it had been occupied by Union soldiers during the Civil War. In 1884, the name of the school was changed to Spelman Seminary in honor of Mr. and Mrs. Harvey Buel Spelman, the parents of Mrs. John D. Rockefeller.

Meanwhile, the future of this separate school for young women was in doubt, as the result of a proposal from the American Baptist Home Mission Society that it be combined with Atlanta Baptist Seminary. Packard and Giles disagreed with the proposed coeducational scheme because it was their experience that in coeducational schools the courses were planned primarily for men, and training for women received only secondary consideration. They also believed that the special education that women required could best be accomplished apart from the distractions caused by constant companionship with men.

The solution to the problem lay in the ability of WABHMS, Packard, and Giles to raise enough money to support the separate school. They began a fund-raising campaign, raising money from Northern Baptists and Georgia black Baptists, and in April 1884, John D. Rockefeller and his family, learning of the serious financial difficulty, donated the remaining balance, thereby ensuring the school's continued existence as a separate school for girls.

The 1883 move and expansion enabled the curriculum to expand from the initial elementary normal course to include a college preparatory department that was equivalent to high school. The industrial department taught cooking, sewing, housekeeping, laundering, and printing and assumed a high priority in the curriculum because of Packard and Giles's desire to make education practical. Spelman's foun-

ders never agonized over the need to offer their black female students a classical education. Ever mindful of the peculiar history of black women in this country and the realities of their everyday lives, the founders' primary aim was to provide training for teachers, missionaries, and church workers. Equally important was the imparting of those practical skills that would make black women good homemakers and mothers.

In 1886, the Nurse Training Department opened, the first black nurse training school in the United States. In 1891, the Missionary Training Department opened. The practical and industrial nature of the Spelman curriculum was in stark contrast to the mostly classical curriculum offered at many colleges for white women during the same era. At Spelman there was a definite emphasis on training for jobs (mainly teaching and missionary work), as well as the building of Christian character. In 1897, Spelman Seminary initiated a College Department, granting its first college degrees in 1901, but the greatest portion of the students' college work was offered on the Morehouse College campus.

In 1900, Rockefeller gave $200,000 for general improvements on the campus, which included the erection of four badly needed buildings as well as a power house with a complete system of heating and lighting. One of the new buildings was MacVicar Hospital, which was needed both as a practice school for the nurses' training program and as a hospital to serve black women patients.

In 1924, Spelman Seminary became Spelman College. When Florence Matilda Read became president in 1927, her task was to develop Spelman into a strong liberal arts college. President Read's first accomplishment was to set in motion the process for securing an endowment for Spelman. In order to conserve limited resources, the Board of Trustees voted to eliminate most of the departments that were outside the college division: the Nurses Training Department and Elementary School were closed, but the high school was retained until 1930 because few public high schools existed for black students in Georgia, and the pool of college-level black females remained small since opportunities for college preparation were still limited.

When the high school finally was discontinued, the aim of Spelman College was to provide to a small number of students a first-rate liberal arts education that would be the equal of any available elsewhere. To achieve this goal, additional college courses in the humanities, fine arts, social sciences, and natural sciences were established, and the college faculty was increased. In 1932, Spelman College received an "A" rating from the Southern Association of Colleges and Secondary Schools. During Florence Read's first year at Spelman, 122 students were enrolled for college work; ten years later the college enrollment totaled 312.

Before 1920, the majority of teachers were unmarried white women from New England, though there were a few black teachers. The earliest black female teachers were former Spelman students. These included Claudia White, a 1901 graduate, who began to teach in the high school in 1902 and, in a joint arrangement with Morehouse, taught German and Latin on the Morehouse campus from 1910 to 1914, and Jane Granderson, also a 1901 graduate, who taught at Spelman from 1902 until her untimely death in 1905. During the 1920s and 1930s, however, black teachers became more prominent on the faculty, both at the high school and college levels.

Gradually the Spelman faculty became more evenly balanced racially, and by 1937, black teachers outnumbered white teachers by two to one; by 1952, there were three times as many black teachers. Women faculty outnumbered men for a longer period. In 1926, there were no men on the faculty, although there had been two in the early years, a white male from 1882 to 1887 and a black male from 1887 to 1897; both taught music. In 1927, two men joined the Spelman faculty, one full-time and one part-time. Ten years later there were twelve men on the Spelman faculty.

Following the stewardship of four white women—Packard (1881–91); Giles (1891–1909); Lucy Tapley (1910–27); and Florence M. Read (1927–53)—Albert E. Manley, then dean of the College of Arts and Sciences of North Carolina College, was elected president on July 1, 1953, bringing an end to more than half a century of New England leadership of the college. On June 15, 1976, Francis Day Rogers, chair of the board of trustees, announced that another black man, Donald Mitchell Steward, associate dean, faculty of arts and sciences, the director of the College of General Studies, and the counselor to the provost at the University of Pennsylvania, would assume the presidency of Spelman College.

Following this announcement, dramatic efforts were taken by some students and faculty members to block the appointment of a man to succeed Dr. Manley to the presidency. Many believed it was time for Spelman to have a black woman president. During the April meeting of the board of trustees, several hundred students and a few faculty and staff members banded together and kept the board of trustees locked in the boardroom for more than twenty hours in a protest move to get them to reconsider Dr. Steward's appointment. The board affirmed its support of Steward, who became the sixth president of the college.

Eleven years later, on April 5, 1987, the board appointed **Johnnetta Betsch Cole** (Robinson), professor of anthropology and director of the Latin American and Caribbean studies program at Hunter College of the City University of New York, as Spelman's seventh president and the first black woman to lead the institution in its 106-year history.

BEVERLY GUY-SHEFTALL

Spikes, Delores (1936–)

"Southern represents hope," said Delores Spikes, president of the Southern University System and former interim chancellor of Southern University at Baton Rouge (1988–91). "It represents a way to open the doors of America to countless young people who would otherwise be shut out."

Delores Spikes was featured in the January 1990 issue of *Ebony* as recipient of the Thurgood Marshall Educational Achievement Award. *Ebony Man* also cited her as one of the twenty most influential black women in America (January 1990). She is the first female in the United States to head a university system, and she was the first female to lead a Louisiana public college or university.

She was born on August 24, 1936, in Baton Rouge, to Mr. and Mrs. Lawrence G. Richard. She married Hermon Spikes, and they have one daughter, Rhonda Kathleen Spikes-Pete, and one granddaughter.

Called one of the twenty most influential black women in America by Ebony Man *magazine, Delores Spikes became the first woman in the United States to head a university system when she was chosen president of the Southern University System.* (PATRICIA KENSCHAFT)

Delores Richard's precollege education was in the public and private schools of Baton Rouge. In 1957, she received a B.S. summa cum laude in mathematics from Southern University. In 1958, the University of Illinois at Urbana awarded her an M.S. in mathematics. After teaching for four years at Mossville School in Calcasieu Parish, she joined the faculty of Southern University in 1961.

In 1971, she became the first black graduate and the first graduate of Southern University to receive a doctorate in mathematics from Louisiana State University. Her Ph.D. was in pure mathematics, with a specialty in commutative ring theory. In 1981, she became part-time assistant to the chancellor of Southern University, along with being full-time professor of mathematics.

She has received numerous awards and prestigious appointments, including being "Alumnus of the Century" at the Southern University Centennial Celebration. In 1989, she received a Thurgood Marshall Educational Achievement Award. She was also appointed to a three-year term on the commission on women in higher education of the American Council on Education.

PATRICIA CLARK KENSCHAFT

Steele, Rebecca (1925–)

Rebecca Walker Steele has had a highly successful career as a choral music director, voice teacher, music educator, singer, and arts administrator. Currently she is director of the Concert Chorale, as well as voice teacher and director of cultural affairs at **Bethune-Cookman College** in Daytona Beach, Florida.

She was born Rebecca Walker on October 18, 1925, the daughter of Edward David and Julia Walker of Lakeland, Florida. At an early age she began playing the piano and singing, talents that were nurtured by her parents, who provided her with the best possible musical training.

She holds a B.S. from Alabama State University, where she studied piano with Hazel Harrison and choral music with Fredrick Hall. She also holds an M.A. in voice, piano, and choral conducting, as well as a master's degree in music education from Columbia University and a Ph.D. in humanities and music, with a special emphasis on multicul-

tural music education, from Florida State University.

She was in great demand as a singer while still a student in New York City and later as a teacher at Florida A & M University, performing throughout the southeast. Particularly popular were her soprano solos from Mozart's *Requiem*, numerous operatic arias, and her interpretations of spirituals.

Rebecca Steele is a dynamic, demanding teacher who accepts nothing but the best from her students. Her motto, "No half-stepping," is evident in the quality of her students, both at Florida A & M and at Bethune-Cookman College. Under her direction, the concert choir at Florida A & M was noted for its performances of major extended choral works, including Verdi's *Requiem* and Bach's *Magnificat*, and for its outstanding renditions of Negro spirituals. While teaching at Florida A & M, Steele introduced opera to many schoolchildren through her production of Verdi's *Rigoletto*, performed by college students.

At Bethune-Cookman, Steele's production of "From Bach to Gospel" features choral works, ensembles, and solos in a wide variety of styles and from many periods. A master of musical interpretation, Steele is noted for her ability to conduct different styles of music and for the beautiful tonal quality and phrasing she produces in her work. Constantly in demand, her choral groups have performed throughout the United States. The Bethune-Cookman Concert Chorale, for example, has performed with the Jacksonville Symphony Orchestra and Lyric Theatre in a production of *Porgy and Bess,* as well as at the Spoleto festival in Charleston, South Carolina.

In addition to her work as a choral director, Steele is an outstanding voice teacher.

Her students at Florida A & M have won many contests, including *The Ted Mack Amateur Hour,* the Florida State Music Teachers Association Collegiate Contest, and state and regional Metropolitan Opera auditions. Her graduates include opera singers, music educators, popular and jazz singers, and music administrators.

Steele's professional affiliations include the Music Educators National Conference, the Florida State Music Teachers Association, the Association of University Professors, the Southern Arts Federation (panelist and member of the Southern Arts Exchange), and the Florida Professional Presenters Consortium. She has served as adjudicator of vocal solo and choral music festivals, clinician for numerous music festivals, and evaluator for the Southern Association of Colleges and Schools.

Steele has received awards from the Music Educators National Conference (certificate of excellence), the Florida A & M University Alumni Association, and the African-American Spiritual Renaissance Festival, as well as numerous service awards from Florida A & M and Bethune-Cookman College.

She lives in Florida with her husband, prominent gourmet chef and food service director, John Steele, and their son, John David Steele.

MARY ROBERTS

Stewart-Lai, Carlotta (1881–1952)

The black experience in Hawaii has remained largely obscure even though a handful of black laborers and professionals migrated to Hawaii during the nineteenth and twentieth centuries in order to improve their economic status and escape the social and political restrictions that plagued black Americans on the mainland. Among these sojourners was Carlotta Stewart-Lai, a black educator who, for more than four decades, taught in the Hawaiian public schools and served as a principal on the islands of Oahu and Kauai. Stewart-Lai's career illustrates that despite the presence of a small black population and considerable discrimination directed at other racial and ethnic minorities, Hawaii was a relatively open community for black females and that economic opportunities were available for black women beyond domestic work and menial labor.

The third child of T. McCants Stewart and Charlotte Pearl Harris, Carlotta Stewart was born in 1881 in Brooklyn, New York, where she attended public school and spent her formative years. She was eighteen when she arrived in Hawaii in 1898, accompanying her father and stepmother. Stewart had hoped to continue her education in Hawaii and begin planning her future. This expectation was realized in 1902, when, as one of eight members in the senior class, she graduated from Oahu College after one year. After graduation, Stewart completed the requirements for a normal (teaching) school certificate, which she received in 1902, and she promptly accepted a teaching position in the practice department of the normal school in July. Stewart remained at the normal school for several years, where she taught English, her major at Oahu College.

Stewart-Lai's teaching career illustrates many of the opportunities and challenges that black professional women faced in Hawaii during the early twentieth century. Her annual salary of $660 in 1902 placed her comfortably in the black middle class, both in Hawaii and on the mainland. Within four years her salary had increased to $900, which she supplemented by typing in her spare time. By 1908, her teaching salary had increased to $100 per month; this not only provided a comfortable standard of living, it also financed extensive travel throughout the islands when her classes were not in session, permitted occasional trips to the mainland by ocean steamer to visit relatives, and allowed her to provide limited financial assistance to her mother and two brothers.

Stewart was highly respected in the community as well as in the classroom. During the 1906 school year she told her brother, McCants, that in addition to teaching, she was busy with classes, vacations, camping, surfing, and frequent parties. She also attended Sunday baseball games on the islands and served as coach of the junior and senior female teams in her local community. Stewart's career ad-

vancement, her acceptance into the larger Hawaiian community, and her strong friendships were pivotal factors in her decision to remain in Hawaii following her father and stepmother's departure in 1905.

Although conditions were neither difficult nor racially oppressive for a black professional woman in Hawaii, there was no substantial black community before World War II, and Stewart saw few black people either in her classrooms or outside. Most of her socializing took place in groups, thus relieving her of the pressure to find a companion with a comparable racial and social background.

Nonetheless, Stewart remained isolated from her family, and following the death of her mother in 1906 she felt particularly dis-

At the age of twenty-eight, Carlotta Stewart-Lai became principal of a multiracial Hawaiian elementary school, a stunning achievement for a black woman in 1909. She is seen here in a 1902 photograph with other members of the senior class of Oahu College. (MOORLAND-SPINGARN)

traught. She had promised to help her mother financially following her divorce from T. McCants Stewart, an obligatio.: that, by her own admission, she had neglected. Yet Stewart was not altogether to blame, for T. McCants Stewart prohibited his three children from contacting their natural mother while they were under his care following his remarriage in 1893. The news of her mother's death triggered a feeling of alienation and depression, and in 1907, Stewart considered returning to the mainland to live permanently for the first time since her arrival in Hawaii.

However, Stewart decided not to return to the mainland. Despite her intermittent loneliness, the depression following the death of her mother, and her financial problems, which stemmed in part from the Panic of 1907, she was an established professional woman in the Hawaiian schools, a status she would have been unlikely to achieve in any Pacific Coast community in the early twentieth century because of racial discrimination. She decided to remain in Hawaii.

Her decision to stay proved to be advantageous, for within two years she had been promoted to principal of an elementary school, with an increase in salary. Her rapid advancement in the space of seven years was an impressive achievement, for although many black women had established teaching careers, and a handful were school administrators by 1909, it was unusual for a black female at the age of twenty-eight to serve as principal of a multiracial school. This achievement was particularly striking in a society in which few black people lived and, therefore, had no political influence to request a job of this magnitude.

Stewart's pupils reflected a true cross-section of Hawaii's school-aged population, which grew rapidly between 1900 and 1940. In 1933, for example, the composition of her pupils included Hawaiians, Japanese, Filipinos, Koreans, and Portuguese; sixteen white Americans also were listed among the student population, but no black students were included. It is unlikely that Stewart had contact with more than a handful of black students prior to World War II, and the majority were probably the children of U.S. military personnel and black laborers who worked on sugar and pineapple plantations.

The number of pupils who attended Stewart's schools when she served as principal varied annually, ranging between 200 and 300 students. The *Hanamaulu School World*, for example, reported that 283 students of various races attended the Hanamaulu School where Stewart served as principal in 1933. Between 1940 and 1944, however, the school's enrollment declined to 256 students. In addition to managing the school, Stewart also supervised several classroom teachers, the school librarian, the cafeteria manager, and taught English. These responsibilities are a firm testament to the confidence that public school officials had in Stewart's administrative ability, but they also indicate how far she had come in her career.

Stewart was not a social reformer, and she never joined any organization designed to promote the advancement of African Americans, Puerto Ricans, Asians, Hawaiians, or women. It is true that Hawaii did not have chapters of the most prominent black national organizations, such as the **National Association for the Advancement of Colored People** (NAACP), the National Urban League, the **National Association of Col-**

ored **Women** (NACW), or the **National Council of Negro Women** during those years, yet Stewart had grown up in a family of black activists. Her brothers, McCants and Gilchrist, both attorneys, were active in civil rights activities in Portland and New York, and her father had challenged successfully several Jim Crow laws in the state of New York and won the praise of Booker T. Washington.

In 1916, as Stewart approached her thirty-fifth birthday, she married Yun Tim Lai, of Chinese ancestry, at Anahola, Kauai County. Lai, five years younger than Stewart, was sales manager of Garden Island Motors, Ltd., an automobile dealership in Lihue, Kauai, when the couple wed.

In 1944, after forty-two years of public service in the Hawaiian schools, Carlotta Stewart-Lai retired. She lived the final years of her life in Kauai on Anahola Bay, before ill health forced her to enter a Honolulu nursing home in 1951. Her health declined rapidly, and on July 6, 1952, she died.

Few black women were employed in teaching or administrative jobs in the western states and territories when Stewart-Lai began teaching at the Normal School in 1902, and fewer still succeeded in moving up the ladder to become principals or administrators before World War II. Thus Carlotta Stewart-Lai was a trailblazer not only for black women in Hawaii but for black women throughout the entire West.

ALBERT S. BROUSSARD

Sudarkasa, Niara (1938–)

A fascination with and commitment to the African continent is one of two continuing motifs in the life of Niara Sudarkasa, born Gloria Marshall on August 14, 1938, in Fort Lauderdale, Florida. The other is a belief in the importance of education to the black community, accompanied by a firm conviction that black colleges provide the best opportunity for providing that education.

Sudarkasa was raised in Florida by her grandparents, who were from the Bahamas. As a result, she was thought of by those around her as a West Indian. Because her family was so large, she grew up thinking that every second person she met would be a cousin.

Her interest in Africa was sparked by a cultural connection she made while at **Oberlin College**. In a course on Caribbean culture, she learned that *esu*, savings associations with which she had been familiar from childhood, were a Yoruba institution. This was the first concrete link between the West Indies and Africa that she had encountered. She became very excited by this evidence of her origins and determined to go to West Africa to explore them further.

Africa was a revelation to Sudarkasa in many ways. She was fascinated by the resemblance, in physical posture and mannerisms, of the Yoruba people to those she had known as a child. She admired the position of women in the culture as market traders and independent workers. Moreover, the sense of being part of a majority was something she had never before experienced. Africa belonged to her in a way that the United States never had. She had always felt that the United States was her country but not her land; Africa was her land.

Her experience in Africa inspired her, among other things, to change her name. She acquired her new last name through marriage. Her new first name was an adaptation of a Swahili word, and it indicates a woman of high purpose.

Having earned an M.A. and Ph.D. in anthropology from Columbia University, Sudarkasa went to work at the University of Michigan, where she became very involved in political activities. She was soon well known as an activist-scholar. She served as the associate vice president for academic affairs at the University of Michigan at Ann Arbor and became the first black woman there to receive tenure.

In 1987, Sudarkasa became the first woman president of Lincoln University, the nation's oldest black college and, for much of its history, an all-male institution. With her strong feelings for the African continent, she leads a school that has a long and distinguished history of association with Africa.

KATHLEEN THOMPSON

Surles, Carol (1946–)

President of Texas Woman's University, Carol Diann Smith Surles received her bachelor's degree in psychology from Fisk University in 1968 and then went to California. There, she served as a social worker with the residents of the small Mexican-American town of Guadalupe and earned her master's degree in counseling from Chapman College in Orange, California, in 1971.

After graduation from Chapman, she served as a professional intern in a White House–sponsored program at Lompoc Federal Correctional Institute before beginning her teaching career as a psychology and language arts instructor at Allan Hancock College on the Vandenberg Air Force Base, where she was also a career counselor. In 1973, she moved to the University of Michigan as a personnel representative and coordinator of the faculty and staff assistance program. While there, she began her doctoral studies.

In 1978, she received her doctorate from Michigan and became director of the equal opportunity and affirmative action programs at the University of Central Florida in Orlando. Over the next nine years, she moved up in the administration of the school until she was associate vice president for human resources. In 1987, she returned to the University of Michigan for two years as vice chancellor of administration and associate professor of management.

In 1989, Surles became vice president for academic affairs at historically black Jackson State University, where she remained until December 1991. In January 1992, she moved back to California to become visiting administrator in residence in the California State University's chancellor's office. That July, she became vice president for administration and business affairs at the Hayward campus.

Surles was appointed president of Texas Woman's University in Denton, Texas, in August 1994.

T

Tate, Merze (1905–)

In 1991, Merze Tate received the American Historical Association's prestigious Distinguished Scholar Award for exceptional teaching and scholarship. Tate taught for more than fifty years on the secondary and college levels before retiring from **Howard University** in 1977. Her experience was primarily in segregated institutions that often gave exceptional educations to African Americans. She was the first African-American woman to receive an advanced degree from Oxford University and she

A legend in the world of foreign relations, Merze Tate served on the faculty of Howard University for thirty-five years, while also acting as consultant to national and international policymakers. (MOORLAND-SPINGARN)

provided excellent instruction to students, who remembered her years later as a wonderful role model and rigorous teacher.

Born in Blanchard, Michigan, on February 6, 1905, Tate walked eight miles daily to attend Battle Creek High School. In 1927, she graduated first in her class from Western Michigan Teachers College in Kalamazoo, where she became the first African American to earn a B.A.

Racial prejudice and Jim Crow practices kept Tate from finding a teaching position in Michigan. However, in 1928 she was hired to teach history at Crispus Attucks High School, a newly opened facility for African-American students in Indianapolis. This academic institution was one of several secondary schools built during the first third of the twentieth century for black students in urban areas throughout the nation. Some of the country's finest African-American scholars began their teaching careers at similar institutions.

Like many African-American educators, Tate spent her summers in New York City, earning her master's degree at Columbia University in 1930. By 1932, she had entered Oxford University, where she earned the Litt.D. in 1935. Her major field of study was international relations.

Afterward Tate began an illustrious college teaching career that spanned more than forty years in historically black institutions. She began with the position of dean of women at Barber College in North Carolina. From there she became the chair of social science at **Bennett College** in Greensboro, North Carolina. In 1941, Tate became the first African-American woman to earn a Ph.D. in government and international relations from Harvard University, writing her dissertation on U.S. disarmament policies. The following year she joined the faculty at Howard University, where she served for thirty-five years.

A significant influence among undergraduate and graduate students, Tate saw the economic and social aspects of society as central to understanding history. A mentor through the years, she has taught outstanding African-American students who themselves have made contributions to public secondary education, higher education, and the history profession. Upon retiring from Howard, she endowed the Tate Seminar in Diplomatic History, an annual lecture hosted by the university.

A prolific writer, Tate is a foreign policy expert whose advice has been sought by the United Nations. Her many books and essays include *The Disarmament Illusion: The Movement for a Limitation of Armaments to 1907* (1942), *The United States and Armaments* (1948), *The United States and the Hawaiian Kingdom: A Political History* (1965), and *Mineral Railways in Africa* (1989).

ROSALYN TERBORG-PENN

Thomas, Lundeana M. (1949–)

From her busy drama department office at Bowling Green State University, Lundeana Thomas runs an organization that connects theatre artists around the country. The Black Theater Network (BTN) is a resource for all who want to see black theater grow, and African Americans take their rightful place in all areas of American theater.

Thomas did not begin her career as a university educator. From the late 1960s to the mid-1970s, she toured as singer, narrator, and entertainer with the Northeast Ohio Gospel Singers and later The Afro-American Chorale, of which she was president. In Youngstown, Ohio, meanwhile, she held jobs as telephone operator; director of the Southside Happening House Community Action Center; and public school teacher of remedial math, reading, and physical coordination. She began to act in and to direct plays ranging from *A Raisin in the Sun* to *Barefoot in the Park* to a version of *Frankenstein*.

Thomas got her B.S. from Youngstown State University in 1976 and that summer was in London, both singing in a club and attending seminars with Jonathan Miller and Simon Gray at the University of London's Birbeck College. Up to 1980 she then remained a Youngstown high school teacher, with skills as diverse as gospel music and forensics. Two years later she earned her theater history and criticism M.A. at Ann Arbor's University of Michigan, where until 1988 she taught drama and communications and where her 1993 paper on Barbara Ann Teer, founder of Harlem's National Black Theatre, earned her a Ph.D.

Two years at Atlanta's **Spelman College**, site of her one-woman performance in the play *Boochie*, preceded her move to Bowling Green, where in 1990 she became assistant professor and BTN's treasurer.

The network's 300 members have become worldwide since its 1986 founding, when they numbered twenty-two. It promotes cohesion in the black theater movement, realization of productions, and sharing ideas and data among the movement's many and far-flung participants. It does so with publications, competitions, honorary and life memberships, conferences, and prizes, such as its annual Young Scholar's Award.

A BTN member from its outset, Thomas launched several reforms as treasurer and secured its nonprofit status. Vice president between 1992 and 1994, she coordinated BTN's work with that of Women in Theatre, a subcommittee of the Association of Theatre in Higher Education, and helped inaugurate the Winona Lee Fletcher Award for Artistic Excellence in Black Theatre in Chicago, 1994.

BTN's annual *Black Theatre Directory* geographically lists African-American artists, scholars, theaters, college programs, and support organizations. Its quarterly *BT News & BTN Job Bulletin* reports current happenings and job information, including auditions and internships. The BTN's *Theatre Annual* prints winning papers by graduates of the BTN Young Scholars Competition. Its volume, *Dissertations Concerning Black Theatre*, catalogs master's and doctoral theses going back to 1900.

"So often," Thomas has said, "on campuses and in the cities there's not a black voice for African Americans. We want to encourage theater that young people can relate to."

GARY HOUSTON

Thornton, Jerry Sue (1947–)

As president of Cuyahoga Community College, the largest community college in Ohio, Dr. Jerry Sue Thornton manages a budget of $140 million, oversees three campuses and two learning centers, and directs more than

In 1992, Jerry Sue Thornton became president of Cuyahoga Community College, the largest community college in Ohio.
(CUYAHOGA COMMUNITY COLLEGE)

2,300 full- and part-time faculty and staff members who in turn serve some 58,000 students.

Thornton received a B.A. in English and Speech and an M.A. in communications from Murray State University in Murray, Kentucky, and a Ph.D. in educational administration from the University of Texas. She began her career as a junior high and high school teacher, moving on to Triton College in River Grove, Illinois, where she became dean of arts and sciences.

Thornton was appointed president of Lakewood Community College in White Bear Lake, Minnesota, in 1985, and remained there until coming to Cuyahoga Community College in 1992. She is a lecturer on the international and national circuits.

MICHAEL NOWAK

W

Wilkerson, Margaret B. (1938–)

"Black women are a prism through which the searing rays of race, class and sex are first focused, then refracted," writes Margaret B. Wilkerson in her introduction to *9 Plays by Black Women*. "The creative among us transform these rays into a spectrum of brilliant colors, a rainbow which illuminates the experience of all mankind." Wilkerson has devoted her life to studying theater, practicing theater, and writing about theater. In a notable academic and professional career that spans nearly three decades, she has provoked and inspired students at the University of California, Berkeley, illuminated the link between theater and society, and celebrated the theatrical richness of African-American experience.

Margaret B. Wilkerson was born on April 3, 1938, in Los Angeles, California, the daughter of George and Gladys Buford. She established her scholarly leanings early, pursuing a broad-based liberal arts education at the University of Redlands, earning a bachelor's degree in history, with distinction, in 1959. She went on to earn a teaching credential at the University of California–Los Angeles in 1961.

Wilkerson taught English and drama at Jordan High School in the Watts area of Los Angeles shortly after leaving school, but her drive to learn and to share her knowledge soon prompted a return to the university. She earned a master's degree in dramatic art from the University of California–Berkeley in 1967, and quickly followed it with doctoral work.

Her pioneering scholarship chronicled the historic achievements of African-American theater artists as well as the contemporary artistic expression of black consciousness on the stage. She earned her Ph.D. in 1972 with a dissertation entitled "Black Theatres in the San Francisco Bay Area and in the Los Angeles Area: A Report and Analysis."

In the years that followed, Wilkerson distinguished herself as an artist as well as a scholar. She founded Kumoja Players Community Theater Group, where she was a director, and merged art and politics with her U.C. Berkeley production of the now-classic Amiri Baraka (LeRoi Jones) play *Dutchman*, among others. She has lectured in the departments of English, dramatic arts, and African-American studies at U.C. Berkeley, and also has written prolifically: theater reviews, essays, magazine articles, and scholarly papers.

In 1973, Wilkerson joined U.C.–Berkeley's Center for the Study, Education and Advancement of Women, moving up through the ranks to the position of director. Over a period of nine years, she coordinated the efforts of the center to provide information, consultation, and counseling on academic areas of concern to women. Meanwhile, in the African American studies department, Wilkerson taught courses in dramatic literature, theater history, and performance. She rose from associate professor to professor and finally to chair, a position she held until 1994.

While Wilkerson's accomplishments during the 1980s were many, the best known is her ground-breaking 1986 anthology, *9 Plays by Black Women*. It was the first published anthology of its kind, shedding new light on such significant writers as Aishah Rahman,

As scholar and as artist, Margaret B. Wilkerson explores and celebrates the African-American experience in the theater. In her introduction to 9 Plays by Black Women *(1986) she writes: "Black women are a prism through which the searing rays of race, class and sex are first focused, then refracted. The creative among us transform these rays into a . . . rainbow which illuminates the experience of all mankind."* (UNIVERSITY OF CALIFORNIA, BERKELEY)

Alice Childers, and Ntozake Shange. It made many theater scholars and artists aware for the first time of the vast wealth of creative work by African-American women. "While preparing this anthology," Wilkerson wrote, "I have come to know many black women writing for the theater, and I have been both amazed and gratified by these artists who celebrate life even as they critique it."

Wilkerson lamented the fact that space limitations did not allow her to share all of the exciting plays that she encountered, but expressed hope that her work would inspire similar volumes. Indeed, in the years since the anthology's publication, a generation of theater artists and scholars have built on the solid foundation constructed by Wilkerson.

In 1995, Wilkerson was appointed chair of the department of dance and dramatic art at U.C.–Berkeley, as well as director of the university's newly established Center for Theater Arts. Her challenge is to forge collaborations between artists and scholars, students and teachers, and academics and professionals in the many disciplines that make up contemporary theater.

"Fragmentation and confusion seem rampant in our society and our world," said Wilkerson at the 1995 opening ceremony for the Center for Theater Arts. "In such an environment, we desperately need spaces where we can critique, reflect, debate, question; places that feed our spirit (both mind and soul) and that sometimes simply soothe; places that allow us to play with possibilities and to confront difficult realities, to revision ourselves and our world—and to do all of these things and more—in community, in concert with others. Theater is such a place."

Wilkerson's awards and honors are many and varied. She was the first recipient of the

Black Theater Network's Winona Lee Fletcher Award for outstanding scholarship. She was named an American Theater Fellow for her distinguished contributions to the American theater by the Kennedy Center in Washington, D.C. She holds an honorary doctorate of humane letters from the University of Redlands and the College of Santa Fe. She has received grants from the Rockefeller Foundation and the Ford Foundation in support of her research. She also has traveled to West Africa as a consultant to the Ford Foundation's Worldwide Workshop on Culture.

Not content to sit on her laurels, Margaret B. Wilkerson is currently writing a literary biography of **Lorraine Hansberry**.

CHRISTINE SUMPTION

Blenda J. Wilson, president of California State University–Northridge, believes that educators today are "preparing the first generation of leaders and professionals who will really live in a global world. . . . What we have here is the making of America's successful future, if we do it well." She faced the ultimate test of her administrative skills after the campus was devastated by an earthquake in January 1994. (CALIFORNIA STATE UNIVERSITY, NORTHRIDGE)

Wilson, Blenda J. (1941–)

When Blenda J. Wilson, president of California State University–Northridge, arrived on campus the morning of January 17, 1994, what she found was devastation. An earthquake measuring 6.6 on the Richter scale had shaken Southern California, with Northridge at the epicenter. Virtually every building on the 353-acre campus was damaged. The parking garage had collapsed, a science building was in flames, the walls of the student dormitories were cracked, and the roof of the university library was dangling precipitously.

To top it off, the telephone lines and computer systems had been incapacitated. But that didn't stop Wilson. She set up temporary offices in a rented recreational vehicle, armed herself with a cellular telephone, and rallied the university community to the task of cleanup and reconstruction. Within one short month, this powerhouse administrator had reopened the university and made a lasting

imprint as a calm, capable, and inspiring leader.

Born January 28, 1941, in Perth Amboy, New Jersey, and raised in Woodbridge, New Jersey, Blenda J. Wilson was one of five children of Horace Lawrence Wilson and Margaret Brogsdale Wilson. Her commitment to education began at an early age. "Blenda was the type that never wanted to miss a day of school," said her mother.

"Once, she had a cold, and I didn't wake her up for school because I thought she should stay home. Would you believe she cried?"

A great lover of books, fascinated by the potential of reading to open up a vast range of knowledge and experience, Wilson pursued a bachelor's degree in English and secondary education from Cedar Crest College and a master's degree in education from Seton Hall University, graduating in 1962. Shortly thereafter, she returned to her hometown of Woodbridge, New Jersey, to teach high school English.

However, it was Wilson's first experience as an administrator that forever changed the course of her career. In 1966, she helped to establish the first Head Start program in the state of New Jersey. She quickly rose through the ranks to the position of executive director at the Middlesex County Economic Opportunities Corporation, supervising resource and advocacy programs in job training, education, health, and welfare. Administration, with its potential to benefit the lives of many, suited her skills and ideals. She never turned back.

In a series of high-level administrative positions at Rutgers University from 1969 to 1972, Wilson focused her primary efforts on supervising the university's affirmative action program and managing the Educational Opportunity Fund programs. "I see public higher education in terms of opportunities for those people who might otherwise not have those chances," she says. Wilson went on to earn a Ph.D. in higher education administration at Boston College in 1979, even as she served as senior associate dean and lecturer on education at Harvard's Graduate School of Education.

In 1984, Wilson's reputation as an educational visionary and an energetic leader brought her to the attention of the Colorado Commission on Higher Education, which appointed her its executive director. She then spent five years coordinating policy for the twenty-eight campuses of the Colorado university system. It was in Colorado that she met her husband, Louis Fair, and they were married in 1985.

In pursuit of further challenge, Wilson moved to Michigan in 1988. She became chancellor and professor of public administration and education at the University of Michigan–Dearborn, and the first woman to head a public university in the state of Michigan. Noted accomplishments during her tenure include the building of bridges between the predominantly white suburb of Dearborn and its African-American neighbors in Detroit, and raising the national profile of the university.

Just four years later, in May 1992, Wilson was appointed president of California State University–Northridge, becoming the first African-American woman to preside over a campus with a student enrollment of more than 28,000. "It's an opportunity for excellence," she says, "in the sense of preparing the first generation of leaders and professionals who will really live in a global world and who really will have to understand different cultures and different people. What we have here is the making of America's successful future, if we do it well."

By all accounts, Blenda J. Wilson does it well. When not cleaning up after earthquakes, she lends her exuberant personality to the task of developing strong relationships between administration, faculty, staff, and students and to strengthening the university's financial position. "An essential quality of leadership is confidence and optimism," she says. She appears to have both in abundance.

CHRISTINE SUMPTION

Y

Yancy, Dorothy Cowser (1944–)

It was a happy reunion between Dorothy Cowser Yancy and Johnson C. Smith University (JCSU) in Charlotte, North Carolina, when she became that school's first woman president in October of 1994. Smith was returning to the college where she had received a B.A. in history and social sciences some thirty years earlier.

Born in Cherokee County, Alabama, on April 18, 1944, Yancy was raised on a farm. She entered college at the age of sixteen. After graduating from JCSU, she earned an M.A. in history at the University of Massachusetts and a Ph.D. in political science at Atlanta University. She then spent twenty-two years as a professor in the School of History, Technology and Society and the School of Management at the Georgia Institute of Technology, where she was the first African American to be promoted and tenured as a full professor.

Yancy came to JCSU in 1994 to serve as interim president. However, she was so energetic in her fund-raising and so popular with both students and faculty that the trustees of the university asked her to stay and accept the position of president.

As a result of her certifications in labor arbitration and mediation she has been ap-pointed to a number of panels in that area, and has been a consultant to governmental agencies, unions, and major U.S. companies.

MICHAEL NOWAK

A distinguished educator, Dorothy Cowser Yancy returned in 1994 to her alma mater, Johnson C. Smith University, to become its president. (JOHNSON C. SMITH UNIVERSITY)

Chronology

BY VALINDA W. LITTLEFIELD

1662

Virginia law establishes that children born in the colony will be held bond or free, according to the condition of their mother.

1746

Lucy Terry [Prince] writes "Bars Fight," the first known poem by an African American in the United States; the poem is not published until 1895.

1773

Phillis Wheatley publishes *Poems on Various Subjects Religious and Moral*, the first book published by a black person in North America and the second published by a woman in North America.

1787

The first African Free School is established in New York, a precursor to secular education for African Americans in New York.

1793

A former slave, Catherine Ferguson, having purchased her freedom, opens Katy Ferguson's School for the Poor in New York, enrolling black and white children from a local almshouse.

1827

The African Dorcas Association is founded by black women in New York City to supply clothing to children in the African Free Schools.

1829

St. Francis of Rome Academy, a boarding school founded by the Oblate Sisters of Providence, opens in Baltimore, Maryland.

1831

The Female Literary Association of Philadelphia and the Afric-American Female Intelligence Society of Boston are founded.

The History of Mary Prince, a West Indian Slave is the first slave narrative published by a black woman in the Americas.

1833

The Philadelphia Library of Colored Persons is established to house books and sponsor concerts, lectures, and debates.

Prudence Crandall, a white Quaker schoolteacher, opens a "High school for young colored Ladies and Misses" in Canterbury, Connecticut, enrolling fifteen students. The townspeople initiate a series of efforts to close the institution, culminating in the burning of the school.

1835

Oberlin College becomes the first college in the United States to admit students without regard to race or sex.

1836

Jarena Lee publishes *The Life and Religious Experiences of Jarena Lee, A Couloured Lady . . .* , the first autobiography by an American black woman.

1838

The Memoirs of Elleanor Eldridge, one of the few narratives of the life of an early nineteenth-century free black woman, is published.

1841

Ann Plato writes *Essays, including Biographies and Miscellaneous Pieces in Prose and Poetry.*

1846

Zilpha Elaw publishes *Memoirs of the Life, Religious Experience, Ministerial Travels and Labors of Mrs. Zilpha Elaw.*

1848

When Boston officials bar Sarah Roberts from a neighborhood white school, and require her to pass five other white schools to attend a school designated for black children, her father, Benjamin Roberts, files the first school integration suit on her behalf. In its 1849 ruling in *Sarah C. Roberts* v. *City of Boston*, the Massachusetts state supreme court upholds the legality of segregation, justifying it with the first recorded use of the "separate but equal" doctrine.

1850

Lucy Sessions earns a literary degree from Oberlin College, becoming the first black woman in the U.S. to receive a college degree.

1852

The **Institute for Colored Youth** is founded in Philadelphia by the Society of Friends as the first coeducational classical high school for African Americans.

The Normal School for Colored Girls is founded in Washington, D.C., by Myrtilla Miner, a white female educator.

1861

Mary Peake opens a one-room day school in Fortress Monroe, Virginia; the American Missionary Association (AMA) would later help support this school.

The Port Royal Commission is begun in the Sea Islands near South Carolina, with Charlotte Forten (Grimké) as the only black teacher in the experiment. She is joined by **Susan King Taylor** in 1864.

1862

Mary Jane Patterson earns a B.A. degree from Oberlin College, making her the first black woman to earn a Bachelor's degree from an accredited U.S. college.

1864

Rebecca Lee [Crumpler] becomes the first African-American woman to graduate from a U.S. college with a formal medical degree, and the first and only black woman to obtain the Doctress of Medicine from the New England Female Medical college in Boston, Massachusetts.

1865

Fanny Jackson [Coppin] is the second African-American woman to receive an A.B. degree, when she graduates from Oberlin.

1866

Sarah Woodson Early is appointed preceptress of English and Latin, and lady principal and matron at Wilberforce University, becoming the first African-American woman on a college faculty.

1867

Rebecca Cole, the second black woman to receive a medical degree in the U.S., graduates from the Women's Medical College of Pennsylvania in Philadelphia.

1869

Howard University Medical School opens it doors to women both black and white; by 1900, 103 women had enrolled, 48 of whom—23 black women and 25 white women—had graduated.

Fanny Jackson [Coppin] is named principal of the Institute for Colored Youth in Philadelphia, becoming the first black woman to head an institution of higher learning in the U.S.

1870

Upon graduation from the New York Medical College for Women, **Susan McKinney Steward** becomes the third black female doctor in the U.S.

1879

Graduating from the School of Nursing, New England Hospital for Women and Children in Boston, **Mary Eliza Mahoney** becomes the first African American in the U.S. to receive a diploma in nursing.

1883

Hartshorn Memorial College for Women is founded in Richmond, Virginia, and becomes (in 1888) the first educational institution in the U.S. chartered as a *college* for black women.

1884

Anna Julia Cooper, Mary Church [Terrell] and Ida Gibbs (Hunt) graduate from Oberlin College.

1886

Lucy Craft Laney opens a grammar school in Augusta, Georgia, which develops into the **Haines Normal and Industrial Institute.**

The first school for black nursing students is established at Spelman Seminary, Atlanta, Georgia.

1889

Maria Louise Baldwin becomes the first African-American female principal in Massachusetts and the Northeast, supervising white faculty and a predominantly white student body at Agassiz Grammar School in Cambridge.

Josephine A. Silone Yates becomes professor and head of the Natural Sciences Department at Lincoln University (Jefferson City, Missouri), earning $1,000 per year.

1892

Mary Moor Booze, Harriet Amanda Miller, and Dixie Erma Williams graduate with B.S. degrees from Hartshorn Memorial College, the first college degrees granted by a black woman's institution.

Anna Julia Cooper publishes *A Voice from the South by a Black Woman of the South.*

1893

Meharry Medical College, founded in 1876 in Nashville, Tennessee, awards its first medical degrees to women: Georgianna Patton and Anna D. Gregg.

1895

Victoria Earle Matthews begins a tour of the South to report on the status of Southern African-American women for the National Federation of the Afro-American Women.

1896

In the precedent-setting *Plessy* v. *Ferguson,* the U.S. Supreme Court rules that "separate but equal" facilities are constitutional, thus signaling the federal government's endorsement of segregation laws.

1897

The First Hampton Negro Conference is held; the annual meeting assesses the conditions and strategies of African Americans. At the first conference, Fanny Jackson Coppin speaks on industrial education; later conferences include sessions organized by state and national women leaders on topics such as women's education, community services, and health issues.

The American Negro Academy is founded to promote scholarly work and fellowship among leading intellectuals; Anna Julia Cooper is the only woman elected to membership.

Elizabeth Evelyn Wright, with the help of Jessie Dorsey, founds the Denmark Indus-

trial School in Denmark, South Carolina (later Voorhees Industrial School, now Voorhees College).

Spelman Seminary opens a College Department, with collegiate courses offered on Atlanta Baptist (Morehouse) campus.

1900

According to a study by W. E. B. DuBois, 252 black women have obtained baccalaureate degrees; 65 of them are Oberlin College graduates.

Pauline Hopkins publishes *Contending Forces: A Romance Illustrative of Negro Life North and South*, a forceful protest novel.

1901

Spelman Seminary grants its first college degrees to Jane Anna Granderson and Claudia Turner White.

1902

Charlotte Hawkins Brown founds the Palmer Institute in Sedalia, North Carolina.

1904

Mary McLeod Bethune establishes the Daytona Educational and Industrial Training School, which becomes **Bethune-Cookman College.**

Virginia W. Broughton publishes *Women's Work, as Gleaned from the Women of the Bible*, an analysis of biblical precedents for gender equality.

1909

Nannie Helen Burroughs is founding president of the **National Training School for Women and Girls** in Washington, D.C.

1910

Sara Winifred Brown, Mary Church Terrell, and others establish the College Alumnae Club.

1915

The first woman to be awarded a certificate by the American Teachers Association, Hannah Pierce Lowe organizes the Organization of Teachers of Colored Children in New Jersey.

1918

Nora Douglas Holt is the first African American to earn an advanced degree in music, receiving an M.Mus. from the Chicago School of Music.

1921

The first black women to earn Ph.D. degrees in the U.S. are **Georgiana R. Simpson,** German, University of Chicago; **Sadie Tanner Mossell [Alexander]**, economics, University of Pennsylvania; and **Eva Dykes,** English philology, Radcliffe College.

1923

Completing the course of study at Carnegie Library School in Philadelphia, **Virginia Proctor Powell [Florence]** becomes the first African-American woman to receive professional training in librarianship.

1924

Spelman Seminary becomes **Spelman College,** now offering college courses on its own campus.

1926

Bennett College, founded as a coeducational institution in 1873, becomes a college for women.

Selena Sloan Butler founds the National Congress of Colored Parents and Teachers.

1929

Lucy Diggs Slowe convenes the first annual conference of deans and advisers to girls in Negro schools, which gives birth to the **Association of Deans of Women and Advisers to Girls in Negro Schools.**

Anna Julia Cooper is named president of Frelinghuysen University in Washington, D.C.

Receiving a degree from Columbia University, Jane Ellen McAlister becomes the first African-American woman in the U.S. to earn a Ph.D. degree in education.

1931

Jane Mathilda Bolin is the first black woman to graduate from Yale University Law School.

1932

Hartshorn Memorial College, the first black woman's college, merges with Virginia Union University.

1934

Receiving a degree from the University of Minnesota, Ruth Winifred Howard becomes the first African-American woman in the U.S. to receive a Ph.D. degree in psychology.

1935

Jessie Jarue Mark is the first African-American woman to earn a Ph.D. degree in botany (Iowa State University).

1936

Flemmie P. Kittrell is the first African-American woman to earn a Ph.D. degree in nutrition (Cornell University).

1939

Tuskegee Institute establishes a school of nurse-midwifery.

Mary T. Washington becomes the first African-American woman Certified Public Accountant, after graduating from Chicago's Northwestern University.

1940

Sixty percent of all black women in the labor force are still employed in domestic service and 10.5 percent are in other service work; only 1.4 percent are in clerical and sales positions and 4.3 percent are in professional positions.

Roger Arliner Young is the first black woman to earn a Ph.D. degree in zoology (University of Pennsylvania).

1941

Charlotte Hawkins Brown's *The Correct thing to Do, to Say, and to Wear* is published.

1942

Margurite Thomas is the first African-American woman to earn a Ph.D. degree in geology (Catholic University).

1943

Mamie Phipps Clark becomes the first black woman to earn a Ph.D. in psychology from Columbia University. Her research into the racial identity formation of black children (with her husband, Kenneth Clark) would be central evidence cited in the 1954 *Brown* v. *Board of Education* Supreme Court decision.

Anne Cooke receives a Ph.D. degree in theater from Yale University.

1947

Receiving a degree from Columbia University, Marie M. Daly becomes the first African-American woman to earn a Ph.D. in chemistry.

1948

In *Ada Lois Sipuel* v. *Board of Regents*, the Supreme Court orders the University of Oklahoma School of Law to admit Sipuel, arguing that a state cannot require African Americans to postpone their education until separate black graduate or professional schools are established.

1949

Marjorie Lee Brown (University of Michigan) and **Evelyn Boyd Granville** (Yale Uiversity) become the first African-American women to earn Ph.D. degrees in mathematics.

1950

Forty-two percent of all black women in the labor force are employed in domestic service and 19.1 percent are in other service work; only 5.4 percent are in clerical and sales positions and 5.7 percent are in professional positions.

Norma Merrick Sklarek graduates from the School of Architecture at Columbia University and in 1954 becomes the first black woman to be licensed as an architect in the U.S.

1951

High school student Barbara Johns initiates a student strike that persuades the National Association for the Advancement of Colored People to make desegregation of schools in Prince Edward County, Virginia, one of the four cases eventually decided by the Supreme Court in its 1954 *Brown* v. *Board of Education* decision, ruling segregated schools unconstitutional.

Mildred Fay Jefferson becomes the first African-American woman to graduate from Harvard University's Medical School. She goes on to serve three terms as president of the National Right to Life Committee.

1954

The *Brown* v. *Board of Education* decision makes segregated schools unconstitutional, with **Constance Baker Motley** playing a major role in preparing the case.

1955

Willa Player becomes president of Bennett College, making her the first black woman president of a college since **Mary McCleod Bethune** founded Bethune College.

1956

Under a Supreme Court order and with the aid of **Ruby Hurley, National Association for the Advancement of Colored People** regional director, **Autherine Lucy [Foster]** enrolls in the University of Alabama in Tuscaloosa, only to be expelled days later by university officials, who cite her statements regarding race relations at the school as grounds for her dismissal.

1957

Nine students, including Minniejean Brown, Elizabeth Eckford, Thelma Mothershed, Melba Pattillo, Gloria Ray, and Carlotta Walls, integrate Central High School in Little Rock, Arkansas, despite violent assaults that eventually are quelled only by the presence of federal troops. **Daisy Bates** and the **Little Rock Nine** receive the National Association for the Advancement of Colored People's Spingarn Medal.

1960

Of all black women in the labor force, 32.5 percent are employed in domestic service; 21.4 percent are in other service positions; 10.8 percent are in clerical and sales, and 6 percent are in professional positions.

1961

Charlayne Hunter [Gault] becomes the first black woman, and Hamilton Holmes the first black man, to be admitted to the University of Georgia in the 175-year history of the University.

1962

Four black mothers begin a sit-in at a Chicago elementary school, protesting de facto segregation, unequal facilities, double shifts, and mobile classrooms.

1970

Of all black women in the labor force, 17.5 percent are employed in domestic service positions; 25.7 percent are in other service positions; 23.4 percent are in sales and clerical positions, and 10.8 are in professional positions.

Activist and educator **Angela Davis** is placed on the FBI's Ten Most Wanted list, arrested after a nationwide police search and charged with murder, kidnapping, and conspiracy. An international campaign to free Davis develops, and in June 1972, a jury, after only thirteen hours of deliberation, finds her not guilty on all counts.

Elaine Jones is the first black women to

graduate from the University of Virginia School of Law. She will become the head of the NAACP Legal Defense and Educational Fund, Inc., in 1993.

1971

Marian Wright Edelman is the first black woman elected to the Yale University Corporation. She remains a member until 1977.

1972

A National Education Association study reveals that African Americans have lost 30,000 teaching positions since 1954 in seventeen Southern and border states because of desegregation and discrimination.

1973

Barbara Sizemore is elected superintendent of schools for the District of Columbia public school system, the first black woman to direct the schools of a major American city.

1976

Mary Frances Berry becomes chancellor of the University of Colorado at Boulder, the first African-American woman to head a major research university.

1979

Jenny Patrick is the first black woman in the U.S. to earn a Ph.D. degree in chemical engineering (Massachusetts Institute of Technology).

1980

Of all black women in the labor force, 6.5 percent are employed in domestic service; 24.3 percent are in other service work; 32.4 percent are in clerical and sales positions, and 14.8 percent are in professional positions.

Marian Wright Edelman becomes the first black person and second woman to chair the Spelman College Board of Trustees.

1983

Christine Darden is the first black woman in the U.S. to earn a Ph.D degree in mechanical engineering (George Washington University).

1987

Johnnetta Cole becomes president of **Spelman College**, the first black woman to head the oldest college for black women still in existence in the United States.

Niara Sudarkasa became the first woman president of Lincoln University, the nation's oldest black college and, for much of its history, an all-male institution.

Gloria Dean Randle Scott becomes president of Bennett College in Greensboro, North Carolina.

Darlene Clark Hine becomes John A. Hannah Distinguished Professor of History at Michigan State University.

1988

Charlayne Hunter-Gault becomes the first black person in the 203-year history of her alma mater, the University of Georgia, to deliver the commencement address. She and Hamilton Holmes were the first blacks to be admitted to the university twenty-five years earlier. Holmes is now a member of the Georgia Foundation, the governing board of the university.

1990

Historian Mary Frances Berry serves as president of the Organization of American Historians, the first black woman to hold this position.

Ruth Simmons becomes the ninth president of Smith College, the first black woman to head a Seven Sisters college.

1991

Nell Irvin Painter is appointed Edwards Professor of American History at Princeton University.

Bibliography

GENERAL BOOKS USEFUL TO THE STUDY OF BLACK WOMEN IN AMERICA

Reference Books

African-Americans: Voices of Triumph. Three volume set: *Perseverance*, *Leadership*, and *Creative Fire*. From the editors of Time-Life Books, Alexandria, Va., 1993.

Estell, Kenneth, ed., *The African-American Almanac*. Detroit, Mich., 1994.

Harley, Sharon. *The Timetables of African-American History: A Chronology of the Most Important People and Events in African-American History*. New York, 1995.

Hine, Darlene Clark. *Hine Sight: Black Women and The Re-Construction of American History*. Brooklyn, N.Y., 1994.

Hine, Darlene Clark, ed., Elsa Barkley Brown and Rosalyn Terborg-Penn, associate eds. *Black Women in America: An Historical Encyclopedia*. Brooklyn, N.Y., 1993.

Hornsby, Alton, Jr. *Chronology of African-American History: Significant Events and People from 1619 to the Present*. Detroit, Mich., 1991.

Kranz, Rachel. *Biographical Dictionary of Black Americans*. New York, 1992.

Lanker, Brian. *I Dream a World: Portraits of Black Women Who Changed America*. New York, 1989.

Logan, Rayford W., and Michael R. Winston, eds. *Dictionary of American Negro Biography*, New York, 1982.

Low, W. Augustus, and Virgil A. Clift, eds. *Encyclopedia of Black America*. New York, 1981.

Salem, Dorothy C., ed. *African American Women: A Biographical Dictionary*. New York, 1993.

Salzman, Jack, David Lionel Smith, and Cornel West. *Encyclopedia of African-American Culture and History*. Five Vols. New York, 1996.

Smith, Jessie Carney, ed., *Notable Black American Women*. Two Vols. Detroit, Mich., Book I, 1993; Book II, 1996.

General Books about Black Women

Giddings, Paula. *When and Where I Enter: The Impact of Black Women on Race and Sex in America*. New York, 1984.

Guy-Sheftall, Beverly. *Words of Fire: An Anthology of African-American Feminist Thought*. New York, 1995.

Hine, Darlene Clark, Wilma King, and Linda Reed, eds. *"We Specialize in the Wholly Impossible:" A Reader in Black Women's History*. Brooklyn, N.Y., 1995.

Jones, Jacqueline. *Labor of Love, Labor of Sorrow: Black Women, Work, and the Family from Slavery to the Present*. New York, 1985.

Lerner, Gerda, ed. *Black Women in White America: A Documentary History*. New York, 1972.

BOOKS THAT INCLUDE INFORMATION ON BLACK WOMEN AND EDUCATION

Anderson, James D. *The Education of Blacks in the South, 1860–1935*. Chapel Hill, N.C., 1988.

Butchart, Ronald E. *Northern Schools, Southern Blacks, and Reconstruction: Freedmen's Education, 1862–1875.* Westport, Conn., 1980.

Bullock, Henry Allen. *A History of Negro Education in the South from 1619 to the Present.* Cambridge, Mass., 1967.

Garvin Fields, Mamie and Fields, Karen. *Lemon Swamp.* New York, 1983.

Kluger, Richard. *Simple Justice: The History of Brown v. Board of Education and Black America's Struggle for Equality.* New York, 1975.

Morris, Robert C. *Reading, 'Riting, and Reconstruction: The Education of the Freedmen in the South, 1861–1870.* Chicago, 1981.

Murray, Pauli. *Proud Shoes: The Story of an American Family.* New York, 1984.

———. *The Autobiography of A Black Activist, Feminist, Lawyer, Priest, and Poet.* Knoxville, Tenn., 1987.

Neverdon-Morton, Cynthia. *Afro-American Women of the South and the Advancement of the Race, 1985–1925.* Knoxville, Tenn., 1989.

New Perspectives on Black Educational History. Franklin, V.P. and James D. Anderson, eds. Boston, 1978.

Weinberg, Meyer. *A Chance to Learn: A History of Race and Education in the United States.* New York, 1977.

Contents of the Set

(ORGANIZED BY VOLUME)

Education

New Era Club
Oblate Sisters of Providence
Phyllis Wheatley Homes and
    Clubs
Porter, Diane M.
Prout, Mary Ann
Rankin, Marlene Owens
Ransom, Emma
Roberts, Ruth Logan
Saddler, Juanita
Saint Frances of Rome Acad-
    emy, Baltimore
Sanctified Church
Saunders, Cecelia Cabaniss
Sigma Gamma Rho Sorority
Sisters of the Holy Family
Smith, Amanda Berry
Smith, Celestine Louise
Southeastern Association of
    Colored Women's Clubs
Sprague, Fredericka and Rosa-
    belle Jones
Stewart, Ella Phillips
Stewart, Sallie Wyatt
Stokes, Ora Brown
Tanneyhill, Ann
Thomas, Cora Ann Pair
Waddles, Charleszetta
Walker, A'Lelia
Walker, Maggie Lena
White Rose Mission, New
    York City
Williams, Fannie Barrier
Williamson, Sarah
Woman's Loyal Union of New
    York and Brooklyn
York, Consuella
Young Women's Christian As-
    sociation
Zeta Phi Beta Sorority

Law and Government

Alexander, Sadie
Anderson, Violette N.
Atkins, Hannah Diggs

Barrett, Jacquelyn H.
Bass, Charlotta Spears
Belton, Sharon Sayles
Berry, Mary Frances
Bethune, Mary McLeod
Black Women Mayors' Caucus
Bolin, Jane Mathilda
Brown, Corrine
Burke, Yvonne Brathwaite
Carson, Julia
Carter, Eunice Hunton
Carter, Pamela Fanning
Chisholm, Shirley
Clayton, Eva
Collins, Barbara-Rose
Collins, Cardiss
Congresswomen
Delco, Wilhelmina R.
Elliott, Daisy
Fauset, Crystal Bird
Federal Judges
Fisher, Ada Lois Sipuel
Guinier, Lani
Hall, Katie
Hamilton, Grace Towns
Harris, Patricia Roberts
Harvard, Beverly
Hedgeman, Anna Arnold
Herman, Alexis M.
Hill, Anita
Ingram, Edith J.
Johnson, Eddie Bernice
Johnson, Norma Holloway
Jones, Elaine
Jones, Star
Jordan, Barbara Charline
Kearse, Amalya Lyle
Kelly, Sharon Pratt Dixon
Kidd, Mae Street
Lafontant-Mankarious, Jewel
    Stradford
Lawson, Marjorie McKenzie
Lee, Sheila Jackson
McKinney, Cynthia
Meek, Carrie
Mitchell, Juanita Jackson
Morris, Carolyn
Moseley-Braun, Carol
Motley, Constance Baker

National Organization of Black
    Elected Legislative Women
National Political Congress of
    Black Women
Norton, Eleanor Holmes
O'Leary, Hazel Rollins
Payton, Carolyn Robertson
Perry, Carrie Saxon
Phillips, Velvalea Rogers
Poe, L. Marian Fleming
Powers, Georgia
Ralston, Elreta Alexander
Ray, Charlotte
Sampson, Edith
Sears-Collins, Leah
Smythe-Haithe, Mabel Murphy
Stout, Juanita Kidd
Taylor, Anna Diggs
Tucker, C. DeLores
Waters, Maxine
Watson, Diane Edith
Welcome, Verda Freeman
Williams, Margaret
Williams, Patricia J.

Theater Arts and Entertainment

Alice, Mary
Allen, Billie
Allen, Debbie
American Negro Theater
Andrews, Regina M. Anderson
Archer, Osceola
Avery, Margaret
Bassett, Angela
Baxter, Karen
Beavers, Louise
Belgrave, Cynthia
Bentley, Gladys
Berry, Halle
Bowman, Laura
Burke, Georgia
Burrill, Mary P.
Burrows, Vinie
Bush, Anita
Canty, Marietta
Carroll, Diahann

Social Activism

Science, Health, and Medicine

Contents of the Set

Index

Page numbers in **boldface** indicate main entries. *Italic* page numbers indicate illustrations.